The Essential Diverticulitis Diet Cookbook For Beginners

1001 Quick & Easy, Healthy Recipes and A Strategic 21 Days Meal Plan to Heal Your Digestive System

Jacqueline Dellinger

CONTENTS

Chapter 3: High-fiber Recipes 39

Introduction

Hi, My name is Jacqueline Dellinger. I am a cookbook author, recipes developer and a former diverticulitis patients which now is full healed. Any kind diagnosis ocan be overwhelming, but intestinal issues are particularly difficult to detect and manage. 4 years back I started having digestive issue constantly but the doctor couldn't treat it. My symptoms are misinterpreted—who among us hasn't had a digestive issue after an overly rich meal or a stressful week at work? My doctor confused the initial stages of diverticulitis with a stomach bug or food poisoning. My symptoms seriously affected my work and life. Because Our brains and digestive systems are highly connected. I was feeling debilitated due to both the symptoms they experience and the lack of information surrounding the condition. While the Internet contains copious information at the click of a button, trying to decipher what intestinal health information is medically sound can feel impossible. I was lucky enough to meet one of friend who suffering some issue few months later. She introduced Diverticulitis Diet to me. I went on the Diverticulitis Diet journey without a doubt. Within a week, I felt a huge relief from my symptoms. After about a month or so, my life was back in normal.Many thanks to my friend and my families supported me all along the journey.

With my love, passion for food and my expertise as recipes developer, I decided to wrote this book—to provide you the most current, medically accurate information you may not have found elsewhere. During my time of healing my diverticulitis, I focus on the love of food.

In this book, you'll find 500+ easy, quick and healthy recipes and 21 days meal plan for your to start. And all the recipes are diverticulitis friendly with flavorful taste. They are super easy to prepare and cook. Even you don't know anything about cooking. The ingredients I used are very common and easy to get. You can get them from any store near your home. You can find out many tips and tricks how to make you diverticulitis diet recipes more tasty and easily.

I even included the information on the diverticulitis. What Is diverticulitis? What Are the Symptoms and Signs? What will causes diverticular Disease, What foods you need to avoid, What foods you need to eat, relationship between diverticular disease and food etc.

I hope you enjoy my diverticulitis diet cookbook and 500+ delicious,mouth-watering recipes! Wish you all the best!!

Chapter 1 Understanding Diverticulitis

People confuse Diverticulitis with other gut-related diseases, which puts them on the wrong track to treat the condition. That is why having a complete understanding of the condition is imperative to take the necessary measure of prevention and treatment.

What Is Diverticulitis?

It is an infection or inflammation of small pouches that can occur in your intestines. These pouches are known as diverticula. Normally, the pouches are harmless. They could show up in your intestines at any point. The medical word for having them is diverticulosis. When they get infected or inflamed, Diverticulitis develops. Diverticulitis might be a minor problem at times. It can, however, be fatal, culminating in a massive infection or intestinal perforation (your doctor will term it a rupture). Symptoms of Diverticulitis can be mistaken for those of other disorders. Your doctor will be able to narrow things down by ruling out alternative options. A physical examination can be the first step.

What Are the Symptoms and Signs?

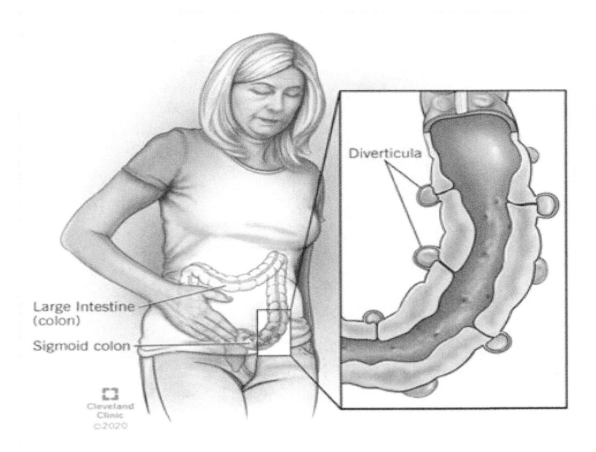

The majority of people who have diverticulosis have no symptoms. Those who do may be suffering from one or more of the following conditions:

Cramps in The Stomach

Stomach Ache

Diarrhea

While a doctor analyzes the cause, he or she will most likely advise you to take some steps to relieve your symptoms, such as taking a pain reliever. They'll want to rule out irritable bowel syndrome and peptic ulcers, both of which can cause similar symptoms.

Diverticular Disease Causes

One possible cause of the disease, which is highly controversial, is the protrusion of such sacs outward from the colon. The main factor, however, is a nutritional deficiency, namely, lack of dietary fiber.

Fiber relaxes stools, and not getting enough of it causes hard stools. As muscles force the feces down, this may put greater pressure or stress on the colon. Diverticula are considered to form as a result of this stress.

Although there is no one known cause of diverticular illness, several factors might raise your chances of getting it, including:

·Genetics

·Immune system dysfunction

·Obesity

·Diet

·A lack of physical activity

·Smoking

·Alterations in the microbiota of the gut

·Steroid medicines

·Diets heavy in red meat and poor in fiber

According to research, some genes will intensify the risk of developing diverticular illness in certain individuals.

Scientists are investigating other elements that may have a role in diverticular illness.

These elements include:

·Germs or feces being trapped in a pocket in the colon

·Alterations in the intestinal microbiome

·In your colon, you may have issues with connective nerves, tissue or muscles.

·Immune system complications

Foods to Avoid

People who follow this diet limit food that are rich in FODMAPS. This comprises, for example, the following foods:

Thick-skinned unpeeled fruits

Full-fat dairy products

Fermented products such as Sauerkraut and kimchi

Meals with a lot of trans fats

Meats that have been red and cured

According to a study, eating a diet strong in processed & red meat may raise your chance of having diverticulitis. A diet rich in fruits, whole grains, and vegetables may help lower the risk of heart disease.

The typical Western diet is heavy in fat, sugar, and carbohydrate but low in fiber. As a result, a person's chance of having diverticulitis may rise.

According to research, eating the following foods may help prevent or lessen the symptoms of diverticulitis:

·Food that has been fried

·Refined grains

·Red meat

Foods to eat

For diverticulitis, a clear liquid diet is recommended.

A clear liquid diet may be recommended if a flare-up is serious or necessitates surgery. You graduate from fluids to a low-residue diet in 1-2 days. "Even if your discomfort does not go away, you continue to eat usual foods." You can't stay on a liquid diet for an extended period of time since you'll get malnourished.

Depending upon your flare-up, you can consume the following foods on a clear liquid diet:

·Clear broths

·Juices that are clear and without pulp

·Jell-O.

·Ice pops.

For diverticulitis, a low-fiber diet is recommended. Eat a low-residue or GI gentle diet for milder forms of diverticulitis. Based on the intensity of the flare-up, a low-fiber diet restricts fiber consumption to 8-12 g per day.

Low-fiber foods to consider include:

Grains: White spaghetti and white bread. These, as well as white crackers & white rice, are low-fiber alternatives.

Get the peeler ready for low-fiber starches. Potatoes with no skin are an option. They may be mashed, roasted, or baked. Puffed rice cereal & corn flakes are two low-fiber cereals that receive a nod of approval.

Eggs, seafood, egg whites, meat & tofu are all good protein sources. Chopped-up chicken, light ground beef, and tender baked fish are the finest choices.

Fruits: Be cautious while eating fruits since they contain a lot of fiber. Canned fruits like peaches, pears, ripe bananas, soft, ripe cantaloupe, applesauce, honeydew are all good choices. You're not consuming the skin, so there's not a lot of fiber. Insoluble fiber, which may aggravate inflamed polyps, is found in the skin. If you're recuperating from a flare-up, cottage cheese and Greek yogurt are big winners in fact they're rich in calcium, minerals, & protein, plus they don't have any fiber. They're also soft, creamy, and easier to swallow if you're sick. Milk and cheese are additional options.

Chapter 2: Clear Fluids Recipes

Fish & Vinegar Broth

Servings: 6
Cooking Time: 12 Hours 5 Minutes
Ingredients:

- 12 C. filtered water
- 2 lb. non-oily fish heads and bones
- ¼ C. apple cider vinegar
- Salt, as required

Directions:

1. In a large pan, add all the ingredients over medium-high heat.
2. Add enough water to cover the veggie mixture and bring to a boil.
3. Now adjust the heat to low and simmer, covered for about 10-12 hours, skimming the foam from the surface occasionally.
4. Through a fine-mesh sieve, strain the broth into a large bowl.
5. Serve hot.

Nutrition:

- Per Serving : Protein 13.4 g | Fiber 0 g | Carbs 0.1 g | Fat 1.7 g

Chicken Clear Soup

Servings: 4
Cooking Time: 30 Minutes
Ingredients:

- ¼ cup of chopped onion
- 4 cups of water
- 3 to 4 smashed garlic cloves
- 2 to 3 sprigs of thyme
- ¼ cup of chopped carrot
- 10.5 oz. of chicken with bones
- ¼ tsp. of black pepper
- 2 bay leaves
- Salt, to taste

Directions:

1. Wash the chicken with bones.
2. Add all the ingredients to a pressure cooker. Cook on high heat for 1 whistle.
3. Turn the heat low & simmer for 10 to 12 minutes.
4. Turn the heat off release the pressure naturally.
5. Strain & serve.

Nutrition:

- Per Serving : Protein 14 g | Fiber 3 g | Carbs 2 g | Fat 11 g

Cucumber Cooler Juice

Servings: 1

Cooking Time: 0 Minutes
Ingredients:

- 1/4 of a peeled lemon
- 2 stalks of celery
- 1/4 of a cantaloupe, peeled & cut into pieces
- Half cucumber, sliced thin

Directions:

1. Add all ingredients to a blender. Pulse until smooth.
2. Strain & serve.

Nutrition:

- Per Serving : Protein 0.1 g | Fiber 1.2 g | Carbs 13 g | Fat 0.2 g

Warm Honey Green Tea

Servings: 4
Cooking Time: 15 Minutes
Ingredients:

- 4 lemon's peel, cut into strips
- 4 lemon slices
- 4 orange's peel, cut into strips
- 4 cups of water
- 4 green tea bags
- 2 tsp. of honey

Directions:

1. In a pan, add the strips & water. Let it come to a boil, turn the heat low.
2. Simmer for 10 minutes. Take the strips out.
3. Add the tea bags, cover & steep as per the package Directions. Discard the tea bags & mix in honey.
4. Serve with a slice of lemon.

Nutrition:

- Per Serving : Protein 0.2 g | Fiber 0.6 g | Carbs 5 g | Fat 0.2 g

Garlic Chicken Soup

Servings: 2
Cooking Time: 20 Minutes
Ingredients:

- 2 lemon wedges
- 3.5 oz. of chicken, thinly sliced
- 2 garlic cloves, thinly sliced
- Salt & pepper to taste
- 2 tsp. of sesame oil
- 6 cups of water
- 1 large carrot, cut into strips
- 3 scallions, diced

Directions:

1. Sauté garlic in a drizzle of oil until crispy.
2. Add the rest of the ingredients with water.

3.　　　Let it come to a boil simmer for 2 to 3 minutes. Strain & serve.

Nutrition:

- Per Serving : Protein 2 g | Fiber 0.3 g | Carbs 11 g | Fat 4 g

Elderberry Tea

Servings: 2
Cooking Time: 5 Mins.

Ingredients:

- 16 oz. water
- 2 tbsp. dried elderberries
- ½ tsp. ground turmeric
- ¼ tsp. ground cinnamon
- 1 tsp. maple syrup

Directions:

1. In a small saucepan, place water and elderberries, turmeric and cinnamon over medium-high heat and bring to a boil.
2. Now adjust the heat to low and simmer for about 15 minutes.
3. Remove from heat and set aside to cool for about 5 minutes.
4. Through a fine mesh strainer, strain the tea into serving mugs and stir in the maple syrup.
5. Serve immediately.

Nutrition:

- Per Serving : Protein 0.1 g | Fiber 1.1 g | Carbs 4.9 g | Fat 0.1 g

Pineapple Juice

Servings: 6
Cooking Time: 0 Minutes

Ingredients:

- 1 cup of water
- ¼ tsp. of black pepper & salt (optional)
- 2 cups of pineapple cubes
- Half" of peeled ginger

Directions:

1. In a blender, add all the ingredients.
2. Pulse until smooth strain & serve chilled.

Nutrition:

- Per Serving : Protein 0.2 g | Fiber 1.1 g | Carbs 12 g | Fat 0.2 g

Spiced Clear Broth

Servings: 4
Cooking Time: 40 Minutes

Ingredients:

- 3 stalks of cilantro
- ⅔ cup of peeled & sliced fresh ginger
- Salt & peppers
- 4 cups of vegetable stock

- 1 tbsp. of sesame seeds

Directions:

1. In a pot, add all ingredients. Boil & then simmer for 5 minutes.
2. Strain & serve.

Nutrition:

- Per Serving : Protein 0 g | Fiber 0 g | Carbs 0 g | Fat 0.2 g

Gooseberry Juice

Servings: 2
Cooking Time: 10 Mins.

Ingredients:

- 1 C. fresh gooseberries, seeds removed and chopped
- 1 C. filtered water

Directions:

1. Place all the ingredients in a high-power blender and pulse until well combined
2. Through a cheesecloth-lined strainer, strain the juice and transfer into 2 glasses.
3. Serve immediately.

Nutrition:

- Per Serving : Protein 0.7 g | Fiber 3.2 g | Carbs 7.6 g | Fat 0.4 g

Grapefruit Gelatin

Servings: 4
Cooking Time: 5 Mins.

Ingredients:

- 1 tbsp. grass-fed gelatin powder
- ¾ C. filtered cold water, divided
- ¼ C. honey
- 1¼ C. fresh grapefruit juice
- Pinch of salt

Directions:

1. In a bowl, soak the gelatin in ¼ C. of cold water. Set aside.
2. In a small pan, add the remaining ½ C. of water and honey over medium heat and bring to a boil.
3. Simmer for about 3 minutes or until honey is dissolved completely.
4. Remove from the heat and stir in the soaked gelatin until dissolved completely.
5. Set aside at room temperature to cool completely.
6. After cooling, stir in the grapefruit juice and salt.
7. Transfer the mixture into serving bowls and refrigerate for about 4 hours or until set.

Nutrition:

- Per Serving : Protein 3.3 g | Fiber 0.8 g | Carbs 23.3 g | Fat 0.1 g

Chinese Fish Soup

Servings: 8
Cooking Time: 40 Minutes
Ingredients:
- 1 lb. of fish
- Potato starch, as needed
- 1 lb. of pickled mustard greens
- 1 lb. of taro
- 12 cups of water
- 1 fish head
- 5 slices of ginger
- 1 tbsp. of chicken powder
- 8 scallions (white part)
- Salt & sugar, to taste

Directions:
1. Coat the fish chunks in potato starch. Fry until golden.
2. Do the same with taro.
3. In a pan, sauté vegetables in oil until tender.
4. Add the rest of the ingredients. Simmer for half an hour.
5. Adjust seasoning, strain & serve.

Nutrition:
- Per Serving : Protein 2 g | Fiber 1 g | Carbs 7 g | Fat 2 g

Lemonade

Servings: 8
Cooking Time: 10 Mins.
Ingredients:
- 8 C. filtered water
- ½ C. fresh lemon juice
- ¼ tsp. pure stevia extract
- Ice cubes, as required

Directions:
1. In a pitcher, place the water, lemon juice and stevia and mix well.
2. Through a cheesecloth-lined strainer, strain the lemonade in another pitcher.
3. Refrigerate for 30-40 minutes.
4. Add ice cubes in serving glasses and fill with lemonade.
5. Serve chilled.

Nutrition:
- Per Serving : Protein 0.1 g | Fiber 0.1 g | Carbs 0.3 g | Fat 0.1 g

Lime & Ginger Tea

Servings: 2
Cooking Time: 5 Mins.
Ingredients:
- 2 C. water
- 2 tbsp. fresh ginger, cut into slices
- 1 tbsp. fresh lime juice
- 1 tbsp. maple syrup

Directions:

1. In a saucepan, add water, ginger and cinnamon over high heat and bring to a boil.
2. Now adjust the heat to low and simmer for about 10 minutes.
3. Remove the saucepan of tea from the and strain into serving mugs.
4. Stir in the lime juice and maple syrup and serve immediately.

Nutrition:
- Per Serving : Protein 0.1 g | Fiber 0.6 g | Carbs 8.6 g | Fat 0.1 g

Big, Clear Vegetable Soup

Servings: 4
Cooking Time: 40 Minutes
Ingredients:
- 1 tbsp. of fish sauce
- ¼ of a Chinese cabbage
- 1 tbsp. of soy sauce
- 1 tbsp. of sake
- 1 cup of dried shiitake mushrooms
- 1 tbsp. of mirin
- salt, to season
- 1 sweet potato, peeled and chopped
- 3 scallions, sliced
- 1 tbsp. of vegetable oil
- 1 tsp. of sesame oil
- 2 carrots, peeled and chopped
- 10 oz. of firm tofu, cubed
- ½ daikon, peeled and chopped

Directions:
1. In a pot, add washed mushrooms with 6 cups of boiling water. Let it rest for 20 minutes.
2. Take the mushroom out & trim the stalks; cut the caps in half.
3. In the liquid, add the mirin, fish sauce, sake & soy sauce.
4. Sauté the vegetables in a different pan in hot oil for 2 minutes.
5. Add to the stock & simmer for 15 minutes.
6. Add tofu & simmer for 10 minutes. Adjust seasoning, strain & serve.

Nutrition:
- Per Serving : Protein 2 g | Fiber 1 g | Carbs 8.0 g | Fat 4.2 g

Citrus Apple Juice

Servings: 2
Cooking Time: 10 Mins.
Ingredients:

- 3 large apples, cored and quartered
- 2 large oranges, peeled and sectioned
- 2 large grapefruit, peeled and sectioned
- ½ of lemon, peeled

Directions:

1. Add all ingredients into a juicer and extract the juice according to the manufacturer's method
2. Through a cheesecloth-lined strainer, strain the juice and transfer into 2 glasses.
3. Serve immediately.

Nutrition:

- Per Serving : Protein 3.6 g | Fiber 14.1 g | Carbs 79.1 g | Fat 1 g

Ginger Zinger Juice

Servings: 6
Cooking Time: 0 Minutes
Ingredients:

- ¼ lemon, peeled
- 5 carrots
- 2 apples, sliced thin
- Half" of fresh ginger

Directions:

1. In a blender, add all the ingredients.
2. Pulse until smooth strain & serve chilled.

Nutrition:

- Per Serving : Protein 0.7 g | Fiber 1.6 g | Carbs 11.9 g | Fat 0.3 g

Simple Black Tea

Servings: 2
Cooking Time: 3 Mins.
Ingredients:

- 2 C. filtered water
- ½ tsp. black tea leaves
- 1 tsp. honey

Directions:

1. In a pan, add the water and bring to a boil.
2. Stir in the tea leaves and turn off the heat.
3. Immediately cover the pan and steep for 3 minutes.
4. Add honey and stir until dissolved.
5. Strain the tea in mugs and serve immediately.

Nutrition:

- Per Serving : Protein 0 g | Fiber 0 g | Carbs 2.9 g | Fat 0 g

Nyquell Herbal Tea

Servings: 1-2
Cooking Time: 0 Minutes

Ingredients:

- 1 tbsp. of dried valerian root
- 1 tbsp. of dried peppermint leaf
- 1 tbsp. of dried chamomile flower
- 1 tbsp. of dried licorice root

Directions:

1. In an air-tight jar, add all the ingredients. Mix & keep in a cool, dry place.
2. To make one cup of tea, add 1 tbsp. of the mixture in a mug, add boiling water & steep for half an hour or more.
3. Strain, add honey to your taste. Serve.

Nutrition:

- Per Serving : Protein 0.1 g | Fiber 1.1 g | Carbs 11 g | Fat 0.3 g

Orange Juice

Servings: 2
Cooking Time: 10 Mins.
Ingredients:

- 8 oranges, peeled and sectioned

Directions:

1. Add the orange sections into a juicer and extract the juice according to the manufacturer's method.
2. Through a cheesecloth-lined strainer, strain the juice and transfer into 2 glasses.
3. Serve immediately.

Nutrition:

- Per Serving : Protein 6.9 g | Fiber 17.7 g | Carbs 86.5 g | Fat 0.9 g

Cherry Limeade

Servings: 8
Cooking Time: 10 Mins.
Ingredients:

- 10 oz. filtered water
- 1/3 C. fresh lime juice
- ½ C. fresh cherry juice
- 1-2 tsp. stevia drops

Directions:

1. In a pitcher, place the water, lime juice, cherry juice and stevia and mix well.
2. Through a cheesecloth-lined strainer, strain the limeade in another pitcher.
3. Refrigerate for 30-40 minutes.
4. Add ice cubes in serving glasses and fill with limeade.
5. Serve chilled.

Nutrition:

- Per Serving : Protein 0.3 g | Fiber 0 g | Carbs 3.1 g | Fat 0 g

Apple Detox Water

Servings: 2
Cooking Time: 10 Mins.
Ingredients:
- 1 apple, cored and thinly sliced
- 1 cinnamon stick.
- 4 C. filtered water

Directions:
1. In a large glass jar, place apple slices, cinnamon stick and pour water on top.
2. Cover the jar with a lid and refrigerate for about 1 hour before serving.
3. Through a cheesecloth-lined strainer, strain the detox water and serve.

Nutrition:
- Per Serving : Protein 0.3 g | Fiber 2.7 g | Carbs 14 g | Fat 0.2 g

Melon Honey Green Tea

Servings: 2
Cooking Time: 0 Minutes
Ingredients:
- 1 bottle of Honey Green Tea (not sweet)
- 6 chunks of honeydew melon, cut into small squares
- 15 fresh mint leaves

Directions:
1. In a bowl, add all ingredients & crush with a spoon.
2. Mix well & strain. Serve with ice.

Nutrition:
- Per Serving : Protein 0.1 g | Fiber 1.1 g | Carbs 11 g | Fat 0.2 g

Sinus Clearing Tea

Servings: 1
Cooking Time: 0 Minutes
Ingredients:
- 2 tbsp. of Pure Honey
- ¼ cup of Lemon Juice/apple cider vinegar
- ¾ cup of Herbal Tea
- Cayenne pepper, to taste
- Hot Water, as needed

Directions:
1. In a pitcher, add hot water & tea, steep as per the package Directions.
2. Strain & add the rest of the ingredients.
3. Mix & serve.

Nutrition:
- Per Serving : Protein 0.1 g | Fiber 1.2 g | Carbs 18.7 g | Fat 0.2 g

Raspberry Juice

Servings: 2
Cooking Time: 10 Mins.

Ingredients:
- 2 C. fresh raspberries
- 1 tbsp. honey
- ¼ C. filtered water

Directions:
1. Add all ingredients in a high-power blender and pulse until well combined.
2. Through a cheesecloth-lined strainer, strain the juice and transfer into 2 glasses.
3. Serve immediately.

Nutrition:
- Per Serving : Protein 1.5 g | Fiber 8 g | Carbs 23.3 g | Fat 0.8 g

Raspberry Popsicles

Servings: 6
Cooking Time: 15 Minutes
Ingredients:
- 1¼ C. cold water
- 1 C. frozen raspberries
- ¼ C. fresh mint leaves
- 24 stevia drops

Directions:
1. Add all the ingredients in a clean blender and pulse until smooth.
2. Through a cheesecloth-lined strainer, strain the mixture.
3. Transfer the mixture into the Popsicle molds and freeze for 4 hours before serving.

Nutrition:
- Per Serving : Protein 0.4 g | Fiber 2.1 g | Carbs 11.2 g | Fat 0.1 g

Hot Apple Cider

Servings: 4
Cooking Time: 25 Minutes
Ingredients:
- 3 cinnamon sticks
- 1 tsp. black peppercorns
- ½ tsp. whole cloves
- 4 C. fresh apple juice
- ½ tbsp. orange zest
- ¼ tsp. ground nutmeg
- 1-2 tsp. maple syrup

Directions:
1. Heat a non-stick saucepan over medium-high heat and toast the cinnamon sticks, peppercorns and cloves for about 3-5 minutes, stirring continuously.
2. Stir in the apple juice, orange zest and nutmeg and bring to a boil.
3. Adjust the heat to low and simmer for about 15-20 minutes.
4. Through a fine-mesh sieve, strain the mixture into serving mugs and serve.

Nutrition:

- Per Serving : Protein 0.1 g | Fiber 0.7 g | Carbs 28.4 g | Fat 0.1 g

Cranberry Juice

Servings: 4
Cooking Time: 10 Mins.
Ingredients:

- 4 C. fresh cranberries
- 1 tbsp. fresh lemon juice
- 2 C. filtered water
- 1 tsp. raw honey

Directions:

1. Add all ingredients in a high-power blender and pulse until well combined.
2. Through a cheesecloth-lined strainer, strain the juice and transfer into 4 glasses
3. Serve immediately.

Nutrition:

- Per Serving : Protein 0 g | Fiber 4 g | Carbs 11.5 g | Fat 0 g

Apple Iced Tea

Servings: 3
Cooking Time: 0 Minutes
Ingredients:

- 4 cups of water
- 1 lemon, thinly sliced
- 2 cinnamon sticks
- 4 cups of clear apple juice
- 2 tea bags (English breakfast)
- Honey, to taste
- 1 red apple, thinly sliced

Directions:

1. Steep the tea bags in boiling water for 15 minutes. Discard the tea bags add the rest of the ingredients.
2. Chill in the fridge & serve.

Nutrition:

- Per Serving : Protein 0.1 g | Fiber 1.2 g | Carbs 18.7 g | Fat 0.2 g

Blueberry, Grapes & Grapefruit Juice

Servings: 2
Cooking Time: 10 Mins.
Ingredients:

- 3 C. fresh blueberries
- 2 C. seedless grapes
- 4 grapefruit, peeled and sectioned

Directions:

1. Add all ingredients into a juicer and extract the juice according to the manufacturer's method.

2. Through a cheesecloth-lined strainer, strain the juice and transfer into 2 glasses.
3. Serve immediately.

Nutrition:

- Per Serving : Protein 3.8 g | Fiber 8.9 g | Carbs 68 g | Fat 1.3 g

Strawberry-basil Iced Tea

Servings: 8
Cooking Time: 10 Minutes
Ingredients:

- Ice, for serving
- 1 pound of strawberries, trimmed & cut into fours
- 1 cup of fresh basil
- 4 cups of water or more
- 8 black-tea bags
- 3/4 cup of sugar

Directions:

1. In a pan, add water and boil. Add tea bags & steep for 5 minutes.
2. In a separate pot, add sugar & water. Stir well on low heat & cook until sugar dissolves.
3. Turn the heat off & add basil. Let it rest for 10 minutes.
4. Add to the strawberries & toss well. Let it rest for 25 minutes.
5. Add the tea to the strawberries let it rest for a few hours in the fridge.
6. Serve chilled after straining.

Nutrition:

- Per Serving : Protein 0.1 g | Fiber 1 g | Carbs 19 g | Fat 0.2 g

Blueberry Gelatin

Servings: 6
Cooking Time: 10 Mins.
Ingredients:

- 1 tbsp. grass-fed gelatin powder
- 1¾ C. fresh blueberry juice, warmed
- ¼ C. hot water

Directions:

1. In a medium bowl, place the gelatin powder.
2. Add just enough warm juice to cover the gelatin and stir well.
3. Set aside for about 2-3 minutes or until it forms a thick syrup.
4. Add the boiling water and stir until gelatin is dissolved completely.
5. Add the remaining juice and stir well.
6. Transfer the mixture into a parchment paper-lined baking dish and refrigerate for 2 hours or until the top is firm before serving.

Nutrition:

- Per Serving : Protein 1 g | Fiber 0 g | Carbs 11.1 g | Fat 0 g

Lemon Gelatin

Servings: 8
Cooking Time: 10 Mins.
Ingredients:
- 3 tbsp. grass-fed gelatin powder
- 3 C. cold water, divided
- 1½ C. boiling water
- 1 C. plus 2 tbsp. fresh lemon juice
- 2 tsp. stevia extract

Directions:
1. In a bowl, soak the gelatin in 1½ C. of cold water. Set aside for about 5 minutes.
2. Add boiling water and stir until gelatin is dissolved.
3. Add the remaining cold water, lemon juice and stevia extract and stir until dissolved completely.
4. Divide the mixture into 2 baking dishes and refrigerate until set before serving.

Nutrition:
- Per Serving : Protein 4.4 g | Fiber 0.1 g | Carbs 0.7 g | Fat 0.3 g

Blueberry Juice

Servings: 2
Cooking Time: 10 Mins.
Ingredients:
- 1½ C. fresh blueberries
- 1 tbsp. fresh lemon juice
- 1 C. filtered water

Directions:
1. Add all ingredients in a high-power blender and pulse until well combined.
2. Through a cheesecloth-lined strainer, strain the juice and transfer into 2 glasses.
3. Serve immediately.

Nutrition:
- Per Serving : Protein 0.9 g | Fiber 2.7 g | Carbs 15.9 g | Fat 0.4 g

Minty Watermelon Popsicles

Servings: 5-6
Cooking Time: 0 Minutes
Ingredients:
- 1 tbsp. of fresh mint leaves
- 1 tbsp. of honey
- 1 ½ cups of coconut water
- 3 cups of sliced watermelon
- 2 tbsp. of lime juice

Directions:
1. Add all ingredients to a blender. Pulse until smooth.
2. Strain well & pour in the molds. Keep in the freezer until they set.
3. Serve.

Nutrition:
- Per Serving : Protein 0.1 g | Fiber 1.1 g | Carbs 11 g | Fat 0.7 g

Fruit-flavored Iced Green Tea

Servings: 6
Cooking Time: 0 Minutes
Ingredients:
- 1 lime, sliced thin
- 8 oz. of strawberries, trimmed
- 8 Green Tea Bags
- Zest of 1 lime
- 2 cups of sugar-free non-pulp Orange Juice
- 8 cups of boiling water

Directions:
1. Steep the tea in boiling water. Take the tea bags out & keep the tea in the fridge.
2. Chop the strawberries in a blender add them to a bowl. Mix with the rest of the ingredients.
3. Pour into ice cube tray, freeze for 2 hours.
4. Pour tea in a glass with fruit ice cubes. Strain & serve.

Nutrition:
- Per Serving : Protein 0.1 g | Fiber 1.2 g | Carbs 7 g | Fat 0.2 g

Veggie Broth

Servings: 10
Cooking Time: 2 Hours 5 Minutes
Ingredients:
- 4 carrots, peeled and chopped roughly
- 4 celery stalks, chopped roughly
- 3 parsnips, peeled and chopped roughly
- 2 large potatoes, peeled and chopped roughly
- 1 medium beet, trimmed and chopped roughly
- 1 large bunch fresh parsley
- 1 (1-inch) piece fresh ginger, sliced
- Filtered water, as required

Directions:
1. In a large pan, add all the ingredients over medium-high heat.
2. Add enough water to cover the veggie mixture and bring to a boil.
3. Now adjust the heat to low and simmer, covered for about 2-3 hours.
4. Through a fine-mesh sieve, strain the broth into a large bowl.
5. Serve hot.

Nutrition:
- Per Serving : Protein 1.9 g | Fiber 3.7 g | Carbs 19 g | Fat 0.2 g

Moroccan Tea

Servings: 1
Cooking Time: 0 Minutes
Ingredients:
- 1 tsp. of ground ginger
- Half tsp. of lemon juice
- 1 ½ cups of boiling water
- 1 to 2 tsp. of honey

Directions:
1. Add all ingredients in a mug.
2. Mix well & serve.

Nutrition:
- Per Serving : Protein 0.2 g | Fiber 0.3 g | Carbs 7 g | Fat 0.2 g

Clear Vegetable Soup

Servings: 3
Cooking Time: 30minutes
Ingredients:
- 1 yellow onion, chopped
- 1 cup of cauliflower florets
- 2 carrots, roughly chopped
- 1 ½ cups of sliced mushrooms
- 12 French beans
- 1 cup of chopped celery stalks
- 1 cup of spring onion
- Water, as needed

Directions:
1. In a pot, add all ingredients. Add enough water to cover the vegetables.
2. Simmer on a medium flame for 30 minutes. Add more water if needed.
3. Strain & add salt pepper. Serve.

Nutrition:
- Per Serving : Protein 5 g | Fiber 5 g | Carbs 19 g | Fat 5 g

Chicken Bone Broth

Servings: 4
Cooking Time: 20 Minutes
Ingredients:
- 2 tbsp. of oil
- ½ cup of green part scallions
- 1 chicken, cut into pieces
- 2 carrots, chopped
- 5 peppercorns
- 2 parsnips, chopped
- 8 cups water
- 1 celery stalk, chopped
- Half tsp. of salt

Directions:
1. Sauté the scallions for 2-3 minutes in hot oil. Add the rest of the ingredients.

2. Let it come to a boil, turn the heat low and simmer for 2 & a half hours.
3. Strain & adjust seasoning. Serve.

Nutrition:
- Per Serving : Protein 3 g | Fiber 1 g | Carbs 13 g | Fat 4.2 g

Apple-cinnamon Tea

Servings:4
Cooking Time: 25 Minutes
Ingredients:
- 1 cup chopped apples, Honey Crisp, Fuji, Granny Smith, or Gala
- 3 cinnamon sticks
- 1 quart water
- 2 bags Earl Grey tea (caffeinated or decaffeinated)
- ⅓ cup honey, plus more if desired

Directions:
1. ⅓ cup honey, plus more if desired
2. In a large saucepan over high heat, place the apples, cinnamon sticks, and water and bring to a boil. Lower the heat to medium and simmer for 15 minutes.
3. Remove from the heat and add the Earl Grey tea bags. Steep for 10 minutes.
4. Using a slotted spoon, remove the tea bags, apples, and cinnamon sticks. Add the honey and stir until it dissolves. Taste and add more honey, if desired. Serve hot.
5. Store leftovers in an airtight container in the refrigerator for up to 5 days. Enjoy cold or reheat in the microwave for 1 minute until hot.

Nutrition:
- Per Serving : Protein 1 g | Fiber 1 g | Carbs 27 g | Fat 1 g

Cranberry Ice Tea

Servings: 7
Cooking Time: 10 Minutes
Ingredients:
- 1¼ C. boiling water
- 2 dandelion tea bags
- 7 C. cold water
- ½ C. unsweetened cranberry juice
- 6 drops grapefruit oil
- 6 drops lemon oil

Directions:
1. In a large glass pitcher, add boiling water and tea bags and brew, covered for about 8-10 minutes.
2. Discard the tea bags and mix in the remaining ingredients.
3. Refrigerate to chill completely before serving.

Nutrition:
- Per Serving : Protein 0 g | Fiber 0 g | Carbs 3.7 g | Fat 0.1 g

Hibachi Clear Soup

Servings: 8
Cooking Time: 90 Minutes
Ingredients:
- 1 onion, diced
- 3" ginger, peeled & chopped
- 4 cups of water
- 1 carrot, chopped
- 1 tbsp. of sesame oil
- 4 cups of beef broth
- 4 minced cloves garlic
- 8 cups of chicken broth

Directions:
1. Sauté the vegetables in hot oil for a few minutes.
2. Add all the liquids & boil.
3. Simmer for 60 minutes. Strain & serve.

Nutrition:
- Per Serving : Protein 3 g | Fiber 1.2 g | Carbs 6.1 g | Fat 2.3 g

Clear Onion Soup

Servings: 6
Cooking Time: 40 Minutes
Ingredients:
- 2 diced onions
- 1 celery stalks, chopped
- 1 cup of sliced button mushrooms
- 1 carrot, diced
- 6 cups vegetable broth
- Salt & pepper, to taste
- ½ tsp. of minced ginger & minced garlic, each
- 1 tsp. of sesame oil
- ½ cup of scallions

Directions:
1. In a pot, sauté the onion for 10 minutes until slightly caramelized.
2. Add the rest of the ingredients simmer for half an hour.
3. Strain & adjust seasoning. Serve.

Nutrition:
- Per Serving : Protein 2 g | Fiber 1 g | Carbs 2 g | Fat 1 g

Ginger Root Tea

Servings: 2
Cooking Time: 10 Minutes
Ingredients:
- 1 tsp. of honey
- 4 thin slices of lemon
- 2 cups of water
- 2" piece of peeled ginger, sliced
- 12 mint leaves

Directions:

1. Boil water, add ginger & lemon. Steep for a few minutes.
2. Add mint leaves & simmer for ten minutes.
3. Turn the heat off, add honey. Mix & strain, serve.

Nutrition:
- Per Serving : Protein 0.2 g | Fiber 0.3 g | Carbs 13 g | Fat 0.1 g

Grapes Juice

Servings: 3
Cooking Time: 10 Mins.
Ingredients:
- 2 C. seedless grapes
- 1½ C. filtered water
- 6-8 ice cubes

Directions:
1. Add all ingredients in a high-power blender and pulse until well combined.
2. Through a cheesecloth-lined strainer, strain the juice and transfer into 3 glasses
3. Serve immediately.

Nutrition:
- Per Serving : Protein 0.4 g | Fiber 10 g | Carbs 10.5 g | Fat 0.2 g

Berries & Carrot Juice

Servings: 2
Cooking Time: 10 Mins.
Ingredients:
- 1½ C. fresh blueberries
- 1½ C. fresh strawberries, hulled
- 1 C. fresh raspberries
- 4 medium carrots, peeled and roughly chopped

Directions:
1. Add all ingredients into a juicer and extract the juice according to the manufacturer's method.
2. Through a cheesecloth-lined strainer, strain the juice and transfer into 2 glasses.
3. Serve immediately.

Nutrition:
- Per Serving : Protein 1.6 g | Fiber 5.9 g | Carbs 21.7 g | Fat 0.6 g

Lemony Grapes Juice

Servings: 3
Cooking Time: 10 Mins.
Ingredients:
- 4 C. seedless white grapes
- 2 tbsp. fresh lemon juice

Directions:
1. Add all ingredients in a high-power blender and pulse until well combined.
2. Through a cheesecloth-lined strainer, strain the juice and transfer into 3 glasses.

3. Serve immediately.
Nutrition:
- Per Serving : Protein 0.9 g | Fiber 1.1 g | Carbs 21.3 g | Fat 0.5 g

Healthy Jell-o

Servings: 8
Cooking Time: 20 Minutes
Ingredients:
- 2 Tbsp. beef gelatin, unflavored
- 2 tbsp. of honey
- 4 cups of clear apple juice

Directions:
1. Add gelatin to half to ¾ cup of the juice. Whisk well & let it rest for 3 to 5 minutes.
2. Add the rest of the juice to a pan simmer on medium heat. Turn the heat off
3. Add honey & gelatin mixture. Mix & pour into the dish.
4. Keep in the fridge for 4 hours. Slice & serve.
Nutrition:
- Per Serving : Protein 0.1 g | Fiber 1 g | Carbs 15 g | Fat 0 g

Chciken Bones & Veggie Broth

Servings: 12
Cooking Time: 10 Hours 25 Minutes
Ingredients:
- 3 tbsp. extra-virgin olive oil
- 2½ lb. chicken bones
- 4 celery stalks, chopped roughly
- 3 large carrots, peeled and chopped roughly
- 1 bay leaf
- 1 tbsp. black peppercorns
- 2 whole cloves
- 1 tbsp. apple cider vinegar
- Warm water, as required

Directions:
1. In a Dutch oven, heat the oil over medium-high heat and sear the bones or about 3-5 minutes or until browned.
2. With a slotted spoon, transfer the bones into a bowl.
3. In the same pan, add the celery stalks and carrots and cook for about 15 minutes, stirring occasionally.
4. Add browned bones, bay leaf, black peppercorns, cloves and vinegar and stir to combine.
5. Add enough warm water to cover the bones mixture completely and bring to a gentle boil.
6. Now adjust the heat to low and simmer, covered for about 8-10 hours, skimming the foam from the surface occasionally.
7. Through a fine-mesh sieve, strain the broth into a large bowl.
8. Serve hot.
Nutrition:

- Per Serving : Protein 5.7 g | Fiber 0.5 g | Carbs 2 g | Fat 4.1 g

Orange & Carrot Juice

Servings: 4
Cooking Time: 10 Mins.
Ingredients:
- 2 lb. carrots, peeled and chopped
- 6 large oranges, peeled and sectioned

Directions:
1. Add the carrots and orange sections into a juicer and extract the juice according to the manufacturer's method.
2. Through a cheesecloth-lined strainer, strain the juice and transfer into 4 glasses.
3. Serve immediately.
Nutrition:
- Per Serving : Protein 3.2 g | Fiber 9 g | Carbs 39.2 g | Fat 0.2 g

Fish & Vegetable Soup

Servings: 4
Cooking Time: 40 Minutes
Ingredients:
- 1 tbsp. of butter
- 1 clove garlic, minced
- 3 ½ cups of chicken broth
- ½ tsp. of dried basil
- 1 cup of sliced carrots
- ¼ cup of diced onion
- 1 cup of green beans
- 1 lb. white fish, cubed
- ½ cup of corn
- ½ tsp. of salt
- ¼ tsp. of dried oregano
- 1/8 tsp. of pepper

Directions:
1. Sauté onion & garlic in butter for 2-3 minutes.
2. Add the rest of the ingredients, except fish. Simmer for 8 minutes.
3. Add fish, cook for 5-7 minutes, strain & serve.
Nutrition:

- Per Serving : Protein 25 g | Fiber 1 g | Carbs 11 g | Fat 4 g

Pineapple Skin Tea

Servings: 16
Cooking Time: 10 Minutes
Ingredients:
- 1 pineapple, peel & core
- 3 tbsp. of grated ginger
- 2 oranges
- 17 cups of water
- 2 tbsp. of grated turmeric
- Half tsp. of Cayenne pepper
- 3 tbsp. of honey
- 2 sprigs of herbs
- 1 lemon
- 2 cinnamon sticks

Directions:
1. Clean the pineapple skin thoroughly. Add to a large pan, add 1-2 tbsp. of vinegar.
2. Soak for half an hour & rinse well. Pat dry & peel & core with a knife.
3. In a pot, add all ingredients (do not add honey yet), mix & place on a medium flame.
4. Simmer for half an hour or more. Strain & add to the pitcher.
5. Serve with the desired amount of honey.

Nutrition:
- Per Serving : Protein 1 g | Fiber 1.2 g | Carbs 14 g | Fat 1 g

Immune Boon Herbal Tea

Servings: 1
Cooking Time: 0 Minutes
Ingredients:
- 1 tbsp. of dried elderberries
- 1 tbsp. of dried echinacea flowers & leaves
- 1 tbsp. of dried ginger root
- 1 tbsp. of dried rose hips
- 1 tbsp. of dried astragalus

Directions:
1. In an air-tight jar, add all the ingredients. Mix & keep in a cool, dry place.
2. To make one cup of tea, add 1 tbsp. of the mixture in a mug, add boiling water & steep for half an hour or more.
3. Strain, add honey to your taste. Serve.

Nutrition:
- Per Serving : Protein 0.2 g | Fiber 1.1 g | Carbs 11 g | Fat 0.2 g

Herbed Beef Broth

Servings: 10
Cooking Time: 6½ Hours
Ingredients:
- 4 lb. beef shanks
- 3 medium carrots, cut into chunks
- 3 celery ribs, cut into chunks
- 2 medium onions, quartered
- ½ C. warm water
- 3 garlic cloves
- 3-4 fresh parsley sprigs
- 1 tsp. dried oregano
- 1 tsp. dried thyme
- 1 tsp. dried marjoram
- 3 bay leaves
- 8-10 whole peppercorns
- Salt, as required
- Cold water, as required

Directions:
1. Preheat the oven to 450 °F.
2. Arrange the beef shanks into a large roasting pan and bake for about 30 minutes.
3. Remove from the oven and place the carrots, celery and onions into the roasting pan with bones.
4. Bake for about 30 minutes.
5. Remove from the oven and drain the fat from pan.
6. With a slotted spoon, transfer the bones and vegetables into a large Dutch oven.
7. Pour the warm water into the roasting pan and with a wooden spoon, stir to loosen browned bits.
8. Transfer the pan juices into the Dutch oven.
9. Add the garlic, herbs, bay leaves, peppercorns and salt and stir to combine.
10. Add enough cold water just to cover the bones mixture.
11. Place the pan over high heat and bring to a boil.
12. Boil for about 30 minutes.
13. Now adjust the heat to low and simmer, uncovered for about 4-5 hours, skimming the foam from the surface occasionally.
14. Through a fine-mesh sieve, strain the broth into a large bowl.
15. Serve hot.

Nutrition:
- Per Serving : Protein 61.6 g | Fiber 1.1 g | Carbs 4.5 g | Fat 11.6 g

Ginger Fish Soup

Servings: 4
Cooking Time: 20 Minutes
Ingredients:
- 1 Tbsp. of cooking oil
- 2" piece of ginger, grated
- 6 cups of chicken stock
- 2 lb. of sole fillets
- 4 Roma tomatoes, diced without seeds
- 2 cups of diced celery
- 1 tsp. + 2 tbsp. of fish sauce
- 2 tsp. of sugar
- 5 shallots, chopped

- 2 cloves of garlic, chopped
- 1 tbsp. of cornstarch

Directions:
1. Toss the fish fillets with fish sauce (1 tsp.) & cornstarch.
2. Sauté the shallots, ginger & garlic for 2 to 3 minutes in hot oil. Add stock, celery & boil.
3. Simmer for 15 minutes. Add fish & tomatoes, cook until done.
4. Strain & adjust seasoning, serve.

Nutrition:
- Per Serving : Protein 2 g | Fiber 0 g | Carbs 6 g | Fat 2 g

Waterelon Juice

Servings: 2
Cooking Time: 10 Mins.
Ingredients:
- 4 C. seedless watermelon, cubed
- ½ tbsp. fresh lime juice

Directions:
1. Add all ingredients into a juicer and extract the juice according to the manufacturer's method.
2. Through a cheesecloth-lined strainer, strain the juice and transfer into 2 glasses.
3. Serve immediately.

Nutrition:
- Per Serving : Protein 1.9 g | Fiber 1.3 g | Carbs 23.5 g | Fat 0.5 g

Mushroom Clear Soup

Servings: 2
Cooking Time: 40 Minutes
Ingredients:
- 4 cups of water
- 7 oz. of button mushrooms, cleaned & sliced
- 1 tbsp. butter
- Few sprigs Thyme
- 1 tsp. of salt

Directions:
1. Sauté the mushrooms in butter for a few seconds.
2. Add the rest of the ingredients.
3. Simmer for half an hour. Strain & adjust seasoning.
4. Serve.

Nutrition:
- Per Serving : Protein 0.1 g | Fiber 1.2 g | Carbs 11 g | Fat 0.2 g

Lemon Tea W Honey & Ginger

Servings: 1
Cooking Time: 0 Minutes
Ingredients:
- Hot water, as need
- Honey, to taste
- 2 to 3 tbsp. of lemon juice

- Fresh chopped ginger, to taste

Directions:
1. In a pan, add water & heat.
2. Add the rest of the ingredients to the mug.
3. Pour hot water & stir, serve.

Nutrition:
- Per Serving : Protein 0.2 g | Fiber 0.2 g | Carbs 14 g | Fat 0.2 g

Chilled Miint Green Tea

Servings: 2
Cooking Time: 10 Mins.
Ingredients:
- 2½ C. boiling water
- 1 C. fresh mint leaves
- 4 green tea bags
- 2 tsp. honey

Directions:
1. In a pitcher, mix together water, mint and tea bags.
2. Cover and steep for about 5 minutes.
3. Through a fine mesh strainer, strain the tea mixture into another pitcher.
4. Refrigerate for at least 3 hours.
5. Discard the tea bags and divide the tea in serving glasses.
6. Stir in honey and serve.

Nutrition:
- Per Serving : Protein 1.5 g | Fiber 3.1 g | Carbs 9.6 g | Fat 0.3 g

Oxtail Soup

Servings: 4
Cooking Time: 3 Hours
Ingredients:
- 2 shallots, chopped
- ½ leek, chopped
- 1 carrot, chopped
- 1 tsp. of Marmite
- 1 oxtail cut
- 1 tsp. of Worcestershire sauce
- 1 stick of celery, chopped
- 1 garlic clove, chopped
- 1 tbsp. of dark sugar
- 1 tsp. of tomato puree
- 4 sprigs thyme
- 4 cups of chicken stock
- 2 bay leaves

Directions:
1. Sauté the oxtail on high flame in a splash of hot oil until seared.
2. Add the rest of the ingredients simmer for 2 to 3 hours.
3. Strain & adjust seasoning. Serve.

Nutrition:

- Per Serving : Protein 5 g | Fiber 1 g | Carbs 17 g | Fat 1.8 g

Homemade Iced Tea

Servings: 8
Cooking Time: 0 Minutes
Ingredients:
- 6 cups of boiling water
- 2 cups of fresh herbs
- 8 tea bags
- 4 cups of clear juice

Directions:
1. Steep the tea bags in boiling water. Take the tea bags out & add the rest of the ingredients.
2. Let it rest for 20 minutes. Strain & serve.

Nutrition:
- Per Serving : Protein 0.1 g | Fiber 1.2 g | Carbs 14 g | Fat 0.2 g

Hibiscus-mint Iced Tea

Servings: 8
Cooking Time: 10 Minutes
Ingredients:
- 4 cups of boiling water
- 4 hibiscus tea bags
- 2 cups of cold water
- Half cup of fresh mint leaves
- 2 cups of apple juice

Directions:
1. In a pot, add mint leaves, tea bags & boiling water. Let it rest for 10 minutes.
2. Take the mint & tea bags out. Add cold water & apple juice. Mix well & serve.

Nutrition:
- Per Serving : Protein 1 g | Fiber 1.3 g | Carbs 12 g | Fat 0.2 g

Grapes & Berries Juice

Servings: 2
Cooking Time: 10 Mins.
Ingredients:
- 1 C. seedless grapes
- ½ C. mixed berries
- 2 tsp. honey
- 1¾ C. filtered water

Directions:
1. Add all ingredients in a high-power blender and pulse until well combined.
2. Through a cheesecloth-lined strainer, strain the juice and transfer into 2 glasses.
3. Serve immediately.

Nutrition:

- Per Serving : Protein 0.6 g | Fiber 1.7 g | Carbs 17.1 g | Fat 0.3 g

Jell-o Jugglers

Servings: 32
Cooking Time: 20 Minutes
Ingredients:
- 4 cups of clear juice
- 4 packets of gelatin

Directions:
1. Add gelatin to one cup of cold juice & let it rest for a few minutes.
2. Simmer the 3 cups of juice & pour on the gelatin mixture stir until dissolved.
3. Pour in a pan. Set in the fridge & serve.

Nutrition:
- Per Serving : Protein 0 g | Fiber 0 g | Carbs 0 g | Fat 0.2 g

Green Goddess Juice

Servings: 1-2
Cooking Time: 0 Minutes
Ingredients:
- 1 pear, cut into 8 wedges
- Half cucumber, slice into fours
- 3 celery stalks
- 1 green apple, cut into 8 wedges

Directions:
1. In a blender, add all the fruits with enough water.
2. Strain the juice & serve.

Nutrition:
- Per Serving : Protein 0.1 g | Fiber 1.4 g | Carbs 12 g | Fat 1.3 g

Thai Fish Soup

Servings: 4
Cooking Time: 40 Minutes
Ingredients:
- 4 scallions, sliced
- 1" piece of ginger, sliced
- 1 lemongrass
- 2 minced garlic cloves
- 2 tbsp. of oil
- 17 oz. of cod fillet, cut into pieces
- 26 oz. of fish stock
- 1tbsp. of coriander, chopped
- 1 lime's juice
- 2 tbsp. of light soy sauce
- 1 shallot, sliced
- 1 tbsp. of caster sugar
- 2 tbsp. of fish sauce
- Salt & black pepper

Directions:

1. Sauté the shallots & scallion in hot oil for 2-3 minutes.
2. Add garlic, lemon grass & ginger for 2-3 minutes.
3. Add the rest of the ingredients cook for 5-7 minutes.
4. Strain & serve.
Nutrition:
- Per Serving : Protein 5 g | Fiber 2 g | Carbs 6 g | Fat 4 g

Lemony Fruit Juice

Servings: 2
Cooking Time: 10 Mins.
Ingredients:
- 2 medium oranges, peeled and sectioned
- 1 C. fresh cranberries
- 2 large red apples, cored and quartered
- 2 large pears, cored and quartered
- ½ of lemon, peeled

Directions:
1. Add all ingredients into a juicer and extract the juice according to the manufacturer's method.
2. Through a cheesecloth-lined strainer, strain the juice and transfer into 2 glasses.
3. Serve immediately.
Nutrition:
- Per Serving : Protein 3.1 g | Fiber 18.4 g | Carbs 89.6 g | Fat 0.9 g

Star Anise & Cinnamon Tea

Servings: 2
Cooking Time: 15 Mins.
Ingredients:
- 7 star anise
- 1 (2-inch) cinnamon stick
- 2-3 C. water

Directions:
1. In a saucepan, add water over medium heat and bring to a rolling boil.
2. Add star anise and cinnamon stick and boil for about 10 minutes.
3. Remove from heat and steep, covered for about 3 minutes.
4. Strain the tea into two serving mugs and stir in the maple syrup.
5. Serve immediately.
Nutrition:
- Per Serving : Protein 0.7 g | Fiber 2.3 g | Carbs 4.4 g | Fat 0.6 g

Berries & Apple Juice

Servings: 2
Cooking Time: 10 Mins.
Ingredients:
- 1 C. fresh blackberries
- 1 C. fresh blueberries
- 1 C. fresh raspberries

- 2 large apples, cored and quartered
Directions:
1. Add all ingredients into a juicer and extract the juice according to the manufacturer's method.
2. Through a cheesecloth-lined strainer, strain the juice and transfer into 2 glasses.
3. Serve immediately.
Nutrition:
- Per Serving : Protein 2.9 g | Fiber 15 g | Carbs 0 g | Fat 1.4 g

Peach Gelatin

Servings: 10
Cooking Time: 5 Mins.
Ingredients:
- 2 tbsp. grass-fed gelatin powder
- 4 C. fresh peach juice, divided
- 2 tbsp. honey

Directions:
1. In a bowl, soak the gelatin in ½ C. of juice. Set aside for about 5 minutes.
2. In a medium pan, add the remaining juice over medium heat and bring to a gentle boil.
3. Remove from the heat and stir in honey.
4. Add the gelatin mixture and stir until dissolved.
5. Transfer the mixture into a large baking dish and refrigerate until set completely before serving.
Nutrition:
- Per Serving : Protein 2.2 g | Fiber 0 g | Carbs 16.1 g | Fat 0 g

Chicken Broth

Servings: 8
Cooking Time: 20 Minutes
Ingredients:
- 1 onion, cut into fours
- 2 carrots, roughly chopped
- 1 parsnip, peeled & chopped
- 2 stalks celery, roughly chopped
- 3 sprigs of parsley
- 4 pounds of whole chicken
- 5 black peppercorns
- 1 leek, chopped
- 16 cups of water
- 3 sprigs of fresh thyme
- 1 bay leaf

Directions:
1. Add all ingredients to a large pot.
2. Let it come to a boil, turn the heat low and simmer for 1 hour.
3. Strain & adjust seasoning.
4. Serve.
Nutrition:

- Per Serving : Protein 2 g | Fiber 1.3 g | Carbs 11 g | Fat 1.2 g

Clear Chicken Soup

Servings: 4
Cooking Time: 30 Minutes
Ingredients:
- 1 tbsp. of butter
- 2 cups of chicken with bones
- Water, as needed
- 2 scallions
- Salt, to taste
- 2 egg
- Black pepper, to taste

Directions:
1. In a pan, melt butter. Sauté the spring onion till it browns.
2. Add chicken & cook until it browns.
3. In a large pan, add water & boil. Add the chicken mixture.
4. Let it simmer for half an hour.
5. Strain & adjust seasoning. Add the whisked egg whites while stirring
6. Add salt & pepper, cook for 2 minutes. Strain & serve.

Nutrition:
- Per Serving : Protein 4 g | Fiber 1.0 g | Carbs 11 g | Fat 0.2 g

Peach Juice

Servings: 2
Cooking Time: 10 Mins.
Ingredients:
- 4 medium peaches, peeled, pitted and chopped
- 1 C. chilled water
- 1 tbsp. fresh lime juice

Directions:
1. Add all ingredients in a high-power blender and pulse until well combined.
2. Through a cheesecloth-lined strainer, strain the juice and transfer into 3 glasses.
3. Serve immediately.

Nutrition:
- Per Serving : Protein 2.8 g | Fiber 4.6 g | Carbs 28.1 g | Fat 0.8 g

Light & Delicious Seafood Soup

Servings: 6
Cooking Time: 40 Minutes
Ingredients:
- 2 tbsp. of olive oil
- 1 white onion, chopped
- 2 celery ribs, chopped
- 1 leek without the dark green part
- Salt and black pepper
- 2 cloves garlic, minced
- 1 pound of deveined & peeled shrimps
- 1 fennel bulb, sliced
- 1 tbsp. of lemon juice
- 5 cups of chicken broth
- 2 tsp. of dried oregano
- ¼ cup of chopped parsley
- Half tsp. of crushed red pepper flakes
- 1 pound scallops, trimmed
- 8 oz. of vegetable stock
- 2 bay leaves
- 2 tsp. of fresh thyme, chopped
- 1 pound of clams

Directions:
1. Wash the leek.
2. In a Dutch oven, add the butter on a medium flame.
3. Sauté the onion, fennel, celery & leek with salt & pepper for 8-10 minutes.
4. Add the garlic, pepper flakes & herbs sauté for 1 minute.
5. Add bay leaves broths & simmer for 10 minutes.
6. Add sea food & simmer for 5-10 minutes.
7. Strain & adjust seasoning. Serve.

Nutrition:
- Per Serving : Protein 6 g | Fiber 1.6 g | Carbs 17 g | Fat 7.2 g

Chilled Fruit Tea

Servings: 6
Cooking Time: 15 Minutes
Ingredients:
- 2 C. lemonade
- 2 peach and mango tea bags
- 2 C. boiling water
- 2 C. chilled pineapple juice
- 1 C. chilled orange juice
- 4½ oz. fresh strawberries, hulled and finely chopped

Directions:
1. In a pitcher, add lemonade and freeze, covered for about 3 hours.
2. In a large pitcher, place tea bags and top with boiling water.
3. Steep, covered for about 5 minutes.
4. Remove the tea bags and add in pineapple juice, orange juice, lemonade and strawberries.
5. Refrigerate to chill.
6. Through a fine mesh strainer, strain the tea and serve immediately.

Nutrition:
- Per Serving : Protein 0.8 g | Fiber 0.7 g | Carbs 25.3 g | Fat 0.3 g

Southern Sweet Iced Tea

Servings: 4
Cooking Time: 0 Minutes
Ingredients:
- Half cup of honey
- 8 cups of water
- 4 black tea bags

Directions:
1. Steep the tea bags in boiling water for 5 minutes.
2. Discard the tea bags add the rest of the ingredients.
3. Stir well & serve.

Nutrition:
- Per Serving : Protein 0.3 g | Fiber 0.2 g | Carbs 11 g | Fat 0.2 g

Raspberry Tea

Servings: 1
Cooking Time: 5 Mins.
Ingredients:
- 1-2 tsp. red raspberry tea leaves
- 1 C. boiling water
- 1 tsp. honey

Directions:
1. In the teapot, place the raspberry leaf tea and top with the boiling water.
2. Cover the pot and steep for 3-5 minutes.
3. Strain the tea into two serving mug and stir in the honey.
4. Serve immediately.

Nutrition:
- Per Serving : Protein 0 g | Fiber 0.3 g | Carbs 5.3 g | Fat 0 g

Apple Tea

Servings: 2
Cooking Time: 8 Minutes
Ingredients:
- 1 C. water
- 4 whole allspice
- 2 black tea bags
- 1 C. fresh apple juice
- 2 tsp. honey

Directions:
1. In a saucepan, add water and allspice and bring to a boil.
2. Add tea bags and remove from the heat.
3. Cover and brew for about 2 minutes.
4. Remove allspice and tea bags.
5. Stir in apple juice and honey and again place the pan over medium heat.
6. Cook for about 2-3 minutes or until heated completely.
7. Strain the tea into mugs and serve immediately.

Nutrition:
- Per Serving : Protein 0.1 g | Fiber 0.3 g | Carbs 19.8 g | Fat 0.2 g

Homemade Chicken Stock

Servings:6
Cooking Time: 2½ To 12½ Hours
Ingredients:
- 1 (2-pound) chicken carcass
- 5 celery stalks, chopped
- 4 carrots, chopped
- 1 white or Spanish onion, chopped
- 2 garlic cloves, crushed
- 2 bay leaves
- 1 teaspoon dried thyme
- 1 teaspoon dried sage
- 1 teaspoon black peppercorns
- Salt

Directions:
1. Salt
2. Preheat the oven to 425°F.
3. On a large baking sheet, spread out the chicken bones, celery, carrots, onion, garlic, and bay leaves. Sprinkle the thyme, sage, and peppercorns over the top. Roast for 20 to 30 minutes, or until the vegetables and bones have a rich brown color.
4. Transfer the roasted bones and vegetables to a large stockpot. Add 6 quarts of water and slowly bring to a boil over high heat. Lower the heat to medium-low and simmer for at least 2 hours and up to 12 hours. (The longer it cooks, the more flavor you will get.)
5. Carefully pour the mixture through a fine mesh strainer into a large bowl. Season with salt and serve hot.
6. Store in airtight containers in the refrigerator for up to 5 days or in the freezer for up to 4 months.

Nutrition:
- Per Serving : Protein 3 g | Fiber 0 g | Carbs 3 g | Fat 1 g

Lime Popsicles

Servings: 12
Cooking Time: 15 Mins.
Ingredients:
- ½ C. honey
- ½ C. fresh lime juice
- 3 C. cold water

Directions:
1. In a large-sized bowl, add honey and lime juice and beat until honey dissolves completely.
2. Add in cold water and mix well.
3. Through a cheesecloth-lined strainer, strain the mixture.
4. Transfer the mixture into the Popsicle molds and freeze for 4 hours before serving.

Nutrition:
- Per Serving : Protein 0 g | Fiber 70 g | Carbs 11.7 g | Fat 0 g

Iced Green Tea With Mint & Ginger

Servings: 4
Cooking Time: 10 Minutes
Ingredients:
- ¼ cup of peeled ginger, sliced
- 1/3 cup of honey
- 3-6 green tea bags
- 1 lemon, divided
- 6 cups of water
- Half cup of mint leaves

Directions:
1. In a pot, add ginger & water. Let it come to a boil, add mint & teabags. Steep for 15 minutes.
2. Strain & add honey.
3. Serve chilled.

Nutrition:
- Per Serving : Protein 0.1 g | Fiber 1.2 g | Carbs 18.7 g | Fat 0.2 g

Citrus Cucumber Sports Drink

Servings: 4
Cooking Time: 10 Mins.
Ingredients:
- 1 lime, sliced
- 1 lemon, sliced
- 1 cucumber, sliced
- 6 C. water
- 3-5 fresh mint leaves

Directions:
1. In a large pitcher, add all ingredients and stir to combine.
2. Through a cheesecloth-lined strainer, strain the punch into another large pitcher.
3. Refrigerate to chill before serving.

Nutrition:
- Per Serving : Protein 0.6 g | Fiber 0.6 g | Carbs 3.5 g | Fat 0.1 g

Easy Miso Soup

Servings: 10
Cooking Time: 20 Minutes
Ingredients:
- 1/3 cup seaweed
- 1 cup of scallions, chopped
- 3 sheets of nori
- 8 cups of water
- ½ cup of white miso paste
- 1 cup of mushrooms
- 2 cups of baby spinach
- 7 oz. of silken tofu, cubed

Directions:
1. In a pot, add water & boil. Add all the ingredients except for miso paste.

2. Cook for 5-7 minutes. Take some water out & mix with miso, add back to the soup.
3. Cook for a few minutes. Strain & Serve.

Nutrition:
- Per Serving : Protein 4 g | Fiber 2 g | Carbs 9 g | Fat 1 g

Strawberry Gelatin

Servings: 8
Cooking Time: 20 Mins.
Ingredients:
- 1 C. water, divided
- 2 lb. fresh strawberries, hulled and quartered
- 1½ C. monk fruit sweetener
- 4 tbsp. grass-fed gelatin powder

Directions:
1. In a large saucepan, add ½ C. of water and strawberries over medium heat and bring to a boil, stirring continuously.
2. Now adjust the heat to medium-low and simmer for about 8-10 minutes, crushing the strawberries with the back of a spoon.
3. Meanwhile, in a small bowl, add remaining water and sprinkle with gelatin powder.
4. Immediately whisk until dissolved and set aside for at least 5 minutes.
5. Through a cheesecloth-lined strainer, strain the strawberry mixture into a bowl, pressing with the back of a spoon.
6. Add more water to the juice to reach 3 C. liquid total.
7. Transfer the juice into clean saucepan over medium heat.
8. Add monk fruit sweetener and stir until dissolved.
9. Immediately Now adjust the heat to low.
10. Stir in the gelatin and cook for about 2 minutes, stirring continuously.
11. Transfer the mixture into a parchment paper-lined baking dish and refrigerate for 4-6 hours or until the top is firm before serving.

Nutrition:
- Per Serving : Protein 3 g | Fiber 1.8 g | Carbs 7 g | Fat 0.3 g

Beef Bones Broth

Servings: 8
Cooking Time: 8 Hours 5 Minutes
Ingredients:
- 2 lb. beef bones
- 1 onion, quartered
- 2 celery stalks, cut into chunks
- 2 carrots, peeled and cut into chunks
- 3 whole garlic cloves, peeled
- 2 bay leaves
- 2 tbsp. apple cider vinegar
- Salt, as require
- 1 tbsp. peppercorns

- Cold water, as required

Directions:
1. In a large-sized Dutch oven, add all ingredients.
2. Add enough cold water just to cover the bones mixture.
3. Place the over high heat and bring to a boil.
4. Now adjust the heat to low and simmer, uncovered for about 8 hours, skimming the foam from the surface occasionally.
5. Through a fine-mesh sieve, strain the broth into a large bowl.
6. Serve hot.

Nutrition:
- Per Serving : Protein 29.9 g | Fiber 0.9 g | Carbs 3.5 g | Fat 8.4 g

Lemon Ginger Detox Tea

Servings: 1-2
Cooking Time: 5 Minutes
Ingredients:
- ¼ tsp. of turmeric
- 2 cups of water
- 1 inch of peeled ginger, sliced thin
- ¼ tsp. of maple syrup
- 1 lemon
- Cayenne pepper, a pinch

Directions:
1. In a pan, add all ingredients. Mix & heat until it starts to steam.
2. Turn the heat off & steep for 5 minutes.
3. Strain & serve.

Nutrition:
- Per Serving : Protein 0.3 g | Fiber 0.6 g | Carbs 2.8 g | Fat 0.2 g

Beet Juice

Servings: 4
Cooking Time: 0 Minutes
Ingredients:
- 2 green apples, diced
- 2 beets, washed & trimmed
- 1 juice of 1 lemon
- 2 carrots, chopped
- 2 cups of water
- 2 peeled clementines
- 7 strawberries, trimmed
- 1" piece of fresh peeled ginger

Directions:
1. In a blender, add all the ingredients.
2. Pulse until smooth, strain & serve chilled.

Nutrition:
- Per Serving : Protein 0.1 g | Fiber 1.4 g | Carbs 14.6 g | Fat 0.3 g

Watermelon Juice

Servings: 4
Cooking Time: 0 Minutes
Ingredients:
- 3 lime wedges
- 4 cups of watermelon cubes
- 1 cup of ice
- 1-2 tbsp. of sugar
- Half tsp. of sea salt

Directions:
1. Add all ingredients to a blender. Pulse until smooth.
2. Strain & serve.

Nutrition:
- Per Serving : Protein 2 g | Fiber 3 g | Carbs 26 g | Fat 1 g

Gingerade

Servings: 2
Cooking Time: 10 Mins.
Ingredients:
- 2 tsp. fresh ginger juice
- 2 tsp. fresh lime juice
- 2 tsp. fresh lemon juice
- 12-14 drops liquid stevia
- 2 C. sparkling water
- Ice cubes, as required

Directions:
1. In a pitcher, mix together the juices and stevia.
2. Through a cheesecloth-lined strainer, strain the mixture into another pitcher.
3. Add the water and fill the pitcher with ice cubes.
4. Serve chilled.

Nutrition:
- Per Serving : Protein 0.2 g | Fiber 0.3 g | Carbs 1.4 g | Fat 0.2 g

Peach Iced Tea

Servings: 4
Cooking Time: 10 Minutes
Ingredients:
- 1 tea sachet (Earl Grey)
- 4 cups of ice
- 2 cups of water
- 2 tea sachets (English breakfast)
- Peach Syrup
- 2 tbsp. of white sugar
- 1 ½ cups of water
- 1 ½ cups of diced peaches

Directions:
1. Steep the teas as per package Directions. Discard the tea bags & cool them in the fridge for half an hour.
2. In a blender, add all the ingredients of peach syrup. Pulse until chopped.

3. Add to a pan heat for 5 minutes. Strain into the tea mix well & serve.

Nutrition:

- Per Serving : Protein 1 g | Fiber 1 g | Carbs 13 g | Fat 1 g

Orange, Cherries & Carrot Juice

Servings: 2
Cooking Time: 10 Mins.

Ingredients:

- 3 oranges, peeled and sectioned
- 2 C. fresh cherries, pitted
- 3 carrots, peeled and roughly chopped

Directions:

1. Add all ingredients into a juicer and extract the juice according to the manufacturer's method.
2. Through a cheesecloth-lined strainer, strain the juice and transfer into 2 glasses.
3. Serve immediately.

Nutrition:

- Per Serving : Protein 5.3 g | Fiber 11.9 g | Carbs 6.4 g | Fat 0.3 g

Antioxidant Blast Juice

Servings: 4
Cooking Time: 0 Minutes

Ingredients:

- 2 beets, trimmed & cut into wedges
- 1 cup of blueberries
- 1 cup of strawberries, halved
- Water, as needed

Directions:

1. Add all ingredients to a blender. Pulse until smooth.
2. Strain & serve.

Nutrition:

- Per Serving : Protein 1.3 g | Fiber 0.4 g | Carbs 12 g | Fat 0.3 g

Mixed Berries Gelatin

Servings: 8
Cooking Time: 5 Mins.

Ingredients:

- 2 C. frozen mixed berries
- 1 1/3 C. Swerve
- 2 C. water, divided
- ½ oz. grass-fed gelatin powder

Directions:

1. In a clean blender, add mixed berries and pulse until chopped finely.
2. Transfer the berry mixture into a small saucepan.
3. Add the sweetener and 1 C. of water and stir to combine.
4. Place the saucepan over medium heat and bring to a boil, stirring continuously.

5. Immediately remove from the heat and through a cheesecloth-lined strainer, strain the strawberry mixture into a bowl, pressing with the back of a spoon.
6. In a bowl, dissolve the gelatin in remaining water.
7. Add 2 C. of strained berry juice and stir to combine.
8. Transfer the mixture into a parchment paper-lined baking dish and refrigerate for 4-6 hours or until the top is firm before serving.

Nutrition:

- Per Serving : Protein 1.8 g | Fiber 1.3 g | Carbs 44.3 g | Fat 0.1 g

Red, White & Blue Finger Jell-o

Servings: 32
Cooking Time: 20 Minutes

Ingredients:

- 1 box of each Berry Blue, strawberry Jell-O
- Boiling water & cold water
- 4 packets of unflavored gelatin
- 1 can of (14 oz.) sweetened condensed milk

Directions:

1. Oil spray a 9 by 13" pan.
2. Mix the one packet of gelatin with blue Jell-O & 2 cups of water (boiling). Mix well.
3. Cool & add to the pan, firm in the fridge for half an hour.
4. Mix one cup of boiling water with condensed milk.
5. Mix the 2 packets of gelatin with a half cup of cold water. Let it rest for a few minutes, add half a cup of boiling water & mix. Add the condensed milk mixture.
6. Cool slightly & pour over the blue Jell-O. Firm in the fridge for half an hour.
7. Do the same procedure for the red layer as you did for the blue layer.
8. Slice & serve.

Nutrition:

- Per Serving : Protein 0.1 g | Fiber 1.2 g | Carbs 18.7 g | Fat 0.2 g

Pear Juice

Servings: 1
Cooking Time: 0 Minutes

Ingredients:

- Water, as needed
- 1 Pear, peeled & cut

Directions:

1. Add all ingredients to a blender. Pulse until smooth.
2. Strain & serve.

Nutrition:

- Per Serving : Protein 0.7 g | Fiber 1.0 g | Carbs 14 g | Fat 0.2 g

Carrot & Lemon Juice

Servings: 2
Cooking Time: 10 Mins.
Ingredients:

- 1 lb. carrots, peeled and chopped
- 2 lemons, peeled and seeded
- 1 C. water

Directions:
1. Add all ingredients in a high-power blender and pulse until well combined.
2. Through a cheesecloth-lined strainer, strain the juice and transfer into 2 glasses.
3. Serve immediately.

Nutrition:

- Per Serving : Protein 2 g | Fiber 6 g | Carbs 23.7 g | Fat 0.1 g

Chicken Bones Broth

Servings: 10
Cooking Time: 5 Hours 50 Minutes
Ingredients:

- 4 lb. chicken bones
- Salt, as required
- 10 C. filtered water
- 2 tbsp. apple cider vinegar
- 1 lemon, quartered
- 3 bay leaves
- 3 tsp. ground turmeric
- 2 tbsp. peppercorns

Directions:
1. Preheat the oven to 400 ºF.
2. Arrange the bones onto a large baking sheet and sprinkle with salt.
3. Roast for about 45 minutes.
4. Remove from the oven and transfer the bones into a large pan.
5. Add the remaining ingredients and stir to combine.
6. Place the pan over medium-high heat and bring to a boil.
7. Now adjust the heat to low and simmer, covered for about 4-5 hours, skimming the foam from the surface occasionally.
8. Through a fine-mesh sieve, strain the broth into a large bowl.
9. Serve hot.

Nutrition:

- Per Serving : Protein 25 g | Fiber 0.1 g | Carbs 0.6 g | Fat 2.6 g

Apple & Orange Juice

Servings: 2
Cooking Time: 10 Mins.
Ingredients:

- 5 apples, cored and quartered
- 1 lemon, peeled
- 1 C. fresh orange juice

Directions:
1. Place all the ingredients in a high-power blender and pulse until well combined
2. Through a cheesecloth-lined strainer, strain the juice and transfer into 2 glasses.
3. Serve immediately.

Nutrition:

- Per Serving : Protein 2.4 g | Fiber 14 g | Carbs 90.6 g | Fat 1.3 g

Lemon-rosemary Iced Tea

Servings: 4
Cooking Time: 15 Minutes
Ingredients:

- 1 cup of lemon juice
- 2 cups of sugar
- 5 cups of water
- 12 sprigs of fresh rosemary
- 1/4 cup of black tea leaves

Directions:
1. In a pan, add herbs, sugar & water. Simmer until sugar dissolves.
2. Turn the heat off. Add tea leaves & steep for 3 minutes.
3. Strain & serve with lemon juice.

Nutrition:

- Per Serving : Protein 1 g | Fiber 1 g | Carbs 104 g | Fat 1 g

Leeks Clear Soup

Servings: 2
Cooking Time: 20 Minutes
Ingredients:

- 4 to 5 cloves of Garlic
- 1 tbsp. of olive oil
- 1 cup of chopped Leeks
- 1 cup of chicken with bones
- Salt & black pepper, to taste
- 4 cups of Water

Directions:
1. Sauté the garlic for 30 seconds in hot oil. Add leeks & mushrooms, sauté for 2 to 3 minutes.
2. Add the rest of the ingredients.
3. Simmer for 10 to 15 minutes. Strain & serve.

Nutrition:

- Per Serving : Protein 0.1 g | Fiber 1.2 g | Carbs 18.7 g | Fat 0.2 g

Raspberry Tea Ice Lollies

Servings: 6
Cooking Time: 0 Minutes
Ingredients:

- 3 raspberry teabag
- 1 lime's juice
- 3.5 oz. of raspberries
- 1 tbsp. of maple syrup

Directions:

1. In a bowl, add all ingredients except for lime juice. Add 350 ml of water (boiling).
2. Stir well & steep for 10 minutes; take the tea bags, add the lime juice.
3. Pour in the molds. Keep in the freezer until they set.
4. Serve.

Nutrition:

- Per Serving : Protein 0.8 g | Fiber 1 g | Carbs 3 g | Fat 0 g

Herbed Pork Bones Broth

Servings: 8
Cooking Time: 9 Hours 5 Mins.
Ingredients:

- 2 lb. pork bones
- 1 onion,
- 4 celery stalks, cut into chunks
- 4 carrots, peeled and cut into chunks
- 3 whole garlic cloves, peeled
- 2 tbsp. apple cider vinegar
- 4 fresh thyme sprigs
- 4 fresh parsley sprigs
- Salt, as required
- Cold water, as required

Directions:

1. Preheat the oven to 450 °F.
2. Arrange the pork bones into a large roasting pan.
3. Bake for about 30 minutes.
4. Transfer the bones and vegetables into a large Dutch oven.
5. Pour the warm water into the roasting pan and with a wooden spoon, stir to loosen browned bits.
6. Transfer the pan juices into the Dutch oven.
7. Add the garlic, herbs, bay leaves, peppercorns and salt and stir to combine.
8. Add enough cold water just to cover the bones mixture.
9. Place the pan over high heat and bring to a boil.
10. Boil for about 30 minutes.
11. Now adjust the heat to low and simmer, uncovered for about 8 hours, skimming the foam from the surface occasionally.
12. Through a fine-mesh sieve, strain the broth into a large bowl.
13. Serve hot.

Nutrition:

- Per Serving : Protein 23.5 g | Fiber 1.2 g | Carbs 4.6 g | Fat 13.1 g

Ginger & Fennel Tea

Servings: 3
Cooking Time: 5 Mins.
Ingredients:

- 2 C. water
- 1 tbsp. fennel seeds, crushed slightly
- 1 (½-inch) piece fresh ginger, peeled and crushed slightly
- 2 tsp. maple syrup

Directions:

1. In a small saucepan, add water over medium heat and bring to a rolling boil.
2. Stir in the fennel seeds and ginger and remove from the heat.
3. Strain the tea into two serving mugs and stir in the maple syrup.
4. Serve immediately.

Nutrition:

- Per Serving : Protein 0.5 g | Fiber 1.6 g | Carbs 7.5 g | Fat 0.5 g

Mutton Soup

Servings: 4
Cooking Time: 1 Hour & 10 Minutes
Ingredients:

- 1 garlic clove
- 4 black peppercorn
- Salt & black pepper, to taste
- 7 oz. of Mutton with bone
- 4 to 5 cups of water
- 1"cinnamon stick
- ½ tsp. of oil

Directions:

1. Sauté the cinnamon, peppercorn & clove in hot oil for a few seconds.
2. Add mutton cook until it is seared.
3. Add the rest of the ingredients. Cook for 60 minutes.
4. Adjust seasoning & strain. Serve.

Nutrition:

- Per Serving : Protein 5 g | Fiber 0.5 g | Carbs 11 g | Fat 5.2 g

Tangerine Gelatin

Servings: 4
Cooking Time: 10 Mins.
Ingredients:
- 1 tbsp. grass-fed tangerine gelatin powder
- 2¼ C. boiling water

Directions:
1. In a large bowl, add the gelatin and boiling water and stir until dissolved completely.
2. Divide in serving bowls and refrigerate until set completely before serving.

Nutrition:
- Per Serving : Protein 2.8 g | Fiber 0 g | Carbs 0.4 g | Fat 0 g

Vietnamese Canh

Servings: 2
Cooking Time: 40 Minutes
Ingredients:
- 1/4 white onion, sliced
- 4 cups of water
- Half tsp. of vegetable oil
- 4 oz. of white fish/shrimp, chopped
- 1 tbsp. of fish sauce
- 1-inch ginger, sliced

Directions:
1. Sauté onion in hot oil for 3 minutes.
2. Add ginger, water & fish sauce. Boil for 5 minutes, turn the heat to low.
3. Add vegetables, cook for 5 minutes.
4. Add seafood & let it cook until done. Strain & serve.

Nutrition:
- Per Serving : Protein 2 g | Fiber 0 g | Carbs 7 g | Fat 2.2 g

Limeade

Servings: 4
Cooking Time: 10 Mins.
Ingredients:
- 2/3 C. fresh lime juice
- 7 C. water
- 1 tsp. stevia extract
- Ice cubes, as required

Directions:
1. In a pitcher, place the water, lime juice and stevia and mix well.
2. Through a cheesecloth-lined strainer, strain the lemonade in another pitcher.
3. Refrigerate for 30-40 minutes.
4. Add ice cubes in serving glasses and fill with lemonade.
5. Serve chilled.

Nutrition:

- Per Serving : Protein 0 g | Fiber 0 g | Carbs 0.4 g | Fat 0 g

Homemade Beef Stock

Servings:6
Cooking Time: 2½ To 12½ Hours
Ingredients:
- 2 pounds beef bones (preferably with marrow)
- 5 celery stalks, chopped
- 4 carrots, chopped
- 1 white or Spanish onion, chopped
- 2 garlic cloves, crushed
- 2 bay leaves
- 1 teaspoon dried thyme
- 1 teaspoon dried sage
- 1 teaspoon black peppercorns
- Salt

Directions:
1. Salt
2. Preheat the oven to 425°F.
3. On a large baking sheet, spread out the beef bones, celery, carrots, onion, garlic, and bay leaves. Sprinkle the thyme, sage, and peppercorns over the top.
4. Roast for 20 to 30 minutes, or until the vegetables and bones have a rich brown color.
5. Transfer the roasted bones and vegetables to a large stockpot. Cover with water and slowly bring to a boil over high heat. Lower the heat to medium-low and simmer for at least 2 hours and up to 12 hours. (The longer it cooks, the more flavor you will get.)
6. Carefully pour the mixture through a fine mesh strainer into a large bowl. Taste and season with salt. Serve hot.
7. Store in airtight containers in the refrigerator for up to 5 days or in the freezer for up to 4 months.

Nutrition:
- Per Serving : Protein 4 g | Fiber 0 g | Carbs 3 g | Fat 1 g

Smooth Sweet Tea

Servings: 8
Cooking Time: 15 Minutes
Ingredients:
- 6 cups of cool water
- ¾ cup of white sugar
- 2 cups of boiling water
- 6 tea bags

Directions:
1. In a pitcher, add tea bags & boiling water. Mix & let it steep for 15 minutes.
2. Take the tea bags out & mix with sugar. Add cool water & keep it in the fridge.
3. Serve chilled.

Nutrition:

- Per Serving : Protein 0.1 g | Fiber 1.2 g | Carbs 18.7 g | Fat 0.2 g

Clear Fish Soup

Servings: 4
Cooking Time: 40 Minutes
Ingredients:
- 2 celery stalks
- 25 oz. of fish (mixed)
- 4 carrots
- 6 potatoes
- 1 onion
- Salt & pepper, to taste
- 2 tomatoes
- 2 tbsp. of oil
- 1 bay leaf

Directions:
1. Clean the fish add to a pot.
2. Add enough water & salt. Boil until half cooked.
3. Take the fish out & add the vegetables (peeled & chopped).
4. Cook until tender. Strain & serve with a drizzle of lemon juice.

Nutrition:
- Per Serving : Protein 2 g | Fiber 1 g | Carbs 11 g | Fat 1.8 g

Mussel Broth

Servings: 6
Cooking Time: 40 Minutes
Ingredients:
- 2 scallions, sliced
- 4 cups of fish stock
- 1 pinch of saffron
- 17 cups of mussels
- 2 tbsp. of olive oil
- ⅜ cup of white wine

Directions:
1. Sauté the scallion in hot oil for 60 seconds.
2. Add mussels with wine place a lid on top. Cook for 5 minutes.
3. Add the rest of the ingredients.
4. Adjust seasoning, strain & serve.

Nutrition:
- Per Serving : Protein 2 g | Fiber 0 g | Carbs 8 g | Fat 0 g

Turmeric Lemon & Ginger Tea

Servings: 4
Cooking Time: 15 Mins.
Ingredients:
- 6 C. water
- ½ of lemon, seeded and chopped roughly
- 1 (1-inch) piece fresh ginger, chopped

- 2 tbsp. maple syrup
- ¼ tsp. ground turmeric

Directions:
1. In a saucepan, add all ingredients over medium-high heat and bring to a boil.
2. Adjust the heat to medium-low and simmer for about 10-12 minutes.
3. Strain into C. and serve hot.

Nutrition:
- Per Serving : Protein 0.2 g | Fiber 0.3 g | Carbs 8 g | Fat 0.1 g

Seafood Stew

Servings: 4
Cooking Time: 60 Minutes
Ingredients:
- 1 shallot, sliced thin
- 1 1/2 cups of chicken stock
- 2 garlic cloves, chopped
- 2 tbsp. of olive oil
- ½ cup of dry white wine
- 1 cup of bottled clam juice
- Canned 1 cup drained tomatoes
- ½ pound of deveined & shelled shrimp
- 1 bay leaf
- 2 thyme sprigs
- ½ tsp. of hot sauce
- Salt and pepper, to taste
- 24 littleneck clams, washed
- 2 tbsp. of chopped parsley
- 3/4 pound of snapper fillets, skinless
- 2 tbsp. of unsalted butter

Directions:
1. In a pot, sauté the garlic & shallots in hot oil for 3 minutes.
2. Add wine & cook until reduced. Add the rest of the ingredients except for clams, snapper & shrimps.
3. Let it come to a boil, turn the heat low. Simmer for 10 minutes.
4. Add the rest of the seafood & cook for 5-7 minutes.
5. Serve.

Nutrition:
- Per Serving : Protein 7 g | Fiber 1.3 g | Carbs 12.1 g | Fat 5.2 g

Herbed Chicken Broth

Servings: 8
Cooking Time: 2 Hours 5 Minutes
Ingredients:
- 1 (3-lb.) whole chicken, cut into pieces
- 5 medium carrots, peeled and cut into 2-inch pieces
- 4 celery stalks with leaves, cut into 2-inch pieces
- 6 fresh thyme sprigs

- 6 fresh parsley sprigs
- Salt, as required
- 9 C. cold water

Directions:

1. In a large pan, add all the ingredients over medium-high heat and bring to a boil.
2. Now adjust the heat to medium-low and simmer, covered for about 2 hours, skimming the foam from the surface occasionally
3. Through a fine-mesh sieve, strain the broth into a large bowl.
4. Serve hot.

Nutrition:

- Per Serving : Protein 49.7 g | Fiber 1.2 g | Carbs 4.3 g | Fat 5.2 g

Chamomile Popsicles

Servings: 10
Cooking Time: 15 Mins.

Ingredients:

- 3 C. boiling water
- 1/3 C. honey
- 4 chamomile tea bags

Directions:

1. In a bowl, add boiling water and beat until honey dissolves completely.
2. Add tea bags and steep, covered for 10 minutes.
3. Through a cheesecloth-lined strainer, strain the mixture.
4. Transfer the mixture into the Popsicle melds and freeze for 4 hours before serving.

Nutrition:

- Per Serving : Protein 0 g | Fiber 0 g | Carbs 9.3 g | Fat 0 g

Apple Lime Sports Drink

Servings: 8
Cooking Time: 10 Mins.

Ingredients:

- 7 C. water
- 1 C. fresh apple juice
- 2-3 tsp. fresh lime juice
- 2 tbsp. honey
- ¼ tsp. salt

Directions:

1. In a large pitcher, add all ingredients and stir to combine.
2. Through a cheesecloth-lined strainer, strain the punch into another large pitcher.
3. Refrigerate to chill before serving.

Nutrition:

- Per Serving : Protein 0.1 g | Fiber 0.1 g | Carbs 7.8 g | Fat 0 g

Finger Jell-o

Servings: 36

Cooking Time: 5 Minutes

Ingredients:

- 3 Jell-O small boxes
- 4 1/2 cups of boiling water
- 4 envelopes of unflavored gelatin

Directions:

1. Boil some water.
2. Mix the gelatin with Jell-O. Add the boiling water & stir for 2 to 3 minutes.
3. Mix & pour into the dish.
4. Keep in the fridge for 4 hours. Slice & serve.

Nutrition:

- Per Serving : Protein 0.1 g | Fiber 1 g | Carbs 15 g | Fat 0 g

Strawberry & Watermelon Juice

Servings: 4
Cooking Time: 10 Mins.

Ingredients:

- 20 oz. seedless watermelon, cubed
- 8 oz. fresh strawberries, hulled
- 6 fresh mint leaves
- 1 tsp. fresh lime juice

Directions:

1. Add all ingredients in a high-power blender and pulse until well combined.
2. Through a cheesecloth-lined strainer, strain the juice and transfer into 4 glasses.
3. Serve immediately.

Nutrition:

- Per Serving : Protein 1.3 g | Fiber 1.8 g | Carbs 15.1 g | Fat 0.4 g

Healthy Fruit Juice

Servings: 1-2
Cooking Time: 0 Minutes

Ingredients:

- 1 cup of grapefruit, peeled
- 2 tbsp. of lemon juice
- 1 tbsp. of honey
- Half cup of ice cubes
- 1 cup of pomegranate seeds
- Half cup of water
- 1 orange

Directions:

1. In a blender, add all the fruits with the rest of the ingredients.
2. Strain the juice & serve.

Nutrition:

- Per Serving : Protein 0.8 g | Fiber 1.6 g | Carbs 10 g | Fat 1.2 g

Strawberry Limeade

Servings: 8
Cooking Time: 10 Mins.
Ingredients:

- 1½ C. fresh strawberries, hulled and sliced
- ¾ C. fresh lime juice
- 1½ tsp. stevia drops
- 5 C. water
- Ice cubes, as required

Directions:

1. Place strawberries and lime juice in a high-power blender and pulse until smooth.
2. Transfer the mixture into a pitcher and stir in stevia and water.
3. Through a cheesecloth-lined strainer, strain the mixture into another pitcher.
4. Add ice cubes in serving glasses and fill with limeade.
5. Serve chilled.

Nutrition:

- Per Serving : Protein 0.2 g | Fiber 0.5 g | Carbs 2.3 g | Fat 0.1 g

Chapter 3: High-fiber Recipes

Blackberry Smoothie

Servings: 2
Cooking Time: 10 Mins.
Ingredients:

- 2 C. frozen blackberries
- 1 small banana, peeled and sliced
- 2 tbsp. fresh lime juice
- 1 tbsp. honey
- 1 tsp. lime zest, grated
- ½ C. fat-free plain yogurt
- 1 C. light coconut milk

Directions:

1. Add all the ingredients in a high-power blender and pulse until creamy.
2. Pour the smoothie into two glasses and serve immediately.

Nutrition:

- Per Serving : Protein 6.1 g | Fiber 10.1 g | Carbs 44.6 g | Fat 7.6 g

Veggies & Avocado Salad

Servings: 4
Cooking Time: 15 Mins.
Ingredients:

- 1 cucumber, peeled and chopped
- 2 small tomatoes, peeled, seeded and chopped
- 1 small avocado, peeled, pitted and chopped
- ½ C. olives, pitted
- 3 C. fresh baby spinach
- 1½ tbsp. extra-virgin olive oil
- ½ tbsp. fresh lemon juice
- ½ tsp. dried oregano, crushed
- Salt and ground black pepper, as required
- 2 tbsp. feta cheese, crumbled

Directions:

1. In a large serving bowl, add all the ingredients except feta and toss to coat well.
2. Top with the feta and serve immediately.

Nutrition:

- Per Serving : Protein 6.7 g | Fiber 10.8 g | Carbs 22.1 g | Fat 36.3 g

Peach & Raspberry Smoothie

Servings: 2
Cooking Time: 10 Mins.
Ingredients:

- 1 C. frozen peaches
- 1 C. frozen raspberries
- 4 tbsp. old-fashioned oat
- ¼ tsp. vanilla extract
- ¼ tsp. ground cinnamon
- 1 C. oat milk
- ½ C. filtered water

Directions:

1. Add all the ingredients in a high-power blender and pulse until creamy.
2. Pour the smoothie into two glasses and serve immediately.

Nutrition:

- Per Serving : Protein 6 g | Fiber 8.3 g | Carbs 40.1 g | Fat 3.1 g

Pork Sausages With Cider Lentils

Servings: 4
Cooking Time: 50 Minutes
Ingredients:

- 2 tbsp. of olive oil
- 8 thick pork sausages
- 1 small bunch of thyme
- 2 onions, diced
- 2 cups of green lentils, rinsed
- 1 1/3 cups of Chicken Stock
- 3 garlic cloves, minced
- 1 apple, peeled & cubed
- 1 bay leaf
- 1 1/3 cups of alcoholic apple cider

Directions:

1. Cook lentils for 15 to 20 minutes in boiling water, drain.
2. Cook sausages in hot oil for 6 to 8 minutes. Take it out on a plate.
3. Sauté garlic & onion in hot oil for 2-3 minutes.
4. Add seasoning, thyme, bay leaf & apple, cook for 3-4 minutes.
5. Add stock cider cook for 7 to 8 minutes.
6. Add the sausage back to the pan cook for 4 to 5 minutes.
7. Serve.

Nutrition:

- Per Serving : Protein 8 g | Fiber 12 g | Carbs 12 g | Fat 7 g

Banana Oat Pancakes

Servings: 3
Cooking Time: 12 Mins.
Ingredients:

- 2 tbsp. flaxseed meal
- 5 tbsp. water
- 1½ C. rolled oats
- ¼ C. unsweetened vegan protein powder
- 1 tsp. baking powder
- ½ tsp. baking soda
- ¼ tsp. salt
- 1½ C. unsweetened almond milk
- 2 tbsp. olive oil
- 2 tsp. vanilla extract

Directions:

1. In a large bowl, add the flaxseed meal and water and mix well.
2. Set aside for about 10 minutes.
3. In another large bowl, add the oats, protein powder, baking powder, baking soda and salt and mix well.
4. In the bowl of flaxseed meal, add the almond milk, oil and vanilla extract and beat until well combined.
5. Add the almond milk mixture into the flour mixture and beat until well combined.

6. Set aside for about 10-12 minutes.
7. Heat a lightly greased wok over medium heat.
8. Add desired amount of mixture and with a spoon, spread into an even layer.
9. Cook about 1-2 minutes per side.
10. Repeat with the remaining mixture.
11. Serve warm.

Nutrition:

- Per Serving : Protein 15.2 g | Fiber 5.9 g | Carbs 31.2 g | Fat 16.3 g

Beans & Oat Falafels

Servings: 3
Cooking Time: 20 Mins.
Ingredients:

- ½ C. pumpkin seeds
- ½ C. oats
- 2 tsp. dried oregano
- 1 tsp. ground coriander
- 1 tsp. ground cumin
- 2 C. canned black beans, rinsed and drained
- 2 tbsp. tomato paste
- 2 tbsp. fresh lime juice
- 1 tbsp. whole-wheat flour
- 2 cucumbers, peeled and sliced

Directions:

1. Preheat your oven to 350 °F. Line a baking sheet with a greased parchment paper.
2. For falafels: in a food processor, add the pumpkin seeds, oats, oregano and spices and pulse until oats are broken down.
3. Add the black beans, tomato paste, lime juice and flour and mix until well combined.
4. Make equal-sized 9 balls from the mixture.
5. Arrange the balls onto the prepared baking sheet in a single layer and gently press each slightly.
6. Bake for approximately 20 minutes.
7. Divide the salad and falafels onto serving plates evenly and serve.

Nutrition:

- Per Serving : Protein 19.4 g | Fiber 14.3 g | Carbs 52.4 g | Fat 15.8 g

Three Veggies Combo

Servings: 4
Cooking Time: 25 Mins.
Ingredients:

- 1 tbsp. olive oil
- 1 small onion, chopped
- 1 tsp. fresh thyme, chopped
- 1 garlic clove, minced
- 8 oz. fresh button mushroom, sliced
- 1 lb. Brussels sprouts, trimmed

- 3 C. fresh spinach
- 4 tbsp. walnuts
- Salt and ground black pepper, as required

Directions:

1. In a large wok, heat the oil over medium heat and sauté the onion for about 3-4 minutes.
2. Add the thyme and garlic and sauté for about 1 minute.
3. Add the mushrooms and cook for about 15 minutes or until caramelized.
4. Add the Brussels sprouts and cook for about 2-3 minutes.
5. Stir in the spinach and cook for about 3-4 minutes.
6. Stir in the walnuts, salt and black pepper and remove from the heat.
7. Serve hot.

Nutrition:

- Per Serving : Protein 8.5 g | Fiber 6.9 g | Carbs 15.8 g | Fat 8.8 g

Buckwheat Porridge

Servings: 4
Cooking Time: 10 Mins.

Ingredients:

- 2 C. buckwheat groats, soaked overnight and rinsed well
- 1½ C. unsweetened almond milk
- 2 tbsp. chia seed
- 1 tsp. vanilla extract
- ¼ C. maple syrup
- 1 tsp. ground cinnamon
- Pinch of salt
- ½ C. mixed fresh berries

Directions:

1. Place the buckwheat groats, almond milk, chia seeds and vanilla extract in a food processor and pulse until well combined.
2. Add the maple syrup, cinnamon, and salt and pulse until smooth.
3. Transfer the mixture into serving bowls and serve immediately topped with berries.

Nutrition:

- Per Serving : Protein 9.6 g | Fiber 11.3 g | Carbs 65.3 g | Fat 5.5 g

Turkey Tortilla Wrap

Servings: 2
Cooking Time: 0 Minutes

Ingredients:

- 2 to 3 tbsp. of Greek yogurt
- 2 tsp. of lemon juice
- ½ avocado
- 4 oz. of sliced turkey
- 2 spinach leaves
- Salt and pepper, to taste

- 2 whole-grain tortillas
- 1 large Roma tomato, sliced thin

Directions:

1. In a food processor, pulse the avocado, pepper, yogurt, salt & lemon juice. Pulse until smooth.
2. Place one tortilla and add some of the yogurt creams with the rest of the ingredients on top.
3. Roll & slice. Serve.

Nutrition:

- Per Serving : Protein 8 g | Fiber 8.9 g | Carbs 12 g | Fat 4.2 g

Vanilla Chia Pudding

Servings: 2
Cooking Time: 10 Mins.

Ingredients:

- 1 C. unsweetened almond milk
- 1/3 C. chia seeds
- 1 tsp. vanilla liquid stevia
- 1 tsp. vanilla extract
- Pinch of salt
- ¼ C. fresh strawberries, hulled and sliced

Directions:

1. Place all the ingredients except the strawberries in a bowl and whisk them until well combined.
2. Refrigerate the mixture for at least 10 minutes before serving.
3. Top the mixture with strawberry slices and serve.

Nutrition:

- Per Serving : Protein 8.6 g | Fiber 16.9 g | Carbs 21.3 g | Fat 13.8 g

Pasta & Chickpeas Curry

Servings: 6
Cooking Time: 40 Mins.

Ingredients:

- 10 oz. whole-wheat pasta
- 1 tbsp. olive oil
- 1 medium onion, chopped
- 3 garlic cloves, minced
- 1 tsp. dried basil, crushed
- 2 lb. ripe tomatoes, peeled, seeded and chopped
- 4 C. cauliflower, cut into bite-sized pieces
- 1 medium bell pepper, seeded and sliced thinly
- 1 C. water
- 1 (15-oz.) can chickpeas, drained and rinsed
- 1 C. fresh baby spinach
- ¼ C. fresh parsley, chopped
- Salt, as required

Directions:

1. In a saucepan of salted boiling water, add the pasta and cook for about 8-10 minutes or according to package's directions.

2. Drain the pasta well and set aside.

3. Heat the oil in a large cast-iron wok over medium heat and sauté the onion for about 4-5 minutes.

4. Add the garlic and basil and sauté for about 1 minute.

5. Stir in the tomatoes, cauliflower, bell pepper and water and bring to a gentle boil.

6. Now adjust the heat to medium-low and simmer, covered for about 15-20 minutes.

7. Stir in the chickpeas and cook for about 5 minutes.

8. Add the spinach and cook for about 3-4 minutes.

9. Stir in the pasta and serve hot.

Nutrition:
- Per Serving : Protein 15.1 g | Fiber 10.3 g | Carbs 58.4 g | Fat 5.9 g

Fruity Ginger Juice

Servings: 2
Cooking Time: 10 Mins.

Ingredients:
- 2 apples, cored and roughly chopped
- 2 pears, cored and roughly chopped
- 2 kiwi fruits, halved
- 1 (¾-inch) piece fresh ginger, peeled and sliced
- ½-¾ C. filtered water

Directions:
1. Add all ingredients in a high-power blender and pulse until well combined.

2. Through a cheesecloth-lined sieve, strain the juice and pour into two glasses.

3. Serve immediately.

Nutrition:
- Per Serving : Protein 2.5 g | Fiber 14.5 g | Carbs 75.7 g | Fat 1.3 g

Kiwi, Apple & Cucumber Juice

Servings: 2
Cooking Time: 10 Mins.

Ingredients:
- 4 kiwi fruit, peeled
- 3 Granny Smith apples, cored and quartered
- 1 large cucumber, roughly chopped

Directions:
1. Add all ingredients into a juicer and extract the juice according to the manufacturer's method.

2. Through a cheesecloth-lined strainer, strain the juice and transfer into 2 glasses.

3. Serve immediately.

Nutrition:
- Per Serving : Protein 3.6 g | Fiber 13.4 g | Carbs 73.9 g | Fat 1.6 g

Pear & Fennel Juice

Servings: 2
Cooking Time: 10 Mins.

Ingredients:
- 3 pears, cored and quartered
- 3 C. fresh kale
- 1 fennel bulb
- 1 (½-inch) piece fresh ginger, peeled

Directions:
1. Add all ingredients into a juicer and extract the juice according to the manufacturer's method.

2. Through a cheesecloth-lined strainer, strain the juice and transfer into 2 glasses.

3. Serve immediately.

Nutrition:
- Per Serving : Protein 5.7 g | Fiber 15 g | Carbs 67.4 g | Fat 0.7 g

Pumpkin Oatmeal

Servings: 4
Cooking Time: 10 Mins.

Ingredients:
- 2¼ C. hot water
- ½ C. pumpkin puree
- ½ C. rolled oats
- 1 tsp. ground cinnamon
- 1 tsp. ground ginger
- ¼ tsp. ground nutmeg
- 2 scoops unsweetened protein powder
- 1 tbsp. maple syrup
- 1 small banana, peeled and sliced

Directions:
1. In a microwave-safe bowl, place water, pumpkin puree, oats and spices and mix well.

2. Microwave on High for about 2 minutes.

3. Remove the bowl of oatmeal from the microwave and stir in the protein powder and maple syrup.

4. Top with banana slices and serve immediately.

Nutrition:
- Per Serving : Protein 29.4 g | Fiber 6 g | Carbs 38.8 g | Fat 2.9 g

Beans With Tomatoes

Servings: 4
Cooking Time: 30 Mins.

Ingredients:
- 1 tbsp. olive oil
- 2 small onions, chopped
- 5 garlic cloves, chopped finely
- 1 tsp. of dried oregano
- 1 tsp. ground cumin
- Salt and ground black pepper, as required
- 2 C. tomatoes, peeled, seeded and chopped
- 2 (13½-oz.) cans black beans, rinsed and drained
- ½ C. homemade vegetable broth

Directions:

1. In a saucepan, heat the olive oil over medium heat and cook the onion for about 5-7 minutes, stirring frequently.
2. Add the garlic, oregano, spices, salt and black pepper and cook for about 1 minute.
3. Add the tomatoes and cook for about 1-2 minutes.
4. Add in the beans and broth and bring to a boil.
5. Now adjust the heat to medium-low and simmer, covered for about 15 minutes.
6. Serve hot.

Nutrition:
- Per Serving : Protein 19.1 g | Fiber 18.8 g | Carbs 54.1 g | Fat 5.1 g

Baked Veggie Stew

Servings: 4
Cooking Time: 55 Mins.
Ingredients:
- 2 tbsp. olive oil, divided
- 1 small onion, chopped and divided
- 2 garlic cloves, minced and divided
- 1 large carrot, peeled and chopped
- 2 parsnips, peeled and chopped
- 1 large sweet potato, peeled and chopped
- ½ C. fresh mushrooms, chopped
- ¼ C. fresh rosemary, chopped
- 1¼ C. vegetable broth
- Salt and ground black pepper, as required

Directions:
1. Preheat your oven to 375 °F.
2. In a large wok, heat 1¼ tbsp. of the oil over medium heat and sauté half of the onion and 1 garlic clove for about 4-5 minutes.
3. Add the carrot, parsnip and sweet potato and sauté for about 4-5 minutes.
4. Transfer the carrot mixture into a large casserole dish evenly.
5. In another wok, heat the remaining oil over medium heat and sauté the remaining onion, garlic, mushrooms and rosemary for about 4-5 minutes.
6. Stir in the broth and bring to a boil.
7. Stir in the salt and black pepper and remove from the heat.
8. Place the mushroom mixture over the vegetable mixture evenly.
9. Bake for approximately 30-40 minutes or until top becomes golden brown.
10. Serve hot.

Nutrition:
- Per Serving : Protein 4 g | Fiber 7.1 g | Carbs 27 g | Fat 8.3 g

Broccoli, Apple & Orange Juice

Servings: 2
Cooking Time: 10 Mins.

Ingredients:
- 2 broccoli stalks, chopped
- 2 large green apples, cored and quartered
- 3 large oranges, peeled and sectioned
- 4 tbsp. fresh parsley

Directions:
1. Add all ingredients into a juicer and extract the juice according to the manufacturer's method.
2. Through a cheesecloth-lined strainer, strain the juice and transfer into 2 glasses.
3. Serve immediately.

Nutrition:
- Per Serving : Protein 3.8 g | Fiber 12.7 g | Carbs 64.7 g | Fat 0.8 g

Kiwi & Orange Salad

Servings: 2
Cooking Time: 10 Mins.
Ingredients:
- For Salad:
- 2 oranges, peeled, seeded and cut into chunks
- 2 kiwi fruit, peeled and cut into chunks
- 2 tbsp. fresh mint leaves, chopped
- 2 tbsp. almonds, toasted and chopped
- For Dressing:
- ½ tsp. fresh ginger, grated finely
- tbsp. raw honey
- 1 tbsp. extra-virgin olive oil
- 1 tbsp. fresh lime juice

Directions:
1. For salad: in a large bowl, add all the ingredients except almonds and mix.
2. For dressing: in another bowl, add all the ingredients and beat until well combined.
3. Place the dressing over salad mixture and toss to coat well.
4. Serve immediately with the garnishing of almonds.

Nutrition:
- Per Serving : Protein 4.1 g | Fiber 7.9 g | Carbs 43.6 g | Fat 10.7 g

Beef & Three Beans Chili

Servings: 8
Cooking Time: 1 Hour
Ingredients:
- 2 lb. lean ground beef
- 1 tbsp. olive oil
- 2½ C. bell pepper, seeded and chopped
- 1½ C. onion, chopped
- 2 garlic cloves, minced
- 1 tbsp. dried oregano, crushed
- 1 tbsp. ground cumin
- 1 (15-oz.) can cannellini beans, rinsed and drained

- 1 (15-oz.) can black beans, rinsed and drained
- 1 (15-oz.) can red kidney beans, rinsed and drained
- 4 C. tomatoes, peeled, seeded and chopped
- Water, as required
- 8 oz. tomato paste
- 2 tbsp. balsamic vinegar

Directions:
1. Heat a large pan over medium heat and cook beef for about 5-8 minutes or until browned completely.
2. With a slotted spoon, transfer the beef into a bowl.
3. Drain the grease from the pan.
4. In the same pan, heat oil over medium-high heat and sauté bell pepper and onion for about 5-6 minutes.
5. Add garlic, thyme and spices and sauté for about 1 minute.
6. Stir in cooked beef, beans, tomatoes and enough water to cover and bring to a boil.
7. Stir in tomato paste and again bring to a boil.
8. Now adjust the heat to low and simmer, covered for about 30-35 minutes.
9. Remove from the heat and immediately stir in vinegar.
10. Serve hot.

Nutrition:
- Per Serving : Protein 47.8 g | Fiber 14.8 g | Carbs 44.9 g | Fat 10.5 g

Baked Pears With Homemade Granola

Servings:8
Cooking Time: 40 Minutes
Ingredients:
- FOR THE GRANOLA
- 1 cup rolled oats
- ¼ cup almonds
- 1 tablespoon chia seeds
- 1 tablespoon hemp seeds
- 1 tablespoon pumpkin or sunflower seeds
- ½ teaspoon ground cinnamon
- Pinch salt
- 1 tablespoon coconut oil, melted
- 2 teaspoons maple syrup
- ¼ teaspoon vanilla extract
- FOR THE PEARS
- 4 Anjou pears
- ½ cup maple syrup
- 1 teaspoon vanilla extract
- ½ teaspoon ground cinnamon

Directions:
1. ½ teaspoon ground cinnamon
2. Preheat the oven to 375°F. Line a baking sheet with parchment paper.

3. In a large bowl, mix together the oats, almonds, chia seeds, hemp seeds, pumpkin seeds, cinnamon, and salt.
4. In a small bowl, mix together the coconut oil, maple syrup, and vanilla. Drizzle the mixture over the oat mixture and stir to combine.
5. Spread the oat mixture out onto the prepared baking sheet. Bake for 10 minutes and stir well. Continue to bake for another 10 minutes. Let cool on a wire rack.
6. Line the baking sheet with another sheet of parchment paper.
7. Cut the pears in half lengthwise. Cut a very small slice off the rounded side of each half, which will help the pears sit flat. Using a melon baller or a spoon, scoop out the core and seeds. Place the pear halves on the prepared baking sheet.
8. Spoon the granola into the pears.
9. In a small bowl, whisk together the maple syrup and vanilla and drizzle it over the pears. Sprinkle the cinnamon over the pear halves.
10. Bake for 15 to 20 minutes, or until the pears are cooked through and tender. Serve immediately.

Nutrition:
- Per Serving : Protein 4 g | Fiber 5 g | Carbs 34 g | Fat 2 g

Mexican Quinoa Wraps

Servings: 6
Cooking Time: 10 Minutes
Ingredients:
- 1 onion, chopped
- 1 cup of uncooked quinoa
- 15 oz. of canned black beans
- 1 red pepper, chopped
- 7 oz. of canned corn

Directions:
1. Cook quinoa. Chop the vegetables.
2. Sauté the vegetables in hot oil for 5 minutes.
3. In each tortilla, add some of the ingredients. Roll & serve.

Nutrition:
- Per Serving : Protein 15 g | Fiber 8 g | Carbs 18.7 g | Fat 22 g

Quinoa & Veggie Stew

Servings: 4
Cooking Time: 1 Hour
Ingredients:
- 2 tbsp. olive oil
- 1 large onion, chopped
- Salt, as required
- 2 C. butternut squash, peeled and cubed
- 3 garlic cloves, minced
- 1 tsp. ground cumin
- 2½ C. tomatoes, peeled, seeded and chopped finely

- ½ C. quinoa, rinsed
- 3 C. water
- 3 C. fresh kale, tough ribs removed and chopped
- 1 tbsp. fresh lime juice

Directions:

1. In a soup pan, heat olive oil over medium heat and cook the onion with few pinches of salt for about 4-5 minutes, stirring occasionally.
2. Add the butternut squash and cook for about 3-4 minutes.
3. Stir in the garlic and spices and cook for about 1 minute.
4. Stir in the tomatoes, quinoa and water and bring to a boil.
5. Now adjust the heat to low and simmer, covered for about 35 minutes.
6. Stir in the kale and cook for about 10 minutes.
7. Serve hot.

Nutrition:

- Per Serving : Protein 6.9 g | Fiber 6.9 g | Carbs 36.2 g | Fat 8.6 g

Avocado & Tomato Sandwich

Servings: 2
Cooking Time: 10 Mins.

Ingredients:

- ¼ C. onion, sliced thinly
- 1 medium tomato, sliced
- 1 small avocado, peeled, pitted and chopped
- 4 romaine lettuce leaves, chopped
- 4 whole-wheat bread slices, toasted
- 2 tbsp. Dijon mustard

Directions:

1. In a large bowl, add the onion, tomato, avocado and lettuce and mix well.
2. Spread Dijon mustard over each bread slice evenly.
3. Divide avocado mixture over 2 slices evenly.
4. Close with remaining 2 slices.
5. With a knife, cut each sandwich in half diagonally and serve.

Nutrition:

- Per Serving : Protein 9.8 g | Fiber 9.2 g | Carbs 32.9 g | Fat 13.7 g

Simple Quinoa Porridge

Servings: 4
Cooking Time: 10 Mins.

Ingredients:

- For Porridge:
- 2 C. unsweetened coconut milk
- 2 C. water
- 2 tbsp. creamy peanut butter
- 1 C. quinoa flakes
- Pinch of salt

- For Topping:
- 2 bananas, peeled and sliced
- 4 tbsp. walnuts, chopped

Directions:

1. In a saucepan, add the coconut milk and water over medium-high heat and bring to a boil.
2. Add the peanut butter and stir until well combined.
3. Stir in the quinoa and salt and cook for about 3-5 minutes, stirring continuously.
4. Remove from the heat and set aside, covered for about 2-3 minutes.
5. Divide the porridge into serving bowls and serve with the topping of banana slices and walnuts.

Nutrition:

- Per Serving : Protein 12 g | Fiber 6.5 g | Carbs 46.1 g | Fat 27.9 g

Pear & Kale Salad

Servings: 4
Cooking Time: 10 Mins.

Ingredients:

- 4 large pears, cored and sliced
- 4 C. fresh baby kale
- ¼ C. walnuts, chopped
- 2 tbsp. olive oil
- 1 tbsp. maple syrup
- Salt, as required

Directions:

1. In a salad bowl, place all ingredients and toss to coat well.
2. Serve immediately.

Nutrition:

- Per Serving : Protein 4.6 g | Fiber 8 g | Carbs 43 g | Fat 11.9 g

Chickpeas With Swiss Chard

Servings: 4
Cooking Time: 15 Mins.

Ingredients:

- 2 tbsp. olive oil
- 1 medium onion, chopped
- 4 garlic cloves, minced
- 1 tsp. dried thyme, crushed
- 1 tsp. dried oregano, crushed
- 1 C. tomato, chopped finely
- 2½ C. canned chickpeas, rinsed and drained
- 5 C. Swiss chard, chopped
- 2 tbsp. water
- 2 tbsp. fresh lemon juice
- Salt and ground black pepper, as required
- 3 tbsp. fresh basil, chopped

Directions:

1. In a wok, heat the olive oil over medium heat and sauté the onion for about 6-8 minutes.
2. Add the garlic and herbs and sauté for about 1 minute.
3. Add the Swiss chard and 2 tbsp. of water and cook for about 2-3 minutes.
4. Add the tomatoes and chickpeas and cook for about 2-3 minutes.
5. Add in the lemon juice, salt and black pepper and remove from the heat.
6. Serve hot with the garnishing of basil.

Nutrition:
- Per Serving : Protein 12 g | Fiber 9 g | Carbs 34 g | Fat 8.6 g

Avocado Chia Pudding Four Ways

Servings:4
Cooking Time: 2 Hours
Ingredients:
- FOR THE PUDDING BASE
- 2 cups milk of choice
- ½ avocado, mashed
- ½ cup chia seeds
- 3 tablespoons honey, plus more as needed
- ½ teaspoon vanilla extract
- FLAVOR OPTIONS
- CHOCOLATE
- ¼ cup unsweetened cocoa powder
- PUMPKIN SPICE
- ½ cup pumpkin puree
- 1 teaspoon ground cinnamon
- ¼ teaspoon ground ginger
- Pinch ground cloves
- APPLE PIE
- ½ cup applesauce
- 1 teaspoon ground cinnamon
- ¼ teaspoon ground ginger
- Pinch ground cloves
- BERRY
- ½ cup berries of choice

Directions:
1. ½ cup berries of choice
2. Put the milk, avocado, chia seeds, honey, and vanilla in a food processor or a blender and puree until smooth. Taste, and add more honey, if desired.
3. Add the ingredients for your choice of flavors and puree.
4. Pour the mixture into bowls or mason jars, cover, and refrigerate for at least 2 hours.

Nutrition:
- Per Serving : Protein 11 g | Fiber 12 g | Carbs 31 g | Fat 11 g

Farro Risotto

Servings:4

Cooking Time: 20 Minutes
Ingredients:
- 1 cup farro
- 1 tablespoon butter or margarine
- ½ cup diced white or Spanish onion
- 2 garlic cloves, minced
- 2½ cups Homemade Chicken Stock or store-bought
- 1 cup chopped fresh spinach
- 1 cup frozen mixed peas and carrots
- ¼ cup whipping cream
- ¼ cup grated Parmesan cheese
- Salt
- Freshly ground black pepper

Directions:
1. Freshly ground black pepper
2. Place the farro in a colander and rinse in cold water.
3. In a large saucepan over medium heat, melt the butter. Add the onion and cook until the onions are translucent, about 3 minutes. Add the garlic and cook for 1 minute.
4. Raise the heat to high, add the stock and farro, and bring to a boil. Lower the heat to medium-low and simmer until all the stock is absorbed, about 15 minutes.
5. Add the spinach, frozen peas and carrots, whipping cream, and Parmesan cheese and stir to combine. Cook until heated through. Taste and season with salt and pepper. Serve hot.

Nutrition:
- Per Serving : Protein 14 g | Fiber 7 g | Carbs 45 g | Fat 12 g

Breakfast Salad

Servings: 1
Cooking Time: 5minutes
Ingredients:
- 1 tbsp. + 1 tsp. olive oil
- 8 blue corn tortilla chips, chopped up
- ¼ avocado, sliced
- 2 tbsp. of chopped cilantro
- 3 tbsp. of salsa verde
- 2 cups of salad greens
- ½ cup of canned kidney beans, rinsed
- 1 egg

Directions:
1. Mix cilantro, salsa & one tbsp. of oil. Add the salad greens & toss.
2. Add the avocado, beans & chips on top.
3. Fry eggs in one tsp. of oil for 2 minutes.
4. Serve the salad with an egg on top.

Nutrition:
- Per Serving : Protein 16 g | Fiber 13 g | Carbs 37 g | Fat 30 g

Chickpeas & Kale Salad

Servings: 3
Cooking Time: 3 Mins.
Ingredients:
- For Salad:
- 1 tsp. olive oil
- 1 (14-oz.) can chickpeas, rinsed and drained
- 2 C. fresh kale, tough ribs removed and torn into pieces
- For Dressing:
- ½ C. cashews, soaked and drained
- 1 small garlic clove, peeled
- 1 tbsp. fresh lemon juice
- ½ tsp. Dijon mustard
- Salt and ground black pepper, as required

Directions:
1. For salad: in a non-stick wok, heat the oil over medium-low heat and cook the chickpeas for about 2-3 minutes, stirring frequently.
2. Remove from the heat and transfer the chickpeas into a bowl. Set aside to cool.
3. Meanwhile, for dressing: in a blender, add all the ingredients and pulse until smooth.
4. In the bowl of chickpeas, add the kale and dressing and toss to coat well.
5. Serve immediately.

Nutrition:
- Per Serving : Protein 13.9 g | Fiber 7.8 g | Carbs 45.2 g | Fat 14.5 g

Blue Corn Waffles Rancheros

Servings: 4
Cooking Time: 50minutes
Ingredients:
- Chipotle Aioli
- 1 egg yolk
- ¼ cup of avocado oil
- ¼ cup of chipotle peppers in adobo
- ⅛ tsp. of salt
- 1 tsp. of lemon juice
- 1 clove garlic, diced
- Tomatillo Salsa
- 1 onion, thickly sliced
- ⅛ tsp. of salt
- ½ jalapeño pepper (optional)
- 8 oz. of tomatillos
- 1 clove garlic
- 1 tbsp. of chopped fresh cilantro
- Waffles & Topping
- ½ cup of masa harina
- 2 tsp. of baking powder
- 1 ¼ cups of blue cornmeal
- ¼ tsp. of salt

- 5 eggs
- 1 cup of milk
- 3 tbsp. butter, melted
- 1 can (15 oz.) black beans, rinsed
- 1 ½ tsp. of maple syrup
- 1 tbsp. of avocado oil

Directions:
1. In a food processor, add all ingredients of aioli except for oil.
2. While running the machine, add the oil slowly & set it aside.
3. Place jalapenos, onion, peeled garlic & tomatillos on a baking sheet & broil for 10 minutes, turning as needed.
4. Cool for a few minutes, add to a food processor with the rest of the ingredients. Pulse until chopped.
5. Let the oven preheat to 200°F.
6. For waffles, add dry & wet ingredients (except for beans) to different bowls & whisk.
7. Add the wet to dry ingredients.
8. Cook waffles on a waffle iron for 2-4 minutes.
9. Serve the waffles with aioli, beans & salsa.

Nutrition:
- Per Serving : Protein 23 g | Fiber 12 g | Carbs 69 g | Fat 38 g

Santa Fe Cobb Salad

Servings:4
Cooking Time: 7 Minutes
Ingredients:
- 4 slices bacon
- 6 cups chopped romaine lettuce
- 4 hard-boiled eggs, sliced
- 2 avocados, sliced
- 1½ cups cherry tomatoes, halved
- 1 cup canned or frozen roasted corn
- 1 cup shelled edamame or canned black beans, rinsed and drained
- ½ cup diced red onion
- 4 ounces crumbled goat cheese
- Ranch, blue cheese, or chipotle ranch dressing
- Hot sauce

Directions:
1. Hot sauce
2. Line a plate with paper towels. In a large sauté pan or skillet over medium heat, cook the bacon until crisp, 5 to 7 minutes. Transfer the bacon to the lined plate. When cool, crumble the bacon into bits and set aside.
3. Divide the romaine between four bowls.
4. Arrange the eggs, avocados, tomatoes, corn, edamame, onion, goat cheese, and bacon bits in neat lines over the lettuce.
5. Lightly drizzle with the desired dressing and a splash of hot sauce.

Nutrition:
- Per Serving : Protein 25 g | Fiber 10 g | Carbs 29 g | Fat 30 g

Moroccan Lamb & Lentil Soup

Servings: 6
Cooking Time: 2 Hours
Ingredients:
- 24 oz. of diced lamb
- 1 onion, chopped
- 2 tsp. of sweet paprika
- 2 tbsp. of olive oil
- 2 tbsp. of tomato paste
- 2 (14 oz.) cans Thick Tomatoes
- 2 garlic cloves, minced
- 11/2 tsp. of ground cumin
- Half tsp. of ground cloves
- 1 bay leaf
- 2 (14 oz.) cans chickpeas, rinsed
- 4 cups of beef stock
- 2 (14 oz.) cans brown lentils, rinsed
- ½ bunch of coriander, chopped

Directions:
1. Season the lamb & cook for 4 to 5 minutes in hot oil; take it out on a plate.
2. Sauté garlic & onion for 3 to 4 minutes.
3. Add lamb, spices, bay leaf & tomato paste. Cook for 1 minute.
4. Add coriander, tomatoes & stock. Simmer for 60 minutes.
5. Add lentils & chickpeas, cook for half an hour.
6. Serve.

Nutrition:
- Per Serving : Protein 13 g | Fiber 9 g | Carbs 18 g | Fat 7 g

Tuna Sandwich

Servings: 2
Cooking Time: 10 Mins.
Ingredients:
- 1 (5-oz.) can water-packed tuna, drained
- 1 medium apple, peeled, cored and cut into small pieces
- 3 tbsp. fat-free plain yogurt
- 1 tsp. mustard
- ½ tsp. honey
- 4 whole-wheat bread slices
- 2 lettuce leaves

Directions:
1. In a bowl, add the tuna, apple, yogurt, mustard and honey and stir to combine well.
2. Spread about ½ C. of the tuna mix over each of 3 bread slices.
3. Top each sandwich with 1 lettuce leaf.

4. Close with the remaining 2 bread slices.
5. With a knife, cut each sandwich in half diagonally and serve.

Nutrition:
- Per Serving : Protein 27.4 g | Fiber 6.8 g | Carbs 42.3 g | Fat 3.4 g

Salmon With Lentils

Servings: 4
Cooking Time: 40 Mins.
Ingredients:
- For Lentils:
- ½ lb. lentils
- 2 tbsp. extra-virgin olive oil
- 2 C. onions, chopped
- 2 C. scallions, chopped
- 1 tsp. fresh parsley, chopped
- Salt and ground black pepper, as required
- 1 tbsp. garlic, minced
- 1½ C. carrots, peeled and chopped
- 1½ C. celery stalks, chopped
- 1 large tomato, peeled, seeded and crushed finely
- 1½ C. homemade chicken broth
- 2 tbsp. balsamic vinegar
- For Salmon:
- 2 (8-oz.) skinless salmon fillets
- 2 tbsp. extra-virgin olive oil
- Salt and ground black pepper, as required

Directions:
1. In a heat-proof bowl, soak the lentils in boiling water for 15 minutes.
2. Drain the lentils completely.
3. In a Dutch oven, heat the oil in over medium heat and cook the onions, scallions, parsley, salt and black pepper for about 10 minutes, stirring frequently.
4. Add the garlic and cook for about 2 more minutes.
5. Add the drained lentils, carrots, celery, crushed tomato and broth and bring to a boil.
6. Now adjust the heat to low and simmer, covered for about 20-25 minutes.
7. Stir in the vinegar, salt and black pepper and remove from the heat.
8. Meanwhile, for salmon: preheat your oven to 450 ºF
9. Rub the salmon fillets with oil and then season with salt and black pepper generously.
10. Heat an oven-proof sauté pan over medium heat and cook the salmon fillets for about 2minutes, without stirring.
11. Flip the fillets and immediately transfer the pan into the oven.
12. Bake for approximately 5-7 minutes or until desired doneness of salmon.
13. Remove from oven and place the salmon fillets onto a cutting board.

14. Cut each fillet into 2 portions.
15. Divide the lentil mixture onto serving plates and top each with 1 salmon fillet.
16. Serve hot.
Nutrition:
- Per Serving : Protein 39.5 g | Fiber 16.5 g | Carbs 51.4 g | Fat 27.9 g

Strawberry French Toasts

Servings: 1
Cooking Time: 5 Mins.
Ingredients:
- 2 egg whites
- ½ tsp. ground cinnamon
- 1½ tsp. vanilla extract
- 2 whole-wheat bread slices
- 2 tsp. olive oil
- 1 C. frozen strawberries
- 1 tbsp. maple syrup
- 3 tsp. fresh lemon juice

Directions:
1. In a bowl, add egg whites, cinnamon and vanilla and beat well.
2. Add bread slices in the egg white mixture and coat from both sides evenly.
3. In a non-stick wok, heat oil over medium heat and cook bread slices for about 5 minutes, flipping once halfway through or until golden brown from both sides.
4. Meanwhile, in a small non-stick pan, add strawberries over low heat and cook for about 2-3 minutes.
5. Stir in maple syrup, lemon juice and remove from heat.
6. Top the French toasts with strawberry mixture and serve.
Nutrition:
- Per Serving : Protein 13.8 g | Fiber 7 g | Carbs 49.9 g | Fat 12 g

Mocha Protein Overnight Oats

Servings: 2
Cooking Time: 0minutes
Ingredients:
- 1 ¼ Cup of Unsweetened Vanilla Almond Milk
- 1 Tsp. of Vanilla Extract
- 1 ½ Tbsp. of Chia Seeds
- 1 Cup of rolled Oats
- 1 Scoop of Coffee Protein Powder
- 1 Tbsp. of Cocoa Powder
- 1 Tsp. of Cinnamon
- 2 Tsp. of maple syrup

Directions:
1. In a mason jar, add all ingredients. Shake well & keep in the fridge overnight.
2. Serve.
Nutrition:

- Per Serving : Protein 5 g | Fiber 6 g | Carbs 32 g | Fat 4 g

Glazed Brussels Sprout

Servings: 3
Cooking Time: 15 Mins.
Ingredients:
- 1 lb. Brussels sprouts, trimmed and halved
- Salt, as required
- 3 tsp. olive oil, divided
- 2 small shallots, sliced thinly
- 2 tsp. fresh orange zest, grated finely
- ¼ tsp. ground ginger
- 2/3 C. fresh orange juice

Directions:
1. Preheat your oven to 400 ºF. Line a roasting pan with parchment paper.
2. In a bowl, add Brussels sprouts, salt, and 1 tsp. of oil and toss to coat well.
3. Transfer the mixture into the prepared roasting pan.
4. Roast for about 10-15 minutes, flipping once halfway through.
5. Meanwhile, for glaze: in a wok, heat oil over medium heat and sauté the shallots for about 5 minutes.
6. Add the orange zest and sauté for about 1 minute.
7. Stir in ginger and orange juice and cook for about 5 minutes.
8. Transfer the roasted Brussels sprouts to a serving plate and top with orange glaze evenly.
9. Serve immediately.
Nutrition:
- Per Serving : Protein 5.9 g | Fiber 6.9 g | Carbs 23.1 g | Fat 3.8 g

Barley & Lentil Stew

Servings: 8
Cooking Time: 55 Mins.
Ingredients:
- 2 tbsp. olive oil
- 2 carrots, peeled and chopped
- 1 large onion, chopped
- 2 celery stalks, chopped
- 2 garlic cloves, minced
- 2 tsp. ground coriander
- 2 tsp. ground cumin
- 1 C. barley
- 1 C. lentils
- 2 C. tomatoes, peeled, seeded and chopped
- 9 C. homemade vegetable broth
- 6 C. fresh spinach, torn
- Ground black pepper, as required

Directions:
1. In a large pan, heat oil over medium heat and sauté carrots, onion and celery for about 5 minutes.

2. Add garlic and spices and sauté for about 1 minute.

3. Add barley, lentils, tomatoes and broth and bring to a boil.

4. Now adjust the heat to low and simmer, covered for about 40 minutes.

5. Stir in spinach and black pepper and simmer for about 3-4 minutes.

6. Serve hot.

Nutrition:

- Per Serving : Protein 16.1 g | Fiber 13.3 g | Carbs 38.9 g | Fat 6.2 g

Scallop Salad

Servings: 6
Cooking Time: 5 Mins.

Ingredients:

- For Scallops:
- 2 tbsp. olive oil
- 1½ lb. sea scallops
- Salt and ground black pepper, as required
- For Dressing:
- 2-3 tbsp. fat-free plain yogurt
- 3 tbsp. Dijon mustard
- Salt and ground black pepper, as required
- For Salad:
- 6 hard-boiled eggs, peeled and sliced
- 3 medium apples, cored and sliced
- 2 C. cabbage, chopped
- 1/3 C. low-fat feta cheese, crumbled

Directions:

1. In a large non-stick sauté pan, heat the olive oil over medium-high heat.

2. Stir in the scallops, salt and black pepper and immediately adjust the heat to high.

3. Cook for about 5 minutes, flipping once halfway through.

4. Transfer the scallops into a bowl and set aside to cool.

5. For dressing: in a bowl, add all ingredients and beat until well combined.

6. For salad: in a large serving bowl, add all the ingredients and mix.

7. Top with scallops and drizzle with dressing.

8. Serve immediately.

Nutrition:

- Per Serving : Protein 27 g | Fiber 5.6 g | Carbs 20.9 g | Fat 12.3 g

Beans & Veggie Bowl

Servings: 2
Cooking Time: 10 Mins.

Ingredients:

- 1 bell pepper, seeded and chopped
- 1 onion, sliced

- ¾ C. canned black beans, rinsed and drained
- ¾ C. canned red kidney beans, rinsed and drained
- ½ C. frozen corn, thawed
- 3 C. lettuce, chopped
- 1 tbsp. fresh lime juice
- ¼ C. salsa

Directions:

1. Divide the beans, corn, veggies and lettuce into serving bowls.

2. Drizzle with lime juice and serve alongside the salsa.

Nutrition:

- Per Serving : Protein 11 g | Fiber 10.2 g | Carbs 39.9 g | Fat 6.5 g

Cherry-mocha Smoothie

Servings: 6
Cooking Time: 0minutes

Ingredients:

- 1 cup of almond Choco milk, unsweetened
- 1 tsp. of instant coffee
- 5.3 to 6-oz. of Greek yogurt
- 1 tsp. of vanilla
- ½ banana
- 1 cup of frozen dark cherries, unsweetened & pitted
- 2 tbsp. of cocoa powder, unsweetened
- 2 tbsp. of almond butter
- 2 cups of ice cubes

Directions:

1. Add all ingredients to a blender. Pulse until smooth.

2. Serve by pouring in a chilled glass.

Nutrition:

- Per Serving : Protein 13 g | Fiber 8 g | Carbs 34 g | Fat 12 g

Squash & Apple Soup

Servings: 4
Cooking Time: 45 Mins.

Ingredients:

- 2 tbsp. olive oil
- 1 C. onion, chopped
- 2 garlic cloves, minced
- 1 tsp. dried thyme
- 3 C. butternut squash, peeled and cubed
- 2 apples, cored and chopped
- 4 C. water
- Salt, as required

Directions:

1. In a soup pan, heat olive oil over medium heat and sauté the onion for about 5 minutes.

2. Add the garlic and thyme and sauté for about 1 minute.

3. Add the squash and apple and ginger and cook for about 1-2 minutes.

4. Stir in the water and bring to a boil.

5. Now adjust the heat to low and simmer covered for about 30 minutes.
6. Stir in the salt and remove from the heat.
7. With a hand blender, puree the soup mixture until smooth.
8. Serve immediately.

Nutrition:
- Per Serving : Protein 1.9 g | Fiber 6.1 g | Carbs 31.4 g | Fat 1.3 g

Mango & Avocado Salad

Servings: 6
Cooking Time: 15 Mins.

Ingredients:
- 2½ C. mango, peeled, pitted and sliced
- 2½ C. avocado, peeled, pitted and sliced
- 1 onion, sliced
- 6 C. fresh baby arugula
- ¼ C. fresh mint leaves, chopped
- 2 tbsp. fresh orange juice
- Salt, as required

Directions:
1. Place all the ingredients in a large serving bowl and gently toss to combine.
2. Cover and refrigerate to chill before serving.

Nutrition:
- Per Serving : Protein 2.6 g | Fiber 6.2 g | Carbs 18.8 g | Fat 12.3 g

Garlic Roasted Salmon

Servings: 6
Cooking Time: 15 Minutes

Ingredients:
- Salt & pepper, to taste
- 1 tbsp. of Garlic Oil
- 2 pounds of salmon fillet, cut into 6 pieces
- 3-4 garlic cloves, minced
- 1 tbsp. of dried oregano

Directions:
1. Let the oven preheat to 450°F.
2. Oil spray a baking sheet.
3. Coat salmon in garlic oil. Add pressed garlic on top & season with salt, oregano & pepper.
4. Bake for 10-12 minutes, serve with rice.

Nutrition:
- Per Serving : Protein 35 g | Fiber 6 g | Carbs 14 g | Fat 19 g

Breakfast Ice Cream

Servings:4
Cooking Time: 10 Minutes

Ingredients:
- 2 cups frozen raspberries or blackberries
- 4 frozen bananas
- ½ avocado
- ¼ cup unsweetened applesauce
- 1 tablespoon chia seeds
- 1 tablespoon honey or maple syrup, plus more as needed

Directions:
1. tablespoon honey or maple syrup, plus more as needed
2. bine the berries, bananas, avocado, applesauce, chia seeds, and honey in a food processor or blender and process until smooth. (It should be the consistency of soft-serve ice cream.) Taste and add more honey if needed. Serve immediately.

Nutrition:
- Per Serving : Protein 4 g | Fiber 11 g | Carbs 45 g | Fat 5 g

Homemade Hummus

Servings:4
Cooking Time: 10 Minutes

Ingredients:
- 1 (15-ounce) can chickpeas
- 2 garlic cloves, roughly chopped
- 4 tablespoons tahini
- 2 tablespoons extra-virgin olive oil
- 1 tablespoon lemon juice
- ½ teaspoon ground cumin
- 2 tablespoons water
- Salt
- Freshly ground black pepper

Directions:
1. Freshly ground black pepper
2. Place the chickpeas, garlic, tahini, olive oil, lemon juice, cumin, and water in a blender or food processor and puree until smooth. Taste and season with salt and pepper.
3. Serve with cut-up vegetables, high-fiber crackers, or whole-wheat pita on the side.

Nutrition:
- Per Serving : Protein 8 g | Fiber 6 g | Carbs 28 g | Fat 16 g

Lentil Burgers With Tomato Sauce

Servings: 4
Cooking Time: 1 Hour 10 Mins.

Ingredients:
- 2 tbsp. olive oil, divided
- 1 medium onion, chopped finely
- 2 garlic cloves, chopped finely
- 2½ C. mushrooms, cut into ½-inch pieces
- ½ tsp. ground coriander
- 1½ C. cooked lentils
- 2 tbsp. tahini
- 1 egg
- ½ C. rolled oats

- ¼ C. sunflower seeds
- 1 tbsp. fresh parsley, chopped
- Non-stick cooking spray
- 4 C. mixed salad greens

Directions:

1. In a large saucepan, heat 1 tbsp. of oil over medium-high heat and cook onion for about 6-8 minutes, stirring occasionally.
2. Transfer onion into a bowl and set aside.
3. In the same pan, heat remaining oil over medium-high heat and sauté garlic for about 30 seconds.
4. Add mushrooms, coriander, salt and pepper and cook for about 5-7 minutes, stirring occasionally.
5. Meanwhile, in a large bowl, add lentils, cooked onion and tahini and with a fork, mash slightly until a rough paste is formed.
6. Add mushrooms, egg, oats, sunflower seeds and parsley and stir to combine well.
7. Refrigerate the mixture for about 30-40 minutes.
8. Make 8 equal-sized patties from mixture.
9. Grease a large flat griddle with cooking spray and heat over medium-high heat.
10. Add the patties and cook for about 5 minutes per side.
11. Serve hot alongside the greens.

Nutrition:

- Per Serving : Protein 13.5 g | Fiber 9.3 g | Carbs 29.1 g | Fat 14.7 g

Oat & Yogurt Bowl

Servings: 2
Cooking Time: 10 Mins.

Ingredients:

- 2 C. water
- 1 C. old fashioned oats
- 6 oz. fat-free plain yogurt
- ½ C. fresh strawberries

Directions:

1. In a saucepan, add water over medium heat and bring to a boil.
2. Stir in the oats and cook about 5 minutes, stirring occasionally.
3. Remove the pan of oats from the heat and stir in half of the yogurt and cinnamon.
4. Divide the oatmeal into serving bowls evenly.
5. Top each bowl with strawberry slices and serve.

Nutrition:

- Per Serving : Protein 9.8 g | Fiber 6.8 g | Carbs 37.6 g | Fat 3.1 g

Beans Enchiladas

Servings: 8
Cooking Time: 20 Mins.

Ingredients:

- 1 (14-oz.) can red kidney beans, drained, rinsed and mashed
- 2 C. low-fat cheddar cheese, grated
- 2 C. tomato sauce
- ½ C. onion, chopped
- ¼ C. black olives, pitted and sliced
- 8 whole-wheat tortillas

Directions:

1. Preheat your oven to 350 °F.
2. In a bowl, add the mashed beans, cheese, 1 C. of tomato sauce, onions and olives and mix well.
3. Place about 1/3 C. of the bean mixture along center of each tortilla.
4. Roll up each tortilla and place enchiladas in a large baking dish.
5. Place the remaining tomato sauce on top of the filled tortillas.
6. Bake for approximately 15-20 minutes.
7. Serve warm.

Nutrition:

- Per Serving : Protein 20.6 g | Fiber 10.3 g | Carbs 46.2 g | Fat 11.2 g

Vegetarian Sushi Bowls

Servings:4
Cooking Time: 50 Minutes

Ingredients:

- FOR THE RICE
- 1 cup brown rice
- 2½ cups water
- 2 tablespoons rice wine vinegar
- 2 tablespoons sugar
- FOR THE TOPPINGS
- 1 English cucumber, thinly sliced
- ¼ cup thinly sliced radishes
- 1 avocado, sliced
- 1 cup shelled edamame
- 3 carrots, thinly sliced
- 2 green onions, finely chopped
- 2 teaspoons black sesame seeds, for garnish

Directions:

1. teaspoons black sesame seeds, for garnish
2. Rinse the rice under warm water in a fine mesh sieve until the water runs clear. Place the rice in a medium saucepan over high heat, cover with the water, and bring to a boil. Lower the heat to medium-low, cover, and cook for 35 to 45 minutes, until all the water has been absorbed. Remove from the heat and let sit, covered, until ready to use.
3. In a small saucepan over medium-high heat, mix together the rice vinegar and sugar and cook until the sugar dissolves, about 5 minutes.
4. Pour the vinegar mixture over the rice and mix to combine.

5. Assemble the sushi bowls by spooning the rice into bowls and topping with the cucumber, radishes, avocado, edamame, carrots, and green onions. Sprinkle the black sesame seeds over the top and serve.

6. Store the assembled bowls covered with plastic wrap in the refrigerator for up to 5 days.

Nutrition:

- Per Serving : Protein 11 g | Fiber 8 g | Carbs 57 g | Fat 10 g

Prosciutto, Kale & Bean Stew

Servings: 4
Cooking Time: 30 Minutes
Ingredients:

- 2 tbsp. of olive oil
- 1 fennel bulb, sliced
- 5 oz. of chicken stock
- 4 thyme sprigs
- 2.8 oz. prosciutto, torn
- 1 can of (14 oz.) cherry tomatoes
- 2 garlic clove, minced
- 2 cans of (14 oz.) butter beans
- 7 oz. of sliced kale

Directions:

1. Sauté the prosciutto in a pan until crispy. Take half of it out.
2. Add oil, salt & fennel. Cook for 5 minutes.
3. Add thyme & garlic cook for 2 minutes.
4. Add stock & simmer.
5. Add all cans & simmer for 15 minutes. Add kale & cook for 1-2 minutes.
6. Serve with crispy prosciutto.

Nutrition:

- Per Serving : Protein 16 g | Fiber 12 g | Carbs 23 g | Fat 9 g

Kiwi, Apple & Grapes Juice

Servings: 2
Cooking Time: 10 Mins.
Ingredients:

- 3 large kiwis, peeled and chopped
- 3 large green apples, cored and quartered
- 2 C. seedless green grapes
- 2 tsp. fresh lime juice

Directions:

1. Add all ingredients into a juicer and extract the juice according to the manufacturer's method.
2. Through a cheesecloth-lined strainer, strain the juice and transfer into 2 glasses.
3. Serve immediately.

Nutrition:

- Per Serving : Protein 6.2 g | Fiber 12.5 g | Carbs 79 g | Fat 2.2 g

Lentil And Chicken Shepherd's Pie

Servings:6
Cooking Time: 1 Hour
Ingredients:

- 4 russet potatoes, quartered
- Salt
- Freshly ground black pepper
- 2 tablespoons vegetable oil, divided
- ½ pound ground chicken, formed into a large patty
- 1 white or Spanish onion, finely chopped
- 2 garlic cloves, minced
- 2 cups finely chopped mushrooms
- 1 cup frozen mixed peas, carrots, and corn
- 1 (15-ounce) can lentils, drained and rinsed
- 1 cup Homemade Chicken Stock or store-bought
- 1 tablespoon cornstarch
- ¼ teaspoon dried thyme
- ¼ teaspoon dried rosemary

Directions:

1. ¼ teaspoon dried rosemary
2. Preheat the oven to 400°F. Grease a 9-by-13-inch baking dish.
3. In a large saucepan over high heat, place the potatoes, cover them with cold water, and bring to a boil. Lower the heat to medium and simmer until the potatoes are soft, about 15 minutes. Drain, and mash them using a potato masher or a hand mixer until smooth. Lightly season with salt and pepper and set aside.
4. In a medium saucepan over medium heat, warm 1 tablespoon of oil. Add the chicken patty and cook until it browns, about 4 minutes. Flip the patty and brown the other side, about 4 more minutes. Break up the chicken into small pieces with a spoon.
5. Add the remaining 1 tablespoon of oil and the onion, garlic, mushrooms, mixed frozen vegetables, lentils, stock, cornstarch, thyme, and rosemary and cook for 2 to 3 minutes.
6. Pour the chicken mixture into the prepared baking dish.
7. Spread the mashed potatoes evenly on top of the chicken mixture.
8. Bake for 25 to 35 minutes, or until the casserole is heated through and the potatoes begin to brown. Serve hot.
9. Store leftovers in an airtight container in the refrigerator for up to 5 days or in the freezer for up to 3 months.

Nutrition:

- Per Serving : Protein 17 g | Fiber 7 g | Carbs 36 g | Fat 6 g

Blueberry & Avocado Smoothie

Servings: 2
Cooking Time: 10 Mins.
Ingredients:
- 2 C. fresh blueberries
- 1 large banana, peeled and sliced
- 1 small avocado, peeled, pitted and chopped
- 1 C. fresh cranberry juice
- ¼ C. ice cubes

Directions:
1. Add all the ingredients in a high-power blender and pulse until creamy.
2. Pour the smoothie into two glasses and serve immediately.

Nutrition:
- Per Serving : Protein 3.7 g | Fiber 12.3 g | Carbs 47.9 g | Fat 12 g

Bean Soup With Kale

Servings: 4
Cooking Time: 30 Minutes
Ingredients:
- 15 oz. of ciabatta bread
- 3 garlic cloves
- 14 oz. of canned cannellini beans, rinsed
- 1 tbsp. of olive oil
- 1 bunch of kale, without thick stems
- 14 oz. of chopped canned tomatoes with paste
- 4 cups of chicken stock

Directions:
1. Let the oven preheat to 350 F.
2. Toss the kale with salt & oil, bake for 10-12 minutes, flipping halfway through.
3. Toast the bread slices. Rub the garlic on hot toasted bread.
4. Sauté the garlic in hot oil, add stock & tomatoes. Boil & add beans, simmer for 10 minutes.
5. Season with salt & pepper.
6. Serve with bread & kale on top.

Nutrition:
- Per Serving : Protein 15.2 g | Fiber 10.6 g | Carbs 44 g | Fat 9.1 g

Apple & Spinach Smoothie

Servings: 2
Cooking Time: 10 Mins.
Ingredients:
- 2 medium apples, peeled, cored and chopped
- 1 banana, peeled and sliced
- 3 C. fresh spinach
- 1 scoop unsweetened protein powder
- 1 C. coconut water
- ¾ C. ice

Directions:
1. Add all the ingredients in a high-power blender and pulse until creamy.
2. Pour the smoothie into two glasses and serve immediately.

Nutrition:
- Per Serving : Protein 14.9 g | Fiber 9.6 g | Carbs 50.5 g | Fat 4.5 g

Quinoa With Mushrooms

Servings: 4
Cooking Time: 30 Mins.
Ingredients:
- ½ tbsp. olive oil
- 1 C. uncooked quinoa, rinsed
- 12 oz. fresh white mushrooms, sliced
- 3 garlic cloves, minced
- 1¾ C. water
- ¼ C. fresh cilantro, chopped
- Salt, as required

Directions:
1. Ina medium saucepan, heat olive oil over medium-high heat and sauté the garlic for about 30-40 seconds.
2. Add the mushrooms and cook on for about 5-6 minutes, stirring frequently.
3. Stir in the quinoa and cook for about 2 minutes, stirring continuously.
4. Add the water and salt and bring to a boil.
5. Now adjust the heat to low and simmer, covered for about 15-18 minutes or until almost all the liquid is absorbed.
6. Serve hot with the garnishing of cilantro.

Nutrition:
- Per Serving : Protein 11.8 g | Fiber 6.2 g | Carbs 41.4 g | Fat 4.1 g

Apple, Pear & Orange Juice

Servings: 2
Cooking Time: 10 Mins.
Ingredients:
- 4 apples, cored and quartered
- 4 pears, cored and quartered
- 2 oranges, peeled, seeded and sectioned
- 6 celery stalks

Directions:
1. Add all ingredients into a juicer and extract the juice according to the manufacturer's method.
2. Through a cheesecloth-lined strainer, strain the juice and transfer into 2 glasses.
3. Serve immediately.

Nutrition:
- Per Serving : Protein 4.8 g | Fiber 29 g | Carbs 128.7 g | Fat 1.7 g

Three Beans Soup

Servings: 12
Cooking Time: 45 Mins.
Ingredients:
- ¼ C. olive oil
- 1 large onion, chopped
- 1 large sweet potato, peeled and cubed
- 3 carrots, peeled and chopped
- 3 celery stalks, chopped
- 3 garlic cloves, minced
- 2 tsp. dried thyme, crushed
- 1 tbsp. ground cumin
- 4 large tomatoes, peeled, seeded and chopped finely
- 2 (16-oz.) cans great Northern beans, rinsed and drained
- 2 (15¼-oz.) cans red kidney beans, rinsed and drained
- 1 (15-oz.) can black beans, drained and rinsed
- 12 C. homemade vegetable broth
- 1 C. fresh cilantro, chopped
- Salt and ground black pepper, as required

Directions:
1. In a Dutch oven, heat the oil over medium heat and sauté the onion, sweet potato, carrot and celery for about 6-8 minutes.
2. Add the garlic, thyme and cumin and sauté for about 1 minute.
3. Add in the tomatoes and cook for about 2-3 minutes.
4. Add the beans and broth and bring to a boil over medium-high heat.
5. Cover the pan with lid and cook for about 25-30 minutes.
6. Stir in the cilantro and remove from heat.
7. Serve hot.

Nutrition:
- Per Serving : Protein 22.7 g | Fiber 18.9 g | Carbs 69.7 g | Fat 5.7 g

Apple-oat Energy Balls

Servings: 6
Cooking Time: 0minutes
Ingredients:
- 1 tsp. of kosher salt
- 1 cup of grated apple
- 2 ½ cups of rolled oats
- ½ cup of shredded coconut, unsweetened
- ¼ cup of honey
- ½ cup of almond butter
- 1 tsp. of ground cinnamon

Directions:
1. In a food processor, add all ingredients. Pulse until smooth.
2. Make it into 12 balls.
3. Serve chilled.

Nutrition:
- Per Serving : Protein 5 g | Fiber 10 g | Carbs 9 g | Fat 6 g

Couscous & Beans Salad

Servings: 4
Cooking Time: 5 Mins.
Ingredients:
- For Salad:
- ½ C. homemade vegetable broth
- ½ C. couscous
- 3 C. canned red kidney beans, rinsed and drained
- 2 large tomatoes, peeled, seeded and chopped
- 5 C. fresh spinach, torn
- For Dressing:
- 1 garlic clove, minced
- 2 tbsp. shallots, minced
- 2 tsp. lemon zest, grated finely
- ¼ C. fresh lemon juice
- 2 tbsp. extra-virgin olive oil
- Salt and ground black pepper, as required

Directions:
1. In a saucepan, add the broth over medium heat and bring to a boil.
2. Add the couscous and stir to combine.
3. Cover the pan and immediately remove from the heat.
4. Set aside, covered for about 5-10 minutes or until all the liquid is absorbed.
5. For salad: in a large serving bowl, add the couscous and remaining ingredients and stir to combine.
6. For dressing: in another small bowl, add all the ingredients and beat until well combined.
7. Pour the dressing over salad and gently toss to coat well.
8. Serve immediately.

Nutrition:
- Per Serving : Protein 15.7 g | Fiber 13.5 g | Carbs 53.2 g | Fat 8.5 g

Chickpeas & Zucchini Chili

Servings: 6
Cooking Time: 1 Hour 10 Mins.
Ingredients:
- 2 tbsp. olive oil
- 1 medium onion, chopped
- 1 large bell pepper, seeded and chopped
- 4 garlic cloves, minced
- 1 tsp. dried thyme
- Salt, as required
- 2 medium zucchinis, chopped
- 3 C. tomatoes, peeled, seeded and chopped
- 3 C. cooked chickpeas
- 2 C. water

Directions:

1. In a saucepan, heat the olive oil over medium heat and sauté the onion and bell pepper for about 8 to 9 minutes.
2. Add the garlic and thyme and salt and sauté for about 1 minute.
3. Add in all remaining ingredients and cook until boiling.
4. Now adjust the heat to low and simmer for about 1 hour or until desired thickness.
5. Serve hot.

Nutrition:
- Per Serving : Protein 8.2 g | Fiber 8.1 g | Carbs 37.3 g | Fat 6.6 g

Spinach & Avocado Smoothie Bowl

Servings: 2
Cooking Time: 10 Mins.

Ingredients:
- 2 C. fresh spinach
- 1 medium avocado, peeled, pitted and chopped roughly
- 2 scoops unsweetened protein powder
- 3 tbsp. maple syrup
- 2 tbsp. fresh lemon juice
- 1 C. milk
- ¼ C. ice cubes

Directions:
1. In a high-speed blender, place all ingredients and pulse until creamy.
2. Pour into 2 serving bowls and serve immediately with your favorite topping.

Nutrition:
- Per Serving : Protein 32.2 g | Fiber 8 g | Carbs 36.2 g | Fat 23.5 g

Charred Kale & Farro Protein Salad

Servings: 2
Cooking Time: 30 Minutes

Ingredients:
- 6 kale leaves, without stems & torn
- Half cup of shaved parmesan
- 1 cup of dry farro, soaked for 12 hours
- Half onion, sliced
- Salt & Pepper
- 1/4 cup of pumpkin seeds
- 2 salmon fillets
- Dressing
- 1 garlic clove, minced
- 2 tbsp. of each olive oil & lemon juice
- 1/4 tsp. of each salt & pepper

Directions:
1. In a pan, add soaked farro add enough water to cover it.
2. Boil & simmer for 20 minutes.
3. Let the oven preheat to 425 F.
4. Coat the salmon in oil season with salt & pepper.
5. Bake for 6 to 10 minutes.

6. In a pan, add a drizzle of oil. Sauté kale for 2-3 minutes until charred.
7. Take it out on a plate, add onion & char them.
8. Toss all of the ingredients except for salmon. Serve with salmon.

Nutrition:
- Per Serving : Protein 11 g | Fiber 10 g | Carbs 13 g | Fat 7 g

Strawberry-banana Breakfast Parfait

Servings:4
Cooking Time: 15 Minutes

Ingredients:
- 2 cups plain Greek yogurt
- 2 tablespoons honey or maple syrup
- ½ teaspoon ground cinnamon
- ½ teaspoon vanilla extract
- 2 cups no-added-sugar muesli or uncooked oats (see Helpful Hints)
- 1 tablespoon chia seeds
- 1 tablespoon pumpkin seeds
- 2 cups sliced strawberries
- 1 banana, sliced

Directions:
1. banana, sliced
2. In a small bowl, mix together the yogurt, honey, cinnamon, and vanilla.
3. Spoon ¼ cup of the yogurt mixture into the bottom of a drinking glass. Top with ¼ cup of the muesli and a thin layer of chia and pumpkin seeds, and sprinkle with strawberry and banana slices. Repeat the layers until the glass is full. Repeat with the rest of the ingredients. Serve immediately.

Nutrition:
- Per Serving : Protein 17 g | Fiber 8 g | Carbs 60 g | Fat 11 g

Chickpeas & Kale Stew

Servings: 4
Cooking Time: 30 Mins.

Ingredients:
- 1 tbsp. olive oil
- 1 large onion, chopped
- 2 garlic cloves, minced
- 3 C. tomatoes, peeled, seeded and chopped finely
- 2 C. water
- 2 C. cooked chickpeas
- 2 C. fresh kale, tough ribs removed and chopped
- 1 tbsp. fresh lime juice
- Salt, as required

Directions:
1. In a soup pan, heat olive oil over medium heat and sauté the onion for about 6 minutes.

2. Stir in the garlic and sauté for about 1 minute.
3. Add the tomatoes and cook for about 2-3 minutes.
4. Add the water and bring to a boil.
5. Now adjust the heat to low and simmer for about 10 minutes.
6. Stir in the chickpeas and simmer for about 5 minutes.
7. Stir in the spinach and simmer for 3-4 minutes more.
8. Stir in the lime juice and seasoning and serve hot.

Nutrition:
- Per Serving : Protein 8.7 g | Fiber 8.4 g | Carbs 40.1 g | Fat 2.1 g

Turkey, Beans & Pumpkin Chili

Servings: 4
Cooking Time: 45 Mins.
Ingredients:
- 2 tbsp. olive oil
- 1 bell pepper, seeded and chopped
- 1 small onion, chopped
- 2 garlic cloves, chopped finely
- 1 lb. lean ground turkey
- 1 (18-oz.) can chickpeas, rinsed and drained
- 1 (15-oz.) pumpkin puree
- 2 C. tomatoes, peeled, seeded and chopped
- 1 tsp. ground cumin
- ½ tsp. ground turmeric
- 1 C. water

Directions:
1. In a large saucepan, heat oil over medium-low heat and sauté bell pepper, onion and garlic for about 5 minutes.
2. Add turkey and cook for about 5 minutes.
3. Add chickpeas, tomatoes, pumpkin, spices and water and stir to combine.
4. Adjust the heat to high and bring to a boil.
5. Now adjust the heat to medium-low and simmer, covered for about 30 minutes, stirring occasionally.
6. Serve hot.

Nutrition:
- Per Serving : Protein 31.3 g | Fiber 10.9 g | Carbs 46 g | Fat 17.3 g

Kiwi & Avocado Smoothie

Servings: 2
Cooking Time: 10 Mins.
Ingredients:
- 1 kiwi, peeled and chopped
- 1 small avocado, peeled, pitted and chopped
- 1 C. cucumber, peeled and chopped
- 2 C. fresh baby kale
- ¼ C. fresh mint leaves
- 2 C. filtered water
- ¼ C. ice cubes

Directions:

1. Add all the ingredients in a high-power blender and pulse until creamy.
2. Pour the smoothie into two glasses and serve immediately.

Nutrition:
- Per Serving : Protein 4.2 g | Fiber 7.1 g | Carbs 20.3 g | Fat 11.4 g

Overnight Steel-cut Oats

Servings:4
Cooking Time: 5 Minutes, Plus 4 Hours Chilling Time
Ingredients:
- FOR THE OATS
- 1 cup steel-cut oats
- ⅔ cup milk or nondairy milk of choice
- 1 tablespoon chia seeds
- 1 tablespoon hemp seeds
- 1 teaspoon ground cinnamon
- FLAVOR OPTIONS
- BERRY
- 1 cup frozen berries of choice
- PUMPKIN SPICE
- 1 tablespoon canned pumpkin puree
- 1 teaspoon ground cinnamon
- Pinch nutmeg
- TROPICAL
- 1 tablespoon shredded coconut
- 1 cup pineapple, diced
- 1 cup mango, diced
- PEACH COBBLER
- 1 cup canned peaches packed in water
- Pinch ground cinnamon
- PEANUT BUTTER–BANANA
- 1 banana, chopped
- 2 tablespoons peanut butter
- APPLE PIE
- 2 apples, Honey Crisp, Fuji, Granny Smith, or Gala, chopped, or 4 tablespoons unsweetened applesauce
- ½ teaspoon ground cinnamon
- Handful pecans

Directions:
1. Handful pecans
2. In a medium airtight container, mix together the oats, milk, chia, hemp, and cinnamon. Gently stir in the toppings of your choice, cover, and refrigerate for at least 4 hours or overnight.
3. Serve cold, but if you prefer your oats hot, place them in a microwave-safe bowl and heat them in the microwave for 2 to 3 minutes, or place them in a small saucepan over low heat until warmed through.

Nutrition:
- Per Serving : Protein 9 g | Fiber 6 g | Carbs 31 g | Fat 5 g

Healthy Chopped Salad

Servings: 4
Cooking Time: 0 Minutes
Ingredients:
- 1 cup of cooked chicken breast, shredded
- 1/4 cup of goat cheese, crumbled
- 1 can of (15.5 oz.) chickpeas, rinsed
- 2 romaine hearts, chopped
- 1 cup of grape tomatoes, halved
- Half cup of BBQ dressing
- 3/4 cup of sweet corn
- 1/3 cup of cilantro
- 1 avocado, diced

Directions:
1. Add all ingredients to a bowl, except for dressing & avocado.
2. Toss & serve with dressing & avocado.

Nutrition:
- Per Serving : Protein 11 g | Fiber 9.8 g | Carbs 7 g | Fat 5 g

Beef & Peach Salad

Servings: 6
Cooking Time: 15 Mins.
Ingredients:
- For Salad:
- 1 lb. cooked beef, cubed
- 4 ripe peaches, pitted and sliced
- 2 cucumbers, chopped
- 2 avocados, peeled, pitted and sliced
- 1 large onion, sliced thinly
- 6 C. fresh baby spinach
- For Dressing:
- ½ C. extra-virgin olive oil
- ¼ C. fresh lemon juice
- 2 tsp. fresh ginger, grated finely
- 1 small garlic clove, minced
- 1 tbsp. honey
- Salt and ground black pepper, to taste

Directions:
1. For salad: in a large serving bowl, add all ingredients and mix.
2. In another bowl, add all dressing ingredients and beat until well combined.
3. Pour dressing over salad and gently toss to coat well.
4. Serve immediately.

Nutrition:
- Per Serving : Protein 27.1 g | Fiber 8.2 g | Carbs 25.7 g | Fat 35.2 g

Orange & Kale Juice

Servings: 2

Cooking Time: 10 Mins.
Ingredients:
- 5 large oranges, peeled and sectioned
- 2 bunches fresh kale

Directions:
1. Add all ingredients into a juicer and extract the juice according to the manufacturer's method.
2. Through a cheesecloth-lined strainer, strain the juice and transfer into 2 glasses.
3. Serve immediately.

Nutrition:
- Per Serving : Protein 10.3 g | Fiber 14 g | Carbs 75.1 g | Fat 0.6 g

Rice With Tofu & Veggies

Servings: 4
Cooking Time: 45 Mins.
Ingredients:
- For Tofu & Rice:
- 1 C. long-grain brown rice, rinsed
- 8 oz. extra-firm tofu, pressed, drained and cut into ¼-inch cubes
- ½ C. green peas
- ½ C. carrots, peeled and chopped finely
- 1 C. scallion, chopped
- 4 garlic cloves, minced
- For Sauce:
- 3 tbsp. creamy peanut butter
- 2 tbsp. fresh lime juice
- 2-3 tbsp. maple syrup
- 1 tbsp. olive oil
- 1 garlic clove, minced

Directions:
1. Preheat your oven to 400°F. Line a baking sheet with lightly greased parchment paper.
2. In a saucepan, add 12 C. of water over high heat and bring to a boil.
3. Stir in the rice and cook, uncovered for about 30 minutes.
4. Remove from the heat and strain the rice.
5. Return the rice to the same pan and set aside, covered for about 10 minutes.
6. Meanwhile, arrange the tofu cubes onto the prepared baking sheet and Bake for approximately 26-30 minutes.
7. For sauce: in a bowl, add all ingredients and beat until well combined.
8. Remove from oven and place the tofu cubes into the bowl of sauce.
9. Stir the mixture well and set aside for about 5 minutes, stirring occasionally.
10. With a slotted spoon, remove the tofu cubes from bowl, reserving the sauce.

11. Heat a large cast-iron wok over medium heat and cook the tofu cubes for about 3-4 minutes, stirring occasionally.

12. With a slotted spoon, transfer the tofu cubes onto a plate. Set aside.

13. In the same pan, add the peas, carrots, scallion and garlic over medium heat and sauté for about 3-4 minutes.

14. Add the cooked rice, tofu and remaining sauce and stir to combine.

15. Adjust the heat to medium-high and cook for about 3-4 minutes, stirring frequently.

16. Serve hot

Nutrition:
- Per Serving : Protein 13.5 g | Fiber 6.1 g | Carbs 54.3 g | Fat 14.5 g

Banana Walnut Bread

Servings: 10
Cooking Time: 50 Mins.
Ingredients:
- 1 C. rye flour
- 1 C. spelt flour
- 1 tsp. ground ginger
- 1 tsp. ground cloves
- 10 burro bananas, peeled and mashed
- ½ C. maple syrup
- ½ C. unsweetened almond milk
- ½ C. olive oil
- ½ C. walnuts, chopped

Directions:
1. Preheat your oven to 350 ºF. Lightly grease and flour a loaf pan.
2. In a bowl, add the flours, ginger and cloves and mix well.
3. Add the bananas, maple syrup, almond milk and oil and beat until well combined.
4. Gently fold in the walnuts.
5. Place the dough into the prepared loaf pan.
6. Bake for approximately 50 minutes or until a wooden skewer inserted in the center of loaf comes out clean.
7. Remove from oven and place the baking sheet onto a wire rack to cool for at least 10 minutes.
8. Then invert the bread onto the rack to cool completely before serving.
9. With a knife, cut the bread loaf into desired-sized slices and serve.

Nutrition:
- Per Serving : Protein 6.3 g | Fiber 8.5 g | Carbs 59.5 g | Fat 16.2 g

Black Bean Burgers

Servings:4
Cooking Time: 1 Hour 15 Minutes
Ingredients:
- FOR THE BURGER

- ½ cup brown rice
- 2 cups cold water
- 1 (15½-ounce) can black beans, drained and rinsed
- 2 green onions, finely chopped
- 1 garlic clove, minced
- 1 large egg
- ¼ cup bread crumbs
- 1 teaspoon Dijon mustard
- ½ teaspoon Italian seasoning
- Salt
- Freshly ground black pepper
- 4 whole-wheat burger buns
- OPTIONAL TOPPINGS
- Sliced onion
- Sliced avocado
- Sliced tomatoes
- Pickle chips
- Mustard
- Mayonnaise
- Ketchup
- Relish
- Lettuce of choice

Directions:
1. Lettuce of choice
2. Preheat the oven to 375°F. Line a baking sheet with parchment paper.
3. Rinse the rice in cold water until the water runs clear. Place the rice and water in a medium saucepan over high heat and bring to a boil. Lower the heat to medium-low, cover, and simmer for 50 minutes. Remove from the heat and let sit, covered, for 5 minutes. Drain any remaining water and fluff the rice with a fork.
4. In a large bowl, mash the black beans with a fork. Add the green onions, garlic, egg, bread crumbs, Dijon mustard, Italian seasoning, and rice and mix well. Season with salt and pepper.
5. Form the mixture into 4 equal patties and place them on the prepared baking sheet.
6. Bake for 20 to 25 minutes, or until heated through.
7. Serve on the buns with the optional toppings on the side.
8. Store the cooked burgers in an airtight container in the refrigerator for up to 5 days or freeze for up to 3 months.

Nutrition:
- Per Serving : Protein 10 g | Fiber 8 g | Carbs 40 g | Fat 3 g

Pear & Blueberry Smoothie

Servings: 2
Cooking Time: 10 Mins.
Ingredients:
- 1 Asian pear, peeled, cored and chopped
- 1 C. frozen blueberries
- 2 Medjool dates, pitted
- 3 tbsp. raw cashews
- 1 tbsp. hemp seeds
- 1¼ C. water

Directions:
1. Add all the ingredients in a high-power blender and pulse until creamy.
2. Pour the smoothie into two glasses and serve immediately.

Nutrition:
- Per Serving : Protein 4.8 g | Fiber 7 g | Carbs 42.1 g | Fat 8.1 g

Freezer Breakfast Burritos

Servings: 6
Cooking Time: 12minutes
Ingredients:
- 1 pack of 14 oz. extra-firm tofu, crumbled
- 1 cup of corn
- 6 whole-wheat (8") tortillas
- 1 tsp. of ground cumin
- 2 tbsp. of oil
- ¼ cup of fresh cilantro
- ¼ tsp. of salt
- 1 can of 15 oz. black beans, rinsed
- 4 scallions, sliced
- ½ cup of salsa

Directions:
1. Sauté the tofu with salt in hot oil (1 tbsp.) for 10-12 minutes. Take it out in a bowl.
2. Add more oil with scallions, beans & corn cook for 3 minutes.
3. Add tofu back to the pan with salsa. Cook for 2 minutes.
4. Serve in warm tortillas after rolling the tortilla. Or freeze for up to three months.

Nutrition:
- Per Serving : Protein 15 g | Fiber 7.7 g | Carbs 44 g | Fat 10 g

Chickpeas & Quinoa Salad

Servings: 8
Cooking Time: 20 Mins.
Ingredients:
- 1¾ C. water
- 1 C. quinoa, rinsed
- Salt, as required
- 2 C. cooked chickpeas
- 2 medium bell peppers, seeded and chopped
- 2 large cucumbers, chopped
- ½ C. onion, chopped
- 3 tbsp. olive oil
- 4 tbsp. fresh basil leaves, chopped

Directions:
1. In a saucepan, add the water over high heat and bring to a boil.
2. Add the quinoa and salt and cook until boiling.
3. Now adjust the heat to low and simmer, covered for about 15-20 minutes or until all the liquid is absorbed.
4. Remove from the heat and set aside, covered for about 5-10 minutes.
5. Uncover and with a fork, fluff the quinoa.
6. In a salad bowl, place quinoa with the remaining ingredients and gently toss to coat.
7. Serve immediately.

Nutrition:
- Per Serving : Protein 7.5 g | Fiber 6.8 g | Carbs 30.5 g | Fat 7.8 g

Apple & Strawberry Salad

Servings: 4
Cooking Time: 15 Mins.
Ingredients:
- For Salad:
- 4 C. mixed lettuce, torn
- 3 apples, cored and sliced
- 1 C. fresh strawberries, hulled and sliced
- ¼ C. pecans, chopped
- For Dressing:
- 3 tbsp. apple cider vinegar
- 3 tbsp. olive oil
- 1 tbsp. maple syrup

Directions:
1. For the salad, place all the ingredients in a large bowl and mix well.
2. For the dressing, place all the ingredients in a bowl and beat until well combined.
3. Pour the dressing over the salad and toss it all to coat well.
4. Serve immediately.

Nutrition:
- Per Serving : Protein 2 g | Fiber 7 g | Carbs 32.4 g | Fat 18.2 g

Fruity Pita Pockets

Servings: 2
Cooking Time: 10 Mins.
Ingredients:

- ½ C. low-fat cottage cheese
- 1 small apple, peeled, corded and chopped
- 1 small pear, peeled, corded and chopped
- 2 whole-wheat pita breads
- 2 tsp. maple syrup

Directions:

1. In a bowl, mix together cottage cheese, apple and pear.
2. Slice the pita bread to make a pocket.
3. Fill the pocket with the fruit mixture and drizzle with maple syrup.
4. Serve immediately.

Nutrition:

- Per Serving : Protein 14.6 g | Fiber 9.6 g | Carbs 67.7 g | Fat 3.1 g

Ground Turkey & Lentil Soup

Servings: 8
Cooking Time: 1 Hour 10 Mins.
Ingredients:

- 2 tbsp. olive oil
- 1½ lb. lean ground turkey
- Salt and ground black pepper, as required
- 1 large carrot, peeled and chopped
- 1 large celery stalk, chopped
- 1 large onion, chopped
- 6 garlic cloves, chopped
- 1 tsp. dried rosemary
- 1 tsp. dried oregano
- 2 large potatoes, peeled and chopped
- 8-9 C. homemade chicken broth
- 4-5 C. tomatoes, peeled, seeded and chopped
- 2 C. dry lentils
- ¼ C. fresh parsley, chopped

Directions:

1. In a large soup pan, heat the olive oil over medium-high heat and cook the turkey for about 5 minutes or until browned.
2. With a slotted spoon, transfer the turkey into a bowl and set aside.
3. In the same pan, add the carrot, celery onion, garlic and dried herbs over medium heat and cook for about 5 minutes.
4. Add the potatoes and cook for about 4-5 minutes.
5. Add the cooked turkey, tomatoes and broth and bring to a boil over high heat.
6. Now adjust the heat to low and cook, covered for about 10 minutes.
7. Add the lentils and cook, covered for about 40 minutes.
8. Stir in black pepper and remove from the heat.

9. Serve hot with the garnishing of parsley.
Nutrition:

- Per Serving : Protein 43 g | Fiber 16.6 g | Carbs 44.6 g | Fat 16.5 g

Vegetarian Breakfast Burritos

Servings:6
Cooking Time: 10 Minutes
Ingredients:

- 1 tablespoon canola oil
- 3 cups canned black beans, drained and rinsed
- 2 tomatoes, diced
- 2 bell peppers, diced
- 1 cup chopped fresh spinach
- 1 bunch green onions, chopped
- 6 large eggs, beaten
- Salt
- Freshly ground black pepper
- 6 whole-grain tortillas
- 1 cup shredded Cheddar cheese
- 1 avocado, diced
- 6 tablespoons salsa, for serving
- 6 tablespoons plain Greek yogurt, for serving

Directions:

1. tablespoons plain Greek yogurt, for serving
2. In a large pan over medium heat, warm the oil until it just begins to shimmer.
3. Add the beans, tomatoes, bell peppers, spinach, and green onions and cook until the vegetables begin to brown and become fragrant, about 2 minutes.
4. Add the eggs and cook, stirring, until the eggs are cooked and are no longer runny, 1 to 2 minutes. Season with salt and pepper to taste.
5. Divide the egg mixture equally among the tortillas, keeping the filling in a line near the middle of the tortilla. Sprinkle with the shredded cheese and diced avocado.
6. To wrap the burritos, take the left and right sides of the tortilla and fold them inward. Take the bottom side and fold it up and over the filling, rolling to wrap it up completely. Repeat with the remaining burritos.
7. Serve warm with 1 tablespoon each of salsa and Greek yogurt per burrito.
8. Store the burritos, wrapped in plastic wrap, in the refrigerator for up to 5 days or in the freezer for up to 3 months. To reheat, defrost frozen burritos in the refrigerator overnight and heat in the microwave or in a 350°F oven until hot, if you like a crispier burrito.

Nutrition:

- Per Serving : Protein 24 g | Fiber 12 g | Carbs 53 g | Fat 22 g

Bean Chili

Servings: 4
Cooking Time: 30 Minutes
Ingredients:
- 1 onion, chopped
- 14 oz. of the canned mixed bean, rinsed
- 1 tbsp. of sunflower oil
- 2 cans of (14 oz.) black beans, rinsed
- 1 tbsp. of brown sugar
- 4 eggs
- 2 cans of (14 oz.) chopped tomatoes with herbs & garlic

Directions:
1. Sauté onion in hot oil for 5 minutes.
2. Add the rest of the ingredients, except for eggs, simmer for 15 to 20 minutes.
3. Make four holes & add one egg in each hole. Simmer for 8-10 minutes.
4. Serve.

Nutrition:
- Per Serving : Protein 24 g | Fiber 15 g | Carbs 48 g | Fat 10 g

Chickpeas & Veggie Stew

Servings: 6
Cooking Time: 1 Hour 5 Mins.
Ingredients:
- 3 C. portabella mushrooms, chopped
- 4 C. water
- 1 C. cooked chickpeas
- 1 C. fresh kale, tough ribs removed and chopped
- 1 C. onion, chopped
- 1 C. bell peppers, seeded and chopped
- ½ C. butternut squash, peeled, seeded and chopped
- 2 tomatoes, peeled, seeded and chopped
- 2 tbsp. olive oil
- 1 tsp. dried oregano
- 1 tsp. dried basil
- Salt, as required

Directions:
1. In a soup pan, add all ingredients over high heat and bring to a rolling boil.
2. Now adjust the heat to low and simmer, covered for about 1 hour, stirring occasionally.
3. Serve hot.

Nutrition:
- Per Serving : Protein 8.8 g | Fiber 7.6 g | Carbs 28.6 g | Fat 6.9 g

Jambalaya

Servings:6
Cooking Time: 40 Minutes
Ingredients:
- 3 teaspoons vegetable oil, divided
- ½ pound large shrimp, peeled and deveined
- 1 boneless, skinless chicken breast, cut into small pieces
- 5 celery stalks, chopped
- 3 green bell peppers, diced
- ½ white or Spanish onion, diced
- 1 garlic clove, minced
- 2 tablespoons Cajun seasoning
- 1½ cups Homemade Chicken Stock or store-bought
- 1 cup brown basmati rice, rinsed
- 1 cup canned crushed tomatoes
- Salt
- Freshly ground black pepper

Directions:
1. Freshly ground black pepper
2. In a large saucepan over medium heat, warm 2 teaspoons of oil. Add the shrimp and cook until pink and golden, 1 to 2 minutes per side. Transfer the shrimp to a plate and set aside.
3. Add the chicken and cook until golden, cooked through, and no longer pink, about 5 minutes. Transfer the chicken to a plate and set aside.
4. Add the remaining 1 teaspoon of oil to the saucepan and warm until just shimmering. Add the celery, bell pepper, onion, garlic, and Cajun seasoning and cook until the onions are translucent, about 3 minutes.
5. Raise the heat to medium-high, add the chicken stock, rice, and crushed tomatoes, and bring to a boil. Lower the heat to medium-low and simmer for 20 to 25 minutes, or until the rice is cooked.
6. Stir in the chicken and shrimp. Taste and season with salt and pepper.
7. Store the jambalaya in an airtight container in the refrigerator for up to 5 days.

Nutrition:
- Per Serving : Protein 1 g | Fiber 17 g | Carbs 4 g | Fat 32 g

Chocolate Chip Zucchini Bread

Servings: 6
Cooking Time: 30minutes
Ingredients:
- 3/4 Cup of Coconut Sugar
- ½ cup of melted Coconut Oil
- 3 eggs
- ½ tsp. of Baking Soda
- 1 Tsp. of Vanilla Extract
- ½ tsp. of Baking Powder
- 1 Cup of Chocolate Chips
- 2 Cups of Whole Wheat Pastry Flour
- 1 Tsp. of Salt
- 2 Cups of Shredded Zucchini, squeezed

Directions:

1. Let the oven preheat to 350°F.
2. Oil spray small loaf pans.
3. Whisk eggs with vanilla, sugar & oil until smooth.
4. Add the dry ingredients & mix.
5. Add chocolate chips & zucchini, add to the small loaf pans.
6. Bake the small loaf pans for 30 to 35 minutes.
7. Serve.

Nutrition:

- Per Serving : Protein 8.1 g | Fiber 8.7 g | Carbs 16.9 g | Fat 8 g

Chickpeas Stuffed Avocado

Servings: 2
Cooking Time: 15 Mins.
Ingredients:

- 1 large avocado
- 1¼ C. cooked chickpeas
- ¼ C. celery stalks, chopped
- 1 scallion (greed part), sliced
- 1 small garlic clove, minced
- 1½ tbsp. fresh lemon juice
- ½ tsp. olive oil
- Salt and ground black pepper, as required
- 1 tbsp. fresh cilantro, chopped

Directions:
1. Cut the avocado in half and then remove the pit.
2. With a spoon, scoop out the flesh from each avocado half.
3. Then, cut half of the avocado flesh in equal-sized cubes.
4. In a large bowl, add avocado cubes and remaining ingredients except for sunflower seeds and cilantro and toss to coat well.
5. Stuff each avocado half with chickpeas mixture evenly.
6. Serve immediately with the garnishing of cilantro.

Nutrition:

- Per Serving : Protein 9.8 g | Fiber 13.8 g | Carbs 0 g | Fat 22.6 g

Banana-nut Oatmeal Cups

Servings: 12
Cooking Time: 30minutes
Ingredients:

- 1 ½ cups of milk
- 1 tsp. of baking powder
- 1 tsp. of vanilla extract
- 2 bananas, mashed
- 3 cups of rolled oats
- ⅓ cup of packed brown sugar
- 2 eggs, whisked
- ½ cup of chopped pecans, toasted
- 1 tsp. of ground cinnamon
- Half tsp. of salt

Directions:
1. Let the oven preheat to 375°F
2. Add all ingredients to a bowl, mix & pour in the oil sprayed muffin tin.
3. Bake for 25 minutes and then serve.

Nutrition:

- Per Serving : Protein 5.2 g | Fiber 4 g | Carbs 26.4 g | Fat 6.2 g

Orange & Avocado Salad

Servings: 3
Cooking Time: 10 Mins.
Ingredients:

- 2 oranges, peeled, seeded and sectioned
- 2 avocados, peeled, pitted and cubed
- 2 tbsp. extra-virgin olive oil
- 3 C. fresh baby arugula
- Pinch of salt and ground black pepper

Directions:
1. Place all ingredients in a salad bowl and gently toss to combine.
2. Serve immediately.

Nutrition:

- Per Serving : Protein 4.2 g | Fiber 12.2 g | Carbs 26.7 g | Fat 35.7 g

Quinoa And Avocado Scramble

Servings:4
Cooking Time: 20 Minutes
Ingredients:

- ⅓ cup quinoa, rinsed
- ⅔ cup water
- 1 teaspoon vegetable oil
- 2 green onions, chopped
- 1 red bell pepper, diced
- Salt
- Freshly ground black pepper
- 4 large eggs, beaten
- ½ cup shredded Cheddar cheese
- ¼ cup chunky salsa
- 1 ripe avocado, peeled, pitted, and cut into slices
- 2 tablespoons fresh lime juice

Directions:
1. tablespoons fresh lime juice
2. In a medium saucepan over high heat, mix together the quinoa and water and bring to a boil. Lower the heat to medium, cover, and continue to cook until the water is absorbed, about 15 minutes. Set aside.
3. In a large saucepan over medium heat, warm the oil until it just begins to shimmer. Add the green onions and peppers and cook until the vegetables begin to brown, 1 to 2 minutes. Lightly season with salt and pepper.

4. Add the eggs and cook, stirring often, until cooked through, 1 to 2 minutes. Remove from the heat.

5. Divide the quinoa equally among four bowls. Top with equal amounts of the egg mixture, shredded cheese, salsa, avocado slices, and a drizzle of lime juice. Serve hot.

Nutrition:

- Per Serving : Protein 12 g | Fiber 5 g | Carbs 18 g | Fat 18 g

Taco Salad

Servings:4
Cooking Time: 15 Minutes

Ingredients:

- 1 teaspoon vegetable oil
- ½ pound lean ground turkey or ground chicken, formed into a large patty
- 2 tablespoons taco seasoning (see Helpful Hint)
- Salt
- Freshly ground black pepper
- 6 cups chopped romaine lettuce
- Toppings
- 2 red or orange bell peppers, diced
- 3 Roma tomatoes, diced
- ½ English cucumber, diced
- ¾ cup green onions, thinly sliced
- 1 (15½-ounce) can black beans, rinsed and drained
- Salsa
- Sour cream or plain Greek yogurt

Directions:

1. Sour cream or plain Greek yogurt

2. In a large sauté pan or skillet over medium heat, warm the oil. Add the turkey patty and cook until browned, about 4 minutes. Flip the turkey and cook until browned, another 4 minutes. Use a spatula to break up the turkey into small pieces. Add the taco seasoning, stir to combine, and cook until completely cooked through, another 5 minutes. Taste, and season with salt and pepper.

3. Place the romaine lettuce in individual bowls. Spoon the taco meat over the lettuce.

4. Place the toppings in individual bowls and set out at the table. Diners can choose whichever toppings they like.

Nutrition:

- Per Serving : Protein 21 g | Fiber 10 g | Carbs 33 g | Fat 7 g

Fruity Chia Pudding

Servings: 4
Cooking Time: 10 Mins.

Ingredients:

- 2/3 C. unsweetened almond milk
- 2 C. frozen blueberries
- ½ of frozen banana, peeled and sliced
- 5 large soft dates, pitted and chopped

- ½ C. chia seeds

Directions:

1. Add all ingredients in a food processor except for chia seeds and pulse until smooth.

2. Transfer the mixture in a bowl. Add chia seeds and stir to combine well.

3. Refrigerate for 30 minutes, stirring after every 5 minutes.

Nutrition:

- Per Serving : Protein 4.1 g | Fiber 8.1 g | Carbs 28 g | Fat 5.9 g

Ginger-garlic Chicken Soup

Servings: 4
Cooking Time: 30 Minutes

Ingredients:

- Half cup of diced yellow onion
- 6 minced cloves garlic
- 3 tbsp. of oil
- 1 pound of chicken thighs, boneless, skinless, cut into half" pieces
- 4 cups of chicken broth
- 1 ½ cups of green papaya, peeled & cubed
- ¼ tsp. of salt & pepper, each
- ¼ cup of fresh ginger, sliced
- 2 cups of chopped bok choy leaves
- 1 tbsp. of fish sauce

Directions:

1. Sauté garlic, onion & ginger in hot oil for 3 minutes.

2. Add both & chicken, cook for 5 minutes.

3. Add papaya, salt, pepper, fish sauce & bok choy. Simmer for 5 minutes.

4. Serve.

Nutrition:

- Per Serving : Protein 27 g | Fiber 4 g | Carbs 14 g | Fat 20 g

Beans With Salsa

Servings: 2
Cooking Time: 11 Mins.

Ingredients:

- 1 tbsp. olive oil
- ½ of small onion, chopped
- 1 garlic clove, minced
- 2 tsp. fresh cilantro, minced
- 1 (16-oz.) can pinto beans, rinsed and drained
- 1/3 C. salsa

Directions:

1. In a large wok, heat oil over medium heat and sauté the onion for about 4-5 minutes.

2. Add the garlic and cilantro and sauté for about 1 minute.

3. Stir in the beans and salsa and cook for about 4-5 minutes or until heated completely.

4. Serve hot.

Nutrition:

- Per Serving : Protein 12.1 g | Fiber 8.6 g | Carbs 38.4 g | Fat 7.1 g

High Fiber Pasta

Servings: 6
Cooking Time: 45minutes

Ingredients:

- 17 oz. of pumpkin, peeled & cubes
- 1 tsp. of olive oil
- ¼ cup of fresh basil, sliced
- 1 garlic clove, minced
- 17 oz. of Whole Meal Spaghetti
- 4 red capsicums, cut into fours without seeds
- 4.4 oz. of olives, halved
- 7 oz. of feta, crumbled
- Salt & black pepper

Directions:

1. Let the oven preheat to 390 F.
2. Oil spray 2 baking trays.
3. In a bowl, toss pumpkin & garlic with oil, salt & pepper. Roast for half an hour on one tray.
4. On the other tray, add capsicum & bake for half an hour.
5. Cook pasta as per package Directions.
6. Slice the capsicum & mix with pasta with the rest of the ingredients.
7. Add salt & pepper. Serve.

Nutrition:

- Per Serving : Protein 5 g | Fiber 8 g | Carbs 14 g | Fat 6 g

Lentils & Pumpkin Soup

Servings: 4
Cooking Time: 50 Mins.

Ingredients:

- 2 tbsp. olive oil
- 2 C. pumpkin, peeled and cubed
- 1 carrot, peeled and chopped
- 1 onion, chopped
- 1 garlic clove, chopped
- 1 C. split lentils, rinsed
- 1½ tsp. dried thyme
- 1 tsp. ground cumin
- Salt and ground black pepper, as required
- 4 C. hot vegetable broth
- 2 tbsp. fresh parsley, chopped

Directions:

1. In a large saucepan, heat the oil over medium heat and cook the pumpkin and carrot for about 10 minutes, stirring occasionally.
2. Add the onion and garlic and cook for about 5 minutes, stirring occasionally.
3. Stir in the lentils, thyme, and cumin and sauté for about 1-2 minutes.

4. Add the water, salt and black pepper and bring to a boil.
5. Adjust the heat to low and simmer, covered for about 20-30 minutes.
6. Remove from the heat and with an immersion blender, blend the soup until smooth.
7. Serve hot with the topping of parsley.

Nutrition:

- Per Serving : Protein 19.3 g | Fiber 19.8 g | Carbs 45.2 g | Fat 9.5 g

Kidney Beans In Tomato Sauce

Servings: 6
Cooking Time: 25 Mins.

Ingredients:

- ¼ C. extra-virgin olive oil
- 1 medium onion, chopped finely
- 2 garlic cloves, minced
- 2 tbsp. fresh ginger, minced
- 1 C. homemade tomato puree
- 1 tsp. ground coriander
- 1 tsp. ground cumin
- Salt and ground black pepper, as required
- 2 large tomatoes, peeled, seeded and chopped finely
- 3 C. canned red kidney beans
- 2 C. water
- ½ C. fresh parsley, chopped

Directions:

1. In a large soup pan, heat oil over medium heat and sauté the onion, garlic, and ginger for about 4-5 minutes.
2. Stir in the tomato puree and spices and cook for about 5 minutes.
3. Stir in the tomatoes, kidney beans, and water and bring to a boil over high heat.
4. Now adjust the heat to medium and simmer for about 10-15 minutes or until desired thickness.
5. Serve hot with the garnishing of parsley.

Nutrition:

- Per Serving : Protein 8.9 g | Fiber 0.4 g | Carbs 28.1 g | Fat 9.9 g

Creamy Potato Soup

Servings:4
Cooking Time: 35 Minutes

Ingredients:

- 3 cups chicken stock
- 4 russet potatoes, scrubbed and cut into small dice (with skin on)
- 2 teaspoons onion powder
- 1 teaspoon garlic powder
- 1 (15½-ounce) can white kidney beans, drained and rinsed
- 1 bunch green onions, chopped, divided
- 1½ cups shredded Cheddar cheese, divided

- ½ cup milk of choice
- Salt
- Freshly ground black pepper

Directions:

1. Freshly ground black pepper
2. In a large stockpot over medium-high heat, mix together the stock, potatoes, onion powder, and garlic powder and bring to a boil. Lower the heat to medium-low and simmer until the potatoes are cooked through, 15 to 20 minutes.
3. In a blender or food processor, puree the beans until smooth. If the mixture is too thick to blend, add water, 1 tablespoon at a time. Set aside.
4. Using an immersion blender, blend the potatoes until your desired consistency. I like mine to have a bit of texture, so I blend only half of the potatoes. Other family members like theirs silky smooth, and they blend smooth.
5. Stir the white bean puree into the potatoes and cook over low heat until heated through, about 15 minutes.
6. Reserve 1 tablespoon of the chopped green onions and 2 tablespoons of the shredded cheese and set aside. Add the remaining green onions, the milk, and the remaining cheese to the soup and stir to combine.
7. Spoon into bowls and serve hot with the reserved green onions and cheese sprinkled over the top for garnish.
8. Leftover soup can be stored in an airtight container in the refrigerator for up to 5 days.

Nutrition:

- Per Serving : Protein 21 g | Fiber 10 g | Carbs 50 g | Fat 14 g

Bean & Meat Loaf

Servings: 4
Cooking Time: 1 Hour & 40 Minutes
Ingredients:

- ¾ cup of a kidney bean, cooked
- 1 tbsp. of Italian herb seasoning
- ½ tsp. of black pepper
- 2 eggs
- 1 tbsp. of tamari
- 1/3 cup of rolled oats
- 2 tbsp. of dried onion flakes
- ½ cup of bell pepper, minced
- 15 oz. of ground beef
- 1 cup of tomato sauce
- ½ cup of celery, minced
- ¾ tsp. of garlic powder

Directions:

1. Let the oven preheat to 350°F.
2. Blend the eggs with tamari, beans, pepper & herb blend.
3. Add the rest of the ingredients to the bean mixture except for a half cup of tomato sauce.
4. Oil spray a loaf pan, add the mixture and top with tomato sauce.

5. Bake for 1-1 ¼ hours.
Nutrition:

- Per Serving : Protein 15 g | Fiber 8.9 g | Carbs 13 g | Fat 8 g

Bean Salad

Servings:4
Cooking Time: 10 Minutes
Ingredients:

- FOR THE DRESSING
- ¼ cup vegetable oil
- 2 tablespoons lime juice
- 1 tablespoon chopped fresh cilantro
- 1 teaspoon honey
- ½ teaspoon Dijon mustard
- 1 garlic clove, minced
- Salt
- Freshly ground black pepper
- FOR THE SALAD
- 1 (15½-ounce) can chickpeas, drained and rinsed
- 1 (15½-ounce) can black beans, drained and rinsed
- 1 (15-ounce) can kidney beans, drained and rinsed
- 1 cup diced cucumber
- ¾ cup canned corn
- 2 tablespoons diced red onion
- ½ avocado, diced

Directions:

1. ½ avocado, diced
2. In a small bowl, whisk together the oil, lime juice, cilantro, honey, Dijon mustard, and garlic. Taste and season with salt and pepper.
3. In a medium bowl, mix together the chickpeas, black beans, kidney beans, cucumber, corn, red onion, and avocado. Add the dressing and lightly toss. Serve immediately.
4. Store the salad in an airtight container in the refrigerator for up to 5 days.

Nutrition:

- Per Serving : Protein 19 g | Fiber 21 g | Carbs 72 g | Fat 20 g

Blueberry Salad

Servings: 2
Cooking Time: 10 Mins.
Ingredients:

- For Salad:
- 3 C. fresh baby arugula
- 1½ C. fresh blueberries
- ¼ C. walnuts, chopped
- For Dressing
- 1 tbsp. olive oil
- 1 tbsp. fresh lime juice
- ½ tsp. maple syrup

- Salt, as required

Directions:

1. For salad: place all ingredients in a salad bowl and mix.
2. For dressing: place all ingredients in another bowl and beat until well combined.
3. Pour the dressing over the salad and toss to coat well.
4. Serve immediately.

Nutrition:

- Per Serving : Protein 5.6 g | Fiber 7.5 g | Carbs 14.9 g | Fat 17 g

Pear & Celery Juice

Servings: 2
Cooking Time: 10 Mins.

Ingredients:

- 4 large pears
- 4 celery stalks
- 1 tsp. honey
- ½ C. filtered water

Directions:

1. Add all ingredients in a high-power blender and pulse until well combined.
2. Through a cheesecloth-lined sieve, strain the juice and pour into two glasses.
3. Serve immediately.

Nutrition:

- Per Serving : Protein 1.8 g | Fiber 13.5 g | Carbs 67.6 g | Fat 0.7 g

Cucumber & Lettuce Smoothie

Servings: 2
Cooking Time: 10 Mins.

Ingredients:

- 1 cucumber, peeled and chopped
- 2 C. lettuce leaves
- ½ C. fresh mint leaves
- 1 tbsp. fresh ginger, grated
- 2 C. water
- 1 tbsp. fresh lime juice
- ¼ C. ice cubes

Directions:

1. Add all the ingredients in a high-power blender and pulse until creamy.
2. Pour the smoothie into two glasses and serve immediately.

Nutrition:

- Per Serving : Protein 3.8 g | Fiber 7 g | Carbs 20.1 g | Fat 1 g

Pasta With Green Peas

Servings: 4
Cooking Time: 30minutes

Ingredients:

- 2 Garlic Cloves
- Half tsp. of Nutmeg
- 12 oz. of Whole Wheat Penne Pasta
- 11 oz. of Peas
- 12 oz. of Broccoli Florets
- 2 tbsp. of Olive Oil
- 4 tbsp. of Fresh Parsley

Directions:

1. Sauté the garlic & nutmeg in hot oil for 30 seconds.
2. Add the parsley, peas & florets with a splash of water, cook for 10 minutes.
3. Add salt & pepper.
4. Cook pasta as per package Directions. Drain & add to the sauce with some of the pasta water.
5. Toss well & serve.

Nutrition:

- Per Serving : Protein 6 g | Fiber 6.2 g | Carbs 19 g | Fat 5 g

Chocolate Smoothie

Servings: 12
Cooking Time: 0minutes

Ingredients:

- ¼ cup of Cacao Bliss
- 2 cups of milk
- ¼ cup of almond butter
- Ice
- 2 bananas, sliced & frozen
- 2 tbsp. of hemp hearts

Directions:

1. Add all ingredients to a blender. Pulse until smooth.
2. Serve by pouring in a chilled glass.

Nutrition:

- Per Serving : Protein 22 g | Fiber 11 g | Carbs 48 g | Fat 31 g

Beef & Broccoli Stir-fry

Servings: 2
Cooking Time: 15 Minutes

Ingredients:

- 2 cups of broccoli, diced
- 1 tsp. of salt
- 1 lb. of flank steak, cubed
- 1 tsp. of pepper
- Sauce
- 1 tbsp. of sesame seed
- ¼ cup of honey
- ½ cup of soy sauce
- 2 cloves of garlic
- 1 tsp. of ginger

Directions:

1. Add all ingredients of sauce in a bowl & mix.
2. Cook beef in hot oil until browned.

3. Add sauce, cook for 2 minutes, add vegetables. Cook until tender.

4. Serve.

Nutrition:

- Per Serving : Protein 72 g | Fiber 7 g | Carbs 20 g | Fat 22 g

Pumpkin Overnight Oats

Servings: 2
Cooking Time: 0minutes
Ingredients:

- 1/4 cup of plain yogurt
- 2/3 cup of almond milk, unsweetened
- 1/4 cup of pumpkin puree
- 1 packet of instant oats
- 1 tsp. of maple syrup
- Half tsp. of pumpkin pie spice

Directions:

1. In a mason jar, add all ingredients. Shake well & keep in the fridge overnight.

2. Serve.

Nutrition:

- Per Serving : Protein 5 g | Fiber 6 g | Carbs 32 g | Fat 4 g

Lentil & Sweet Potato Soup

Servings: 4
Cooking Time: 50 Mins.
Ingredients:

- 1 tbsp. olive oil
- 1 C. onion, chopped
- ½ C. carrots, peeled and chopped
- ½ C. celery, chopped
- 2 garlic cloves, minced
- 4 C. homemade vegetable broth
- 2½ C., peeled and chopped
- 1 C. lentils, rinsed
- 1½ tbsp. fresh lemon juice
- Salt and ground black pepper, as required
- 2 tbsp. fresh cilantro, chopped

Directions:

1. In a large Dutch oven, heat the oil over medium heat and sauté the onion, carrot and celery for about 5-7 minutes.

2. Add the garlic and sauté for about 1 minute.

3. Add the sweet potatoes and cook for about 1-2 minutes.

4. Add in the broth and bring to a boil.

5. Now adjust the heat to low and simmer, covered for about 5 minutes.

6. Stir in the lentils and gain bring to a boil over medium-high heat

7. Now adjust the heat to low and simmer, covered for about 25-30 minutes or until desired doneness.

8. Stir in the lemon juice, salt and black pepper and remove from the heat.

9. Serve hot with the garnishing of cilantro.

Nutrition:

- Per Serving : Protein 19.3 g | Fiber 19.7 g | Carbs 61 g | Fat 5.6 g

Chickpeas In Tomato Sauce

Servings: 6
Cooking Time: 25 Mins.
Ingredients:

- 3 tbsp. olive oil
- 1 medium onion, chopped finely
- 2 garlic cloves, minced
- 1 tsp. ground cumin
- Salt, as required
- 2 large tomatoes, peeled, seeded and chopped finely
- 3 C. cooked chickpeas
- 2 C. water
- ¼ C. fresh parsley, chopped

Directions:

1. In a saucepan, heat the oil over medium heat and sauté the onion and garlic for about 6-8 minutes.

2. Stir in the spices and salt and cook for about 1-2 minutes.

3. Stir in the tomatoes, chickpeas and water and bring to a boil over high heat.

4. Now adjust the heat to medium and simmer for 10-15 minutes or until desired thickness.

5. Serve hot with the garnishing of parsley.

Nutrition:

- Per Serving : Protein 8.3 g | Fiber 7.8 g | Carbs 27.7 g | Fat 3.3 g

Quinoa, Beans & Mango Salad

Servings: 6
Cooking Time: 15 Mins.
Ingredients:

- For Dressing:
- 2 tbsp. fresh lime juice
- 2 tbsp. maple syrup
- 1 tbsp. Dijon mustard
- ½ tsp. ground cumin
- Salt and ground black pepper, as required
- ¼ C. extra-virgin olive oil
- For Salad:
- 2 C. fresh mango, peeled, pitted and cubed
- 2 tbsp. fresh lime juice, divided
- 2 avocados, peeled, pitted and cubed
- Pinch of salt
- 1 C. cooked quinoa
- 2 (14-oz.) cans black beans, rinsed and drained
- 1 small onion, chopped
- ½ C. fresh cilantro, chopped

- 6 C. romaine lettuce, shredded

Directions:

1. For dressing: in a blender, add all the ingredients except oil and pulse until well combined.
2. While the motor is running, gradually add the oil and pulse until smooth.
3. For salad: in a bowl, add the mango and 1 tbsp. of lime juice and toss to coat well.
4. In another bowl, add the avocado, a Pinch of salt and remaining lime juice and toss to coat well.
5. In a large serving bowl, add the mango, avocado and remaining salad ingredients and mix.
6. Place the dressing and toss to coat well.
7. Serve immediately.

Nutrition:

- Per Serving : Protein 18.1 g | Fiber 19.7 g | Carbs 71.5 g | Fat 24.4 g

Strawberry Oat Smoothie

Servings: 2
Cooking Time: 10 Mins.

Ingredients:

- 1½ C. frozen strawberries
- 1 medium banana, peeled and sliced
- ¼ C. old-fashioned oats
- 1 C. fat-free plain yogurt
- ¾ C. unsweetened almond milk

Directions:

1. Add all the ingredients in a high-power blender and pulse until creamy.
2. Pour the smoothie into two glasses and serve immediately.

Nutrition:

- Per Serving : Protein 10 g | Fiber 6.1 g | Carbs 37.9 g | Fat 4 g

Apple-cinnamon Baked Oatmeal Squares

Servings:9
Cooking Time: 35 Minutes

Ingredients:

- 1½ cups milk
- 2 large eggs
- ½ cup brown sugar
- ½ cup unsweetened applesauce
- 4 tablespoons (½ stick) butter, melted
- 2 teaspoons ground cinnamon
- 1½ teaspoons baking powder
- 1 teaspoon vanilla extract
- Pinch salt
- 3 cups rolled oats
- 2 apples, Honey Crisp, Fuji, Granny Smith, or Gala, peeled and finely diced

- 1 tablespoon chia seeds
- 2¼ cups plain or vanilla Greek yogurt

Directions:

1. ¼ cups plain or vanilla Greek yogurt
2. Preheat the oven to 350°F.
3. In a large mixing bowl, whisk together the milk, eggs, brown sugar, applesauce, butter, cinnamon, baking powder, vanilla, and salt until well combined.
4. Add the oats, apples, and chia seeds and mix to incorporate.
5. Pour the oatmeal mixture into an 8-by-8-inch baking dish and spread out evenly. Bake for 30 to 35 minutes, or until the oatmeal is set. Let cool on a wire rack for 5 minutes.
6. Cut into 9 squares and serve with ¼ cup of Greek yogurt each for a complete meal.

Nutrition:

- Per Serving : Protein 12 g | Fiber 4 g | Carbs 40 g | Fat 12 g

Lentil Curry

Servings:4
Cooking Time: 1 Hour 15 Minutes

Ingredients:

- 1½ cups brown basmati rice
- 2½ cups cold water
- 2 teaspoons vegetable oil
- 1 white or Spanish onion, diced small
- 1 garlic clove, minced
- 2 tablespoons curry powder
- 1 teaspoon garam masala
- 1 cup dried red lentils, rinsed
- 2½ cups vegetable or chicken stock
- 1 (6-ounce) can tomato paste
- 1 cup coconut milk
- 1 teaspoon soy sauce
- ½ teaspoon lime juice
- ½ teaspoon honey
- Salt
- Freshly ground black pepper
- ½ cup plain Greek yogurt

Directions:

1. ½ cup plain Greek yogurt
2. Rinse the rice in cold water until the water runs clear. Place the rice and water in a medium saucepan over high heat and bring to a boil. Lower the heat to medium-low, cover, and simmer for 50 minutes. Remove from the heat and let sit, covered, for 5 minutes. Fluff with a fork and set aside.
3. In a large sauté pan or skillet over medium heat, warm the oil. Add the onions, garlic, curry powder, and garam masala and cook until the onions are translucent, about 3 minutes. Add the lentils and cook for another 2 minutes. Raise the heat to medium-high, add the stock and tomato

paste, and bring to a boil. Lower the heat to medium-low and simmer for 10 to 15 minutes.

4. Add the coconut milk, soy sauce, lime juice, and honey, stir to combine, and simmer for 5 minutes. Taste and season with salt and pepper. Garnish with a dollop of plain Greek yogurt.

5. Serve hot over the brown rice.

Nutrition:

- Per Serving : Protein 23 g | Fiber 12 g | Carbs 100 g | Fat 18 g

Bulgur Porridge

Servings: 2
Cooking Time: 15 Mins.
Ingredients:

- 2/3 C. fat-free milk
- 1/3 C. bulgur, rinsed
- Pinch of salt
- 1 ripe banana, peeled and mashed
- 1 large apple, peeled, cored and chopped

Directions:

1. In a saucepan, add the almond milk, bulgur and salt over medium-high heat and bring to a boil.

2. Now adjust the heat to low and simmer for about 10 minutes.

3. Remove the pan of bulgur from heat and immediately stir in the mashed banana.

4. Serve warm with the topping of chopped apple.

Nutrition:

- Per Serving : Protein 6.5 g | Fiber 8.5 g | Carbs 50.6 g | Fat 2.4 g

Orange & Kale Salad

Servings: 2
Cooking Time: 10 Mins.
Ingredients:

- For Salad:
- 3 C. fresh kale, tough ribs removed and torn
- 2 oranges, peeled and segmented
- 2 tbsp. fresh cranberries
- For Dressing:
- 2 tbsp. olive oil
- 2 tbsp. fresh orange juice
- ½ tsp. maple syrup
- Salt, as required

Directions:

1. For salad: place all ingredients in a salad bowl and mix.

2. For dressing: place all ingredients in n another bowl and beat until well combined.

3. Pour the dressing over salad and toss to coat well.

4. Serve immediately.

Nutrition:

- Per Serving : Protein 4.8 g | Fiber 7 g | Carbs 35.7 g | Fat 14.3 g

Sweet Corn Oatmeal

Servings: 4
Cooking Time: 10minutes
Ingredients:

- 2 cups of corn kernels
- 1 tbsp. of maple syrup
- 1 cup of milk
- ⅛ tsp. of ground nutmeg
- 2 cups of rolled oats
- 1 tbsp. of unsalted butter
- 1 tsp. of kosher salt
- ¼ tsp. of vanilla extract
- 3 cups of water
- ¼ cup of yogurt
- 1 cup of sliced peaches

Directions:

1. In a pan, heat butter, cook corn syrup for 3 minutes.
2. Add salt & oats. Cook for 2 minutes.
3. Add milk, water & nutmeg, cook for 5 minutes.
4. Add vanilla & yogurt mix.
5. Divide the oats into 4 bowls, top with yogurt & serve.

Nutrition:

- Per Serving : Protein 11 g | Fiber 6 g | Carbs 51 g | Fat 1.6 g

Prosciutto Pizza With Corn & Arugula

Servings: 4
Cooking Time: 40 Minutes
Ingredients:

- 2 tbsp. of olive oil, divided
- 1 clove garlic, minced
- 1 oz. of sliced prosciutto, torn
- 1 cup of mozzarella cheese, shredded
- 1 pound of whole-wheat pizza dough
- ¼ tsp. of ground pepper
- 1 cup of fresh corn
- 1 ½ cups of arugula
- ½ cup of torn fresh basil

Directions:

1. Let the grill preheat to medium.
2. Roll the dough. Mix the garlic with 1 tbsp. of oil.
3. Oil spray the grill & grill the dough for 1-2 minutes.
4. Flip & spread garlic oil, add corn, cheese & prosciutto.
5. Grill for 2-3 minutes. Add the rest of the ingredients,
6. Slice & serve.

Nutrition:

- Per Serving : Protein 18 g | Fiber 4 g | Carbs 53 g | Fat 19 g

Beef & Lentil Chili

Servings: 6
Cooking Time: 45 Mins.
Ingredients:

- 1 tbsp. olive oil
- 2 lb. lean ground beef
- 2 C. onion, chopped
- 1 C. bell pepper, seeded and chopped
- 1 C. celery stalk, chopped
- 4 garlic cloves, chopped finely
- 1 tsp. dried oregano, crushed
- 2 tsp. ground cumin
- Salt and ground black pepper, as required
- 2 bay leaves
- 3 C. tomatoes, peeled, seeded and chopped finely
- 1 C. homemade chicken broth
- 1 C. water
- 1 C. dried lentils

Directions:

1. I a large pan, heat oil over medium-high heat and cook beef for about 4-5 minutes, breaking the lumps with a wooden spoon.
2. Add onion, red pepper, celery, oregano, salt and black pepper and cook for about 4-5 minutes.
3. Add bay leaves, tomatoes, broth and water and bring to a boil.
4. Now adjust the heat to medium and simmer, covered for about 20 minutes, stirring occasionally.
5. Meanwhile, in another large pan of water, add the lentils and bring to a boil.
6. Simmer for about 15 minutes, stirring occasionally.
7. Drain the lentils and transfer into chili.
8. Simmer for about 10 minutes, stirring occasionally.
9. Discard bay leaves and serve hot.

Nutrition:

- Per Serving : Protein 56.8 g | Fiber 12.4 g | Carbs 29.6 g | Fat 12.8 g

Chickpeas & Avocado Toast

Servings: 2
Cooking Time: 7 Mins.
Ingredients:

- 1½ tbsp. extra-virgin olive oil, divided
- 1 (16-oz.) can chickpeas, rinsed, drained and pat dried
- 1 tsp. ground turmeric
- 1 tsp. fresh lemon juice
- Salt and ground black pepper, as required
- 1 avocado, peeled, pitted and chopped roughly
- 2 whole-wheat bread slices, toasted
- ¼ C. tomatoes, peeled, seeded and chopped
- ½ tsp. fresh parsley, chopped

Directions:

1. In a wok, heat 1 tbsp. of oil over medium heat and cook the chickpeas for about 3-4 minutes, stirring continuously.
2. Stir in the turmeric and cooking for about 2-3 minutes or until chickpeas are toasted.
3. Remove from the heat and stir in the lemon juice, salt and black pepper. Set aside.
4. In a bowl, add the chopped avocado with a Pinch of salt and black pepper and with a fork, mash well.
5. Arrange 1 bread slices onto each serving plate.
6. Spread mashed avocado on one side of each bread slice and top with chickpeas.
7. Garnish with parsley and serve.

Nutrition:

- Per Serving : Protein 5.8 g | Fiber 17.8 g | Carbs 72.9 g | Fat 32.9 g

Satisfying Salad

Servings: 3
Cooking Time: 0minutes
Ingredients:

- 1 onion
- 1 garlic clove
- 10 walnuts, chopped
- 1 cup of sliced cabbage
- Half lemon's juice
- 1 cup of sliced lettuce
- 10 olives
- 1 red pepper
- 1 cup of canned white beans
- 1 tsp. of balsamic vinegar
- Half cup of canned corn
- 1 carrot
- 1 tbsp. of olive oil

Directions:

1. Chop the vegetables to your liking.
2. Add all the ingredients to a bowl, mix well & serve.
3. Adjust seasoning & serve.

Nutrition:

- Per Serving : Protein 13 g | Fiber 10 g | Carbs 38 g | Fat 23 g

Chicken & Fruit Salad

Servings: 4
Cooking Time: 15 Mins.
Ingredients:

- For Vinaigrette:
- 2 tbsp. apple cider vinegar
- 2 tbsp. extra-virgin olive oil
- Salt and ground black pepper, as required
- For Salad:
- 2 C. cooked chicken, cubed
- 8 C. lettuce, torn
- 2 apples, peeled, cored and chopped

- 2 C. fresh strawberries, hulled and sliced
- ¼ C. almonds, chopped

Directions:

1. For vinaigrette: in a small bowl, add all ingredients and beat well.
2. For salad: in a large salad bowl, mix together all ingredients.
3. Place vinaigrette over chicken mixture and toss to coat well.
4. Serve immediately.

Nutrition:

- Per Serving : Protein 22.8 g | Fiber 6.1 g | Carbs 25.6 g | Fat 12.7 g

High-fiber Mac And Cheese

Servings:4
Cooking Time: 20 Minutes

Ingredients:

- 2½ cups whole-wheat or high-fiber elbow macaroni
- 1 tablespoon olive oil
- 1 cup canned brown or green lentils, rinsed, drained
- 3 tablespoons butter or margarine
- 3 tablespoons all-purpose flour
- 1 teaspoon onion powder
- ¼ teaspoon Dijon mustard
- Pinch ground nutmeg
- 1¾ cups half-and-half or whipping cream
- 1½ cups shredded sharp Cheddar cheese
- Salt
- Freshly ground black pepper

Directions:

1. Freshly ground black pepper
2. Bring a large saucepan of water to a boil over high heat and cook the macaroni until al dente, according to the package instructions, about 8 minutes. Drain the pasta and toss with the olive oil to prevent the noodles from sticking.
3. Puree the lentils in a blender or food processor until smooth. If the mixture is too thick, add water 1 tablespoon at a time and continue to puree until smooth. Set aside.
4. In a large saucepan over medium heat, melt the butter. Add the flour, onion powder, Dijon mustard, and nutmeg, and cook, stirring constantly, for 1 minute. Slowly whisk in the half-and-half and bring to a boil. Lower the heat to medium-low and simmer, whisking constantly, for 2 minutes.
5. Remove from the heat, add the lentil puree and shredded cheese, and stir until the cheese is melted. Taste and season with salt and pepper. Add the macaroni to the sauce and stir until completely combined. Serve hot.

Nutrition:

- Per Serving : Protein 26 g | Fiber 10 g | Carbs 72 g | Fat 40 g

Chickpeas & Couscous Burgers

Servings: 4
Cooking Time: 10 Mins.

Ingredients:

- 1 C. water
- 1/3 C. dry couscous
- 1½ C. broccoli florets
- 2 tsp. olive oil
- ½ C. onion, chopped
- ½ C. scallion, chopped
- 2 tsp. ground cumin
- ¼ tsp. ground turmeric
- 1 tbsp. tahini
- 1 (15-oz.) can chickpeas, rinsed and drained
- ½ C. panko breadcrumbs
- 4 C. fresh kale, tough ribs removed and chopped

Directions:

1. Preheat your oven to 400 ºF. Line a baking sheet with foil paper.
2. In a small pan, mix together water and couscous over medium heat and bring to a boil.
3. Immediately remove from heat and set aside, covered for about 10 minutes or until all the liquid is absorbed.
4. Meanwhile, in a saucepan of boiling water, arrange a steamer basket.
5. Place the broccoli in steamer basket and steam, covered for about 5-7 minutes. Drain the broccoli well.
6. Meanwhile, in a wok, heat the oil over medium heat and sauté the onion and scallion for about 3-5 minutes.
7. Stir in the cumin and turmeric and remove from heat.
8. In a food processor, add the couscous, broccoli, onion mixture, tahini and chickpeas and pulse until well combined.
9. Transfer the mixture into a bowl.
10. Add the breadcrumbs and stir to combine.
11. Make equal-sized patties from mixture.
12. Arrange the patties onto the prepared baking sheet in a single layer.
13. Bake for approximately50 minutes, flipping once halfway through.
14. Serve alongside the kale.

Nutrition:

- Per Serving : Protein 12.8 g | Fiber 8.3 g | Carbs 44.2 g | Fat 7.1 g

Chicken, Beans & Spinach Chili

Servings: 10
Cooking Time: 55 Mins.

Ingredients:

- 2 tbsp. olive oil
- 3 lb. ground chicken
- 1 C. onion, chopped
- 4 garlic cloves, minced
- 1 tsp. fresh ginger, minced

- 2 tsp. dried thyme, crushed
- 2 tsp. ground cumin
- 3 (15-oz.) cans black beans, rinsed and drained
- 4 C. fresh baby spinach
- 6 tomatoes, peeled, seeded and chopped
- 1 (8-oz.) can tomato paste
- 3 C. water

Directions:
1. In a large Dutch oven, heat oil over medium heat and cook chicken for about 4-5 minutes.
2. Add onions, garlic, ginger, thyme and spices and stir fry for about 4-5 minutes.
3. Stir in remaining ingredients and bring to a gentle boil.
4. Now adjust the heat to low and simmer, covered for about 30-40 minutes, stirring occasionally.
5. Serve hot.

Nutrition:
- Per Serving : Protein 53 g | Fiber 13.6 g | Carbs 39.7 g | Fat 12.6 g

Quinoa & Sweet Potato Burgers

Servings: 6
Cooking Time: 22 Mins.
Ingredients:
- 1 tbsp. olive oil
- 1 medium onion, chopped
- Salt, as required
- ½ tsp. fresh ginger, minced
- 3 garlic cloves, minced
- 1 tbsp. fresh thyme, chopped
- 2 C. cooked quinoa
- 2 medium baked sweet potatoes, peeled and mashed
- Ground black pepper, as required
- 3-4 tbsp. olive oil
- 8 C. fresh baby spinach

Directions:
1. In a wok, heat olive oil over medium-low heat and sauté onion and salt for about 4-5 minutes.
2. Add ginger, garlic and thyme and sauté for about 1 minute.
3. Remove from heat and set aside to cool slightly.
4. In a bowl, add quinoa, sweet potato, onion mixture, salt and black pepper and mix until well combined.
5. Make 12 equal-sized patties from mixture.
6. In a large wok, heat oil over medium heat and cook 6 patties for about 3-4 minutes per side.
7. Serve hot alongside the spinach.

Nutrition:
- Per Serving : Protein 10.3 g | Fiber 7.8 g | Carbs 54.4 g | Fat 13.1 g

Lentil Tomato Salad

Servings: 4

Cooking Time: 0 Minutes
Ingredients:
- 1/4 cup of white wine vinegar
- 15 oz. of canned lentils, rinsed
- Salt, to taste
- 1 1/2 cups of cherry tomatoes, halved
- 1/8 cup of chopped chives

Directions:
1. Add all ingredients to a bowl. Toss well & serve.

Nutrition:
- Per Serving : Protein 10 g | Fiber 9 g | Carbs 24 g | Fat 1 g

Warm Fruity Cheese Bowl

Servings: 2
Cooking Time: 8 Mins.
Ingredients:
- 1 apple, peeled, cored and chopped
- ½ C. frozen unsweetened cherries
- tsp. pure maple syrup
- 2 tbsp. fresh lemon juice
- 2-3 tbsp. water
- 1 C. fresh raspberries
- ½ tsp. orange zest, grated finely
- ½ tsp. ground cinnamon
- 1 tsp. vanilla extract
- 1½ C. low-fat cottage cheese
- 3 tbsp. almonds, chopped

Directions:
1. In a saucepan, add the apple, cherries, maple syrup, lemon juice and water and stir to combine.
2. Place the pan over medium heat and bring to a boil, stirring occasionally.
3. Add the raspberries, orange zest and spices and stir to combine.
4. Now adjust the heat to low and simmer, covered for about 5-8 minutes, stirring occasionally.
5. Remove from the heat and immediately stir in the vanilla extract.
6. Cover the pan and set aside for about 5 minutes.
7. Uncover the pan and stir the mixture well.
8. Meanwhile, in a bowl, add the cottage cheese and almonds and mix well.
9. Divide the cheese mixture into 2 serving bowls.
10. Top with warm fruity mixture and serve.

Nutrition:
- Per Serving : Protein 26.7 g | Fiber 8.9 g | Carbs 38.5 g | Fat 8.6 g

Carrot, Beet & Apple Juice

Servings: 2
Cooking Time: 10 Mins.
Ingredients:
- 3 large carrots, peeled and chopped
- 3 medium red beetroots, trimmed, peeled and chopped
- 1 large red apple, cored and quartered
- 1 large green apple, cored and quartered

Directions:
1. Add all ingredients into a juicer and extract the juice according to the manufacturer's method.
2. Through a cheesecloth-lined strainer, strain the juice and transfer into 2 glasses.
3. Serve immediately.

Nutrition:
- Per Serving : Protein 4.3 g | Fiber 13.8 g | Carbs 71.8 g | Fat 0.9 g

Teff Porridge

Servings: 2
Cooking Time: 20 Mins.
Ingredients:
- 2 C. water
- ½ C. teff grain
- Pinch of salt
- 1 tbsp. maple syrup
- 2 tbsp. walnuts, chopped

Directions:
1. In a small pan, place the water and salt over medium-high heat and bring to a boil.
2. Slowly add the teff grain, stirring continuously.
3. Now adjust the heat to low and cook, covered for about 15 minutes or until the amaranth has thickened, stirring twice.
4. Stir in the maple syrup and remove from the heat.
5. Serve hot with the topping of walnuts.

Nutrition:
- Per Serving : Protein 6.9 g | Fiber 7.1 g | Carbs 41.4 g | Fat 2.9 g

Raspberry & Banana Smoothie Bowl

Servings: 2
Cooking Time: 10 Mins.
Ingredients:
- 3 C. fresh raspberries, divided
- 2 frozen bananas, peeled
- ½ C. unsweetened almond milk
- 1 tbsp. hemp seeds

Directions:
1. In a blender, add the raspberries, bananas, and milk and pulse until smooth.
2. Transfer the smoothie into two serving bowls evenly.
3. Top each bowl with berries and serve immediately.

Nutrition:
- Per Serving : Protein 5 g | Fiber 15.4 g | Carbs 49.7 g | Fat 4.2 g

Banana Oat Smoothie

Servings: 2
Cooking Time: 10 Mins.
Ingredients:
- 1½ frozen bananas, peeled and sliced
- ½ C. old-fashioned oats
- 2 tbsp. peanut butter
- 1 tbsp. chia seeds
- 1½ tbsp. honey
- 1½ C. unsweetened almond milk
- ¼ C. ice cubes

Directions:
1. Add all the ingredients in a high-power blender and pulse until creamy.
2. Pour the smoothie into two glasses and serve immediately.

Nutrition:
- Per Serving : Protein 9.1 g | Fiber 7.3 g | Carbs 52.8 g | Fat 13.5 g

Lamb Dhal Makhani

Servings: 4
Cooking Time: 30minutes
Ingredients:
- 1 brown onion, chopped
- 10 oz. of lamb mince
- 2 tsp. of ground cumin
- 14 oz. of canned red kidney beans, rinsed
- 1 tbsp. of vegetable oil
- 1-inch piece of fresh ginger, grated
- 14 oz. of canned lentils, rinsed
- 2 garlic cloves, minced
- 1 cinnamon stick
- 2 tbsp. of tomato paste
- 14 oz. of can tomato puree

Directions:
1. Sauté the onion & mince in hot oil for 6-8 minutes.
2. Add cumin, garlic, ginger & cinnamon. Cook for 1 minute.
3. Add tomato paste cook for 2 minutes. Add the rest of the ingredients to boil.
4. Simmer for 10 minutes. Discard the cinnamon & serve.

Nutrition:
- Per Serving : Protein 9 g | Fiber 7 g | Carbs 13 g | Fat 4 g

Black Beans Soup

Servings: 6
Cooking Time: 55 Mins.
Ingredients:
- 2 tbsp. extra-virgin olive oil
- 3 celery stalks, chopped finely
- 2 medium onions, chopped
- 1 large carrot, peeled and chopped
- 6 garlic cloves, minced
- 4 tsp. ground cumin
- 3 (15-oz.) cans black beans, rinsed and drained
- 6 C. homemade vegetable broth
- 2 tbsp. fresh lime juice
- Salt and ground black pepper, as required
- ¼ C. fresh cilantro, chopped

Directions:
1. In a large Dutch oven, heat the oil over medium heat and sauté the celery, onions, carrot and a little salt and cook for about 10-15 minutes, stirring occasionally.
2. Stir in the garlic, cumin and sauté for about 1 minute.
3. Add the beans and broth and stir to combine.
4. Adjust the heat to medium-high and bring to a boil.
5. Adjust the heat to low and simmer for about 30 minutes.
6. Remove from the heat and set aside to cool slightly.
7. In a blender, add about 4 C. of the soup and pulse until smooth.
8. Return the pureed soup into the pan with remaining soup over medium heat and cook for about 2-3 minutes.
9. Stir in the lime juice, salt and black pepper and remove from the heat.
10. Serve hot with the topping of cilantro.

Nutrition:
- Per Serving : Protein 24.7 g | Fiber 20 g | Carbs 57.9 g | Fat 7.6 g

Creamy White Bean And Spinach Soup

Servings: 4
Cooking Time: 40 Minutes
Ingredients:
- 1 large onion, diced
- Half cup of dried navy beans, soaked for 12 hours
- 1 tbsp. of Dijon mustard
- 1 tbsp. of olive oil
- 2 cloves garlic, minced
- 4 cups of spinach

Directions:
1. In a pot, add sauté the garlic & onion in hot olive oil for 5 minutes.
2. Add water (2 cups) & beans, boil. Simmer on low for 45 minutes.

3. Add mustard & spinach, pulse with a stick blender until smooth.
4. Serve.

Nutrition:
- Per Serving : Protein 5 g | Fiber 7 g | Carbs 17 g | Fat 4 g

Breakfast Sandwich

Servings: 1
Cooking Time: 0minutes
Ingredients:
- 1 toasted bagel thin
- 1 slice of Monterey Jack cheese
- 2 tbsp. of sliced thinly red onion
- ¼ avocado, sliced
- 1 tbsp. of garlic mayonnaise
- 2 tbsp. of alfalfa sprouts
- 1 fried egg

Directions:
1. In between the bagel, add the rest of the ingredients.
2. Top with the other half & serve.

Nutrition:
- Per Serving : Protein 19 g | Fiber 9 g | Carbs 30 g | Fat 36 g

Quinoa Black Bean Salad

Servings: 6
Cooking Time: 30 Minutes
Ingredients:
- 1 red onion cut, largely chopped
- 3 tbsp. of lime juice
- 1 clove garlic, minced
- 1 1/4 pounds of peeled sweet potatoes, largely cubed
- 1 tsp. of smoked paprika
- Half tsp. of kosher salt
- 1 1/2 cups of cooked quinoa
- 4 tbsp. of olive oil
- Zest of 2 limes
- 3/4 cup of cilantro
- 2 tsp. of maple syrup
- 1 can of (15 oz.) black beans, rinsed
- 1 bell pepper, diced

Directions:
1. Let the oven preheat to 400 F.
2. Toss the potatoes & onion in oil (1tbsp.), salt & paprika and bake for 25 minutes.
3. In a bowl, whisk the oil (3 tbsp.), garlic, lime juice, maple syrup & zest.
4. Add the rest of the ingredients to a bowl, add dressing, toss & serve.

Nutrition:
- Per Serving : Protein 8 g | Fiber 23 g | Carbs 49 g | Fat 11 g

Three Flours Bread

Servings: 10
Cooking Time: 1 Hour
Ingredients:
- 3 C. quinoa flour
- 2 C. chickpeas flour
- 1 C. spelt flour
- 3 C. water
- 3 tbsp. fresh lime juice
- 1 tbsp. salt

Directions:
1. Preheat your oven to 350 ºF. Lightly grease a bread loaf pan.
2. In a bowl, place all ingredients and with a wooden spoon, mix until thick dough forms.
3. Pour the mixture into prepared loaf pan evenly.
4. Bake for approximately ¾-1 hour or until a wooden skewer inserted in the center of loaf comes out clean.
5. Remove from oven and place the baking sheet onto a wire rack to cool for at least 10 minutes.
6. Then invert the bread onto the rack to cool completely before serving.
7. With a knife, cut the bread loaf into desired-sized slices and serve.

Nutrition:
- Per Serving : Protein 10.8 g | Fiber 6.1 g | Carbs 42.7 g | Fat 3.3 g

Pasta With Mushrooms

Servings: 4
Cooking Time: 25 Mins.
Ingredients:
- 12 oz. spelt pasta
- 4 tbsp. olive oil
- 1 lb. fresh white mushrooms, sliced
- 2 garlic cloves, minced
- 1¼ C. unsweetened coconut milk
- 2 tbsp. fresh parsley, chopped
- 1½ tbsp. fresh lime juice
- Salt and ground black pepper, as required

Directions:
1. In a saucepan of salted boiling water, cook the pasta for about 8-10 minutes or according to manufacturer's directions.
2. Meanwhile, in a large wok, heat 2 tbsp. of the oil over medium heat and sauté the mushroom and garlic for about 4-5 minutes.
3. Add in the milk and bring to a boil.
4. Add the parsley, lime juice, salt and black pepper and cook for about 4-5 minutes.
5. Divide the pasta onto serving plates.
6. Top with mushroom sauce and serve.

Nutrition:
- Per Serving : Protein 16.5 g | Fiber 8.8 g | Carbs 66.6 g | Fat 25.2 g

Fruity Muffins

Servings: 6
Cooking Time: 20 Mins.
Ingredients:
- ½ C. hot water
- ¼ C. flaxseed meal
- 1 banana, peeled and sliced
- 1 apple, peeled, cored and chopped roughly
- 2 C. rolled oats
- ½ C. walnuts, chopped
- ½ C. raisins
- ¼ tsp. baking soda
- 2 tbsp. ground cinnamon
- ½ C. unsweetened almond milk
- ¼ C. maple syrup

Directions:
1. Preheat your oven to 350 ºF. Line a 12 cups muffin tin with paper liners.
2. In a bowl, add water and flaxseed and beat until well combined. Set aside for about 5 minutes.
3. In a blender, add the flaxseed mixture and remaining all ingredients and pulse until smooth and creamy.
4. Transfer the mixture into prepared muffin cups evenly.
5. Bake for approximately 20 minutes.
6. Remove the muffin tin from oven and place onto a wire rack to cool for about 10 minutes.
7. Then invert the muffins onto the wire rack to cool completely before serving.

Nutrition:
- Per Serving : Protein 8 g | Fiber 8 g | Carbs 50.8 g | Fat 9.9 g

Apple, Pear & Carrot Juice

Servings: 2
Cooking Time: 10 Mins.
Ingredients:
- 2 medium apples, cored and quartered
- 2 medium pears, cored and quartered
- 4 large carrots, peeled and roughly chopped
- 4 celery stalks

Directions:
1. Add all ingredients into a juicer and extract the juice according to the manufacturer's method.
2. Through a cheesecloth-lined strainer, strain the juice and transfer into 2 glasses.
3. Serve immediately.

Nutrition:
- Per Serving : Protein 2.6 g | Fiber 15.4 g | Carbs 75.6 g | Fat 0.8 g

Lentils & Crispy Brussel Sprouts

Servings: 6
Cooking Time: 35 Minutes
Ingredients:

- 2 shallots, cut into wedges
- 2 ½ tbsp. of olive oil
- 1 garlic clove, sliced
- 4 large Portobello mushrooms
- ½ cup of dried puy lentils washed
- 8 oz. Brussels sprouts halved
- 0.8 oz. butter, chopped
- 1 tsp. of thyme leaves
- 2 tbsp. of cider vinegar
- ½ cup of pecans halved
- 1 radicchio, torn leaves
- 2 tbsp. of fresh parsley, chopped

Directions:
1. Let the oven preheat to 400°F.
2. Toss the shallots & sprouts with salt, pepper & oil (1 tbsp.).
3. Toss the mushrooms with salt, thyme, pepper & oil (1 tbsp.).
4. Place on two different baking trays.
5. Roast for 25 minutes. Cook lentils as per package Directions.
6. Toast pecans in the rest of the oil, add garlic & radicchio. Cook for 3-4 minutes.
7. Add lentils, shallots & sprouts. Add vinegar, salt, pepper & parsley.
8. Toss & serve with mushrooms.

Nutrition:
- Per Serving : Protein 11.8 g | Fiber 12.2 g | Carbs 11 g | Fat 27 g

Tofu With Veggies

Servings: 4
Cooking Time: 42 Mins.
Ingredients:

- 1 (14-oz.) package extra-firm tofu, pressed, drained and cubed
- 2 tbsp. olive oil, divided
- 3 tbsp. maple syrup
- 2 tbsp. creamy peanut butter
- 2 tbsp. fresh lime juice
- 1 lb. green beans, trimmed
- 2-3 small bell peppers, seeded and cubed
- 2 scallion greens, chopped

Directions:
1. Preheat your oven to 400 °F. Line a baking sheet with parchment paper.
2. Arrange the tofu cubes onto the prepared baking sheet in a single layer.

3. Bake for approximately 25-30 minutes.
4. Meanwhile, in a small bowl, add 1 tbsp. of the oil, maple syrup, peanut butter and lime juice and beat until well combined. Set aside
5. Remove from oven and place the tofu cubes into the bowl of sauce.
6. Stir the mixture well and set aside for about 10 minutes, stirring occasionally.
7. With a slotted spoon, remove the tofu cubes from bowl, reserving the sauce.
8. Heat a large cast-iron wok over medium heat and cook the tofu cubes for about 5 minutes, stirring occasionally.
9. With a slotted spoon, transfer the tofu cubes onto a plate. Set aside.
10. In the same wok, add the remaining oil, green beans, bell peppers and 2-3 tbsp. of reserved sauce and cook, covered for about 4-5 minutes.
11. Adjust the heat to medium-high, and stir in the cooked tofu remaining reserved sauce.
12. Cook for about 1-2 minutes, stirring frequently.
13. Stir in the scallion greens and remove from the heat.
14. Serve hot.

Nutrition:
- Per Serving : Protein 17.2 g | Fiber 7.2 g | Carbs 32 g | Fat 19.9 g

Chickpeas & Squash Stew

Servings: 4
Cooking Time: 1¼ Hours
Ingredients:

- 2 tbsp. olive oil
- 1 large onion, chopped
- 4 garlic cloves, minced
- 4 large tomatoes, seeded and chopped finely
- 1 lb. butternut squash, peeled, seeded and chopped
- 1½ C. water
- 1 C. cooked chickpeas
- 2 tbsp. fresh lime juice
- Salt, as required
- 2 tbsp. fresh parsley, chopped

Directions:
1. In a soup pan, heat the olive oil over medium heat and sauté the onion for about 4-6 minutes.
2. Add the garlic and sauté for about 1 minute.
3. Add the tomatoes and cook for about 2-3 minutes.
4. Add the squash and water and bring to a boil.
5. Now adjust the heat to low and simmer, covered for about 50 minutes.
6. Add the chickpeas and cook for about 10 minutes.
7. Stir in lime juice and salt and remove from heat.
8. Serve hot with the garnishing of parsley.

Nutrition:

- Per Serving : Protein 5.2 g | Fiber 8.6 g | Carbs 21.5 g | Fat 1.8 g

Lentil & Pumpkin & Kale Soup

Servings: 6
Cooking Time: 45 Mins.
Ingredients:
- 1 tbsp. olive oil
- 2 medium carrots, peeled and chopped
- 1 C. onion, chopped
- 4 garlic cloves, minced
- 1 tsp. fresh ginger, minced
- Salt and ground black pepper, as required
- 3 C. pumpkin, peeled, seeded and cubed
- 6-7 C. vegetable broth
- 1¼ C. lentils, rinsed and drained
- 4 C. fresh kale, tough ribs removed and chopped
- 2 tbsp. fresh lemon juice

Directions:
1. In a large soup pan, heat oil over medium heat and sauté the carrots, onion, garlic and ginger for about 3-5 minutes.
2. Add the sweet potatoes and cook for about 3-4 minutes, stirring occasionally.
3. Add the lentils and broth and stir to combine.
4. Adjust the heat to medium-high and bring to a boil.
5. Adjust the heat to low and simmer for about 20-25 minutes.
6. Stir in the kale and simmer for about 4-5 minutes.
7. Stir in the lemon juice and serve hot.

Nutrition:
- Per Serving : Protein 17.7 g | Fiber 17.2 g | Carbs 40.4 g | Fat 4.6 g

Barley With Chorizo & Tomatoes

Servings: 4
Cooking Time: 30 Minutes
Ingredients:
- 6 cups + ¼ cup of boiling water
- 1 tbsp. of olive oil
- 1 cup of pearl barley
- 17 oz. of chorizo, thinly sliced
- 10.5 oz. of baby brussels sprouts, halved or quartered
- 1 red onion, sliced
- 1/4 cup of chopped parsley
- Half tsp. of Paprika
- Half tsp. of ground cumin
- 8.8 oz. Roma tomatoes, halved
- 2 garlic cloves, minced

Directions:
1. Add water (6 cups) & barley to a pan simmer for 25 minutes. Drain.
2. In a pan, cook chorizo in oil for 2-3 minutes. Take it out on a plate.

3. Add garlic, cumin, onion & paprika to a pan cook for 3 minutes.
4. Add chorizo & cook for 2-3 minutes, add sprouts & cook for 3 to 4 minutes.
5. Add water & cook for 2 minutes.
6. Add barely & mix well. Add tomato, serve.

Nutrition:
- Per Serving : Protein 17 g | Fiber 13 g | Carbs 47 g | Fat 15 g

Date & Almond Smoothie

Servings: 2
Cooking Time: 10 Mins.
Ingredients:
- 1 C. Medjool dates, pitted and chopped
- ½ C. almonds, chopped
- 1½ C. unsweetened almond milk
- ¼ C. ice cubes

Directions:
1. Add all the ingredients in a high-power blender and pulse until creamy.
2. Pour the smoothie into two glasses and serve immediately.

Nutrition:
- Per Serving : Protein 8 g | Fiber 10.8 g | Carbs 73.4 g | Fat 14.9 g

Southwest Chicken

Servings: 4
Cooking Time: 40 Minutes
Ingredients:
- 4 chicken breast halves, skinless & boneless
- 1 can of 9 oz. kernel corn, drained
- 1 pinch of ground cumin
- 1 can of 10 oz. diced tomatoes
- 1 tbsp. of vegetable oil
- 1 can of 15 oz. black beans, rinsed

Directions:
1. Cook chicken in hot oil until browned.
2. Add the corn, tomatoes & beans. Simmer for half an hour.
3. Serve with cumin.

Nutrition:
- Per Serving : Protein 35 g | Fiber 7.5 g | Carbs 27 g | Fat 6 g

Pear & Brussels Sprout Salad

Servings: 4
Cooking Time: 15 Mins.
Ingredients:
- For Salad:
- 2 large pears, peeled, cored and sliced
- 2 C. Brussels sprout, trimmed and sliced thinly
- 4 C. fresh salad greens, chopped finely
- ½ C. almonds, chopped
- For Dressing:
- 1 tbsp. shallot, minced
- 3 tbsp. apple cider vinegar
- 3 tbsp. extra-virgin olive oil
- 1 tbsp. pure maple syrup
- 2 tsp. Dijon mustard
- Ground black pepper, as required

Directions:
1. For salad: in a large serving bowl, add all the pears, Brussels sprout and salad greens and mix.
2. For dressing: in another bowl, add all the ingredients and beat until well combined.
3. Pour the dressing over salad and toss to coat well.
4. Top with almonds and serve immediately.

Nutrition:
- Per Serving : Protein 10.4 g | Fiber 15.6 g | Carbs 19.58 g | Fat 34 g

Rice & Beans Pilaf

Servings: 4
Cooking Time: 1 Hour.
Ingredients:
- 2 tbsp. olive oil
- 2 garlic cloves, minced
- 2 C. fresh mushrooms, sliced
- 1¼ C. brown rice, rinsed
- 2 C. homemade vegetable broth
- Salt and ground black pepper, as required
- 1 bell pepper, seeded and chopped
- 4 scallions, chopped
- 1 (16-oz.) can red kidney beans, drained and rinsed
- 2 tbsp. fresh parsley, chopped

Directions:
1. In a large pan, heat the oil over medium heat and sauté the onion for about 4-5 minutes.
2. Add the garlic and mushrooms and cook for about 5-6 minutes.
3. Stir in the rice and cook for about 1-2 minutes, stirring continuously.
4. Stir in the broth, salt and black pepper and bring to a boil.
5. Now adjust the heat to low and simmer, covered for about 35 minutes, stirring occasionally.

6. Add in the bell pepper and beans and cook for about 5-10 minutes or until all the liquid is absorbed.
7. Serve hot with the garnishing of parsley.
Nutrition:
- Per Serving : Protein 18.5 g | Fiber 11.6 g | Carbs 76.7 g | Fat 10.1 g

Banana-chocolate French Toast

Servings: 3
Cooking Time: 6minutes
Ingredients:
- 2 eggs, whisked
- ⅛ tsp. of salt
- ¾ tsp. of vanilla extract
- ¼ cup of milk
- ½ tsp. of sugar
- 1 cup of sliced thin banana
- 6 slices of whole-grain bread
- 1 ½ tsp. of powdered sugar
- 4 ½ tbsp. of Nutella spread
- 2 tsp. of canola oil

Directions:
1. Add 5 first ingredients in a bowl & mix.
2. Spread Nutella on 3 bread slices, place banana slices on top.
3. Place the 3 slices on top.
4. Heat oil in a skillet. Add the sandwiches to the milk mixture & flip to coat well.
5. Add to the pan cook for 2 minutes on one side.
6. Slice & serve.
Nutrition:
- Per Serving : Protein 5 g | Fiber 6 g | Carbs 53 g | Fat 13.8 g

Vegetable Stir-fry

Servings:6
Cooking Time: 25 Minutes
Ingredients:
- ¼ cup soy sauce
- 2 tablespoons sesame oil
- 1 tablespoon pineapple or orange juice
- 1 tablespoon cornstarch
- 1 cup brown rice
- 1¾ cups water
- 2 carrots, chopped
- 1 cup broccoli florets
- 1 cup cauliflower florets
- 2 teaspoons vegetable oil
- 1 small white or Spanish onion, thinly sliced
- 2 garlic cloves, minced
- 2 cups shelled edamame
- 1 cup quartered button mushrooms

- 1 cup sugar snap peas
- 1 bell pepper, diced

Directions:

1. bell pepper, diced
2. In a small bowl, mix together the soy sauce, sesame oil, pineapple juice, and cornstarch until smooth.
3. In a medium saucepan over high heat, mix the rice with the water and bring to a boil. Lower the heat to medium-low, cover, and cook for 10 minutes. Remove from the heat and let sit, covered, for an additional 10 minutes. Set aside.
4. Bring a medium saucepan of water to a boil over medium-high heat. Add the carrots, broccoli, and cauliflower and cook until tender-crisp, about 3 minutes. Drain and set aside.
5. In a large sauté pan or skillet over medium heat, warm the vegetable oil. Add the onion and cook for 3 minutes. Add the garlic, edamame, mushrooms, snap peas, bell pepper, carrots, broccoli, and cauliflower and cook until the vegetables are tender, about 5 minutes.
6. Pour the sauce over vegetables, stir, and cook for 5 more minutes.
7. Serve the stir-fry over the rice.

Nutrition:

- Per Serving : Protein 12 g | Fiber 5 g | Carbs 39 g | Fat 8 g

Pear & Kale Juice

Servings: 2
Cooking Time: 10 Mins.

Ingredients:

- 6 pears, cored and quartered
- 3 celery stalks
- 3 C. fresh kale
- 2 tbsp. fresh parsley

Directions:

1. Add all ingredients into a juicer and extract the juice according to the manufacturer's method.
2. Through a cheesecloth-lined strainer, strain the juice and transfer into 2 glasses.
3. Serve immediately.

Nutrition:

- Per Serving : Protein 5.1 g | Fiber 15.2 g | Carbs 50.5 g | Fat 0.9 g

Apple, Grapefruit & Kale Juice

Servings: 2
Cooking Time: 10 Mins.

Ingredients:

- 2 large apples, cored and sliced
- 4 medium carrots, peeled and chopped
- 2 medium grapefruit, peeled and seeded
- 1 C. fresh kale
- 1 tsp. fresh lemon juice

Directions:

1. Add all ingredients in a high-power blender and pulse until well combined.
2. Through a cheesecloth-lined strainer, strain the juice and transfer into 2 glasses.
3. Serve immediately.

Nutrition:

- Per Serving : Protein 4.2 g | Fiber 11.7 g | Carbs 67 g | Fat 0.7 g

Lentil & Spinach Soup

Servings: 6
Cooking Time: 1¼ Hours

Ingredients:

- 2 tbsp. olive oil
- 2 carrots, peeled and chopped
- 2 celery stalks, chopped
- 2 sweet onions, chopped
- 3 garlic cloves, minced
- 1½ C. lentils, rinsed
- 2 C. tomatoes, peeled, seeded and chopped finely
- ¼ tsp. dried basil, crushed
- ¼ tsp. dried oregano, crushed
- ¼ tsp. dried thyme, crushed
- 1 tsp. ground cumin
- ½ tsp. ground coriander
- 6 C. vegetable broth
- 3 C. fresh spinach, chopped
- Salt and ground black pepper, as required
- 2 tbsp. fresh lemon juice

Directions:

1. In a large soup pan, heat the oil over medium heat and sauté the carrot, celery, and onion for about 5 minutes.
2. Add the garlic and sauté for about 1 minute.
3. Add the lentils and sauté for about 3 minutes.
4. Stir in the tomatoes, herbs, spices, and broth and bring to a boil.
5. Now adjust the heat to low and simmer partially covered for about 1 hour or until desired doneness
6. Stir in the spinach, salt, and black pepper and cook for about 4 minutes.
7. Stir in the lemon juice and remove from the heat.
8. Serve hot.

Nutrition:

- Per Serving : Protein 5.3 g | Fiber 13.7 g | Carbs 63.6 g | Fat 1.5 g

Stuffed Sweet Potatoes

Servings:4
Cooking Time: 1 Hour
Ingredients:

- 2 cups quinoa, rinsed
- 1⅓ cups water
- 4 medium sweet potatoes, scrubbed
- 1 tablespoon vegetable oil
- ½ red onion, diced
- 4 cups fresh spinach
- 1 red bell pepper, diced
- 1 cup diced zucchini
- 1 garlic clove, minced
- 1 (15½-ounce) can chickpeas, drained and rinsed
- Salt
- Freshly ground black pepper
- 2 tablespoons tahini
- 1 tablespoon lemon juice
- Pinch ground cumin
- 4 Roma tomatoes, diced
- 1 cup crumbled feta cheese

Directions:
1. cup crumbled feta cheese
2. In a medium saucepan over high heat, mix together the quinoa and water and bring to a boil. Lower the heat to medium, cover, and continue to cook until the water is absorbed, about 15 minutes. Set aside.
3. Preheat the oven to 400°F. Line a baking sheet with parchment paper.
4. Pierce the sweet potatoes with a fork several times and place them on the prepared baking sheet. Bake for 35 to 45 minutes, or until a knife inserted into a sweet potato meets no resistance.
5. In a large sauté pan or skillet over medium heat, warm the oil. Add the red onion and cook until translucent, about 3 minutes. Add the spinach, red bell pepper, zucchini, and garlic and cook for 5 minutes.
6. Add the quinoa and chickpeas and stir to combine. Taste and season with salt and pepper. Set aside and keep warm.
7. In a small bowl, mix together the tahini, lemon juice, and cumin to make the dressing. If it is too thick to drizzle, thin it out with more lemon juice or water.
8. Cut the potatoes in half, about ¾ of the way through. Squeeze the ends to open them up a bit. Stuff the potatoes with the vegetable and quinoa mixture. Top with the feta cheese and diced tomatoes, and drizzle with the tahini dressing. Serve warm.
9. To store, wrap each stuffed potato individually in plastic wrap and refrigerate for up to 5 days.

Nutrition:
- Per Serving : Protein 28 g | Fiber 17 g | Carbs 125 g | Fat 24 g

Gingerbread Pancakes

Servings:4
Cooking Time: 25 Minutes
Ingredients:

- ½ cup whole-wheat flour
- ¼ cup sugar
- 1½ teaspoons baking powder
- ½ teaspoon baking soda
- ½ teaspoon salt
- 1 cup canned lentils, rinsed
- 2 large eggs
- ¼ cup molasses
- ¼ cup milk of choice
- 3 tablespoons canola oil
- 1 teaspoon ground ginger
- 1 teaspoon ground cinnamon
- ½ teaspoon ground cloves
- 1 teaspoon vegetable oil or cooking spray

Directions:
1. teaspoon vegetable oil or cooking spray
2. In a medium bowl, sift together the flour, sugar, baking powder, baking soda, and salt. Set aside.
3. Place the lentils in a blender or food processor and puree until completely smooth. Add water 1 tablespoon at a time to thin enough to puree.
4. In a separate large bowl, whisk together the eggs, molasses, milk, canola oil, ginger, cinnamon, and cloves.
5. Mix the flour mixture into the lentil mixture and stir until smooth.
6. Set a large sauté pan or skillet over medium heat. Lightly grease with the vegetable oil. Spoon ¼ cup of batter into the skillet and cook until bubbles start to form around the edges, 2 to 3 minutes. Flip and cook until golden brown, another 2 to 3 minutes. Serve with desired toppings.
7. Store leftovers in the refrigerator for up to 5 days or in the freezer for up to 4 months. To reheat, heat in the microwave until hot.

Nutrition:
- Per Serving : Protein 10 g | Fiber 6 g | Carbs 49 g | Fat 15 g

Rice & Lentil Casserole

Servings: 6
Cooking Time: 1 Hour
Ingredients:

- 2½ C. water, divided
- 1 C. lentils
- ½ C. wild rice
- 1 tsp. olive oil
- 1 small onion, chopped
- 3 garlic cloves, minced
- 1/3 C. zucchini, peeled, seeded and chopped

- 1/3 C. carrot, peeled and chopped
- 1/3 C. celery stalk, chopped
- 1 large tomato, peeled, seeded and chopped
- 8 oz. tomato sauce
- 1 tsp. ground cumin
- 1 tsp. dried oregano, crushed
- 1 tsp. dried basil, crushed
- Salt and ground black pepper, as required

Directions:

1. In a saucepan, add 1 C. of the water and rice over medium-high heat and bring to a rolling boil.
2. Now adjust the heat to low and simmer, covered for about 20 minutes.
3. Meanwhile, in another pan, add the remaining water and lentils over medium heat and bring to a rolling boil.
4. Now adjust the heat to low and simmer, covered for about 15 minutes.
5. Transfer the cooked rice and lentils into a casserole dish and set aside.
6. Preheat your oven to 350 ºF.
7. Heat the oil in a large wok over medium heat and sauté the onion and garlic for about 4-5 minutes.
8. Add the zucchini, carrot, celery, tomato and tomato paste and cook for about 4-5 minutes.
9. Stir in the cumin, herbs, salt and black pepper and remove from the heat
10. Transfer the vegetable mixture into the casserole dish with rice and lentils and stir to combine.
11. Bake for approximately 30 minutes.
12. Remove from the heat and set aside for about 5 minutes.
13. Cut into equal-sized 6 pieces and serve.

Nutrition:

- Per Serving : Protein 11.3 g | Fiber 12 g | Carbs 34.5 g | Fat 1.5 g

Veggie Pie

Servings: 8
Cooking Time: 1 Hour 20 Mins.

Ingredients:

- For Topping:
- 5 C. water
- 1¼ C. yellow cornmeal
- For Filing:
- 1 tbsp. extra-virgin olive oil
- 1 large onion, chopped
- 1 medium bell pepper, seeded and chopped
- 2 garlic cloves, minced
- 1 tsp. dried oregano, crushed
- 2 C. fresh tomatoes, peeled, seeded and chopped
- 2½ C. cooked pinto beans
- 2 C. boiled corn kernels

Directions:

1. Preheat your oven to 375 ºF. Lightly grease a shallow baking dish.
2. In a saucepan, add the water over medium-high heat and bring to a boil.
3. Slowly add the cornmeal, stirring continuously.
4. Now adjust the heat to low and cook covered for about 20 minutes, stirring occasionally.
5. Meanwhile, prepare the filling. In a large wok, heat the oil over medium heat and sauté the onion and bell pepper for about 3-4 minutes.
6. Add the garlic, oregano, and spices and sauté for about 1 minute
7. Add the remaining ingredients and stir to combine.
8. Now adjust the heat to low and simmer for about 10-15 minutes, stirring occasionally.
9. Remove from the heat.
10. Place half of the cooked cornmeal into the prepared baking dish evenly.
11. Place the filling mixture over the cornmeal evenly.
12. Place the remaining cornmeal over the filling mixture evenly.
13. Bake for 45-50 minutes or until the top becomes golden brown.
14. Remove the pie from oven and set it aside for about 5 minutes before serving.

Nutrition:

- Per Serving : Protein 16.6 g | Fiber 13.3 g | Carbs 65 g | Fat 3.9 g

Veggie Pancakes

Servings: 2
Cooking Time: 12 Mins.

Ingredients:

- 1 C. water
- 1 C. chickpea flour
- 1 tsp. ground turmeric
- Salt and ground black pepper, as required
- 1 bell pepper, seeded and chopped finely
- 3 scallions, chopped finely
- 1 tbsp. olive oil

Directions:

1. In a food processor, add the water, flour, turmeric, salt and black pepper and pulse until well combined.
2. Transfer the mixture into a bowl and set aside for about 3-5 minutes.
3. Add the bell pepper and scallion and mix well.
4. In a wok, heat the oil over medium heat.
5. Add half of the mixture and spread in an even layer.
6. Cook for about 5-6 minutes, flipping once after 3 minutes.
7. Repeat with the remaining mixture.
8. Serve warm.

Nutrition:

- Per Serving : Protein 10.2 g | Fiber 9.7 g | Carbs 33 g | Fat 6.7 g

Beans & Sweet Potato Chili

Servings: 6
Cooking Time: 2 Hours 10 Mins.
Ingredients:
- 2 tbsp. olive oil
- 1 onion, chopped
- 2 small bell peppers, seeded and chopped
- 4 garlic cloves, minced
- 1 tsp. ground cumin
- 1 medium sweet potato, peeled and chopped
- 3 C. tomatoes, peeled, seeded and chopped finely
- 4 C. canned red kidney beans, rinsed and drained
- 2 C. homemade vegetable broth
- Salt and ground black pepper, as required

Directions:
1. In a large pan, heat the oil over medium-high heat and sauté the onion and bell peppers for about 3-4 minutes.
2. Add the garlic and spices and sauté for about 1 minute.
3. Add the sweet potato and cook for about 4-5 minutes.
4. Add the remaining ingredients and bring to a boil.
5. Now adjust the heat to medium-low and simmer covered for about 1½-2 hours.
6. Season with salt and black pepper and remove from the heat.
7. Serve hot.
Nutrition:
- Per Serving : Protein 13.1 g | Fiber 11.2 g | Carbs 40.8 g | Fat 7.2 g

High-fiber Bran Muffins

Servings:12
Cooking Time: 18 Minutes
Ingredients:
- 1 cup wheat bran
- 1 cup whole-wheat flour
- ¾ cup sugar
- 2 teaspoons baking powder
- 1 teaspoon baking soda
- 1 teaspoon ground cinnamon
- ½ teaspoon salt
- 1 large egg
- 1 cup plain Greek yogurt
- ½ cup canola oil
- 1 tablespoon chia seeds
- ½ cup berries of choice

Directions:
1. ½ cup berries of choice
2. Preheat the oven to 375°F. Place muffin liners in a 12-cup muffin tin.

3. In a large bowl, mix together the wheat bran, flour, sugar, baking powder, baking soda, cinnamon, and salt. Set aside.
4. In a small bowl, whisk together the egg, yogurt, canola oil, and chia seeds.
5. Form a well in the center of the dry ingredients. Pour the yogurt mixture into it and mix just until incorporated. Be careful not to overmix, or the muffins will be tough.
6. Fold in the berries. Divide the batter evenly among the muffin cups.
7. Bake for 15 to 18 minutes, or until a toothpick inserted into the center of a muffin comes out clean.
8. The muffins can be stored in an airtight container at room temperature for up to 5 days or frozen for up to 3 months.
Nutrition:
- Per Serving : Protein 5 g | Fiber 4 g | Carbs 24 g | Fat 11 g

Matcha Avocado Smoothie

Servings: 2
Cooking Time: 10 Mins.
Ingredients:
- ½ of medium avocado
- 1 pack unsweetened acai puree
- 2 tbsp. almond butter
- 2 tbsp. matcha green tea powder
- 4-5 drops liquid stevia
- 1½ C. unsweetened almond milk

Directions:
1. Add all the ingredients in a high-power blender and pulse until creamy.
2. Pour the smoothie into two glasses and serve immediately.
Nutrition:
- Per Serving : Protein 7.1 g | Fiber 7.5 g | Carbs 12.9 g | Fat 27.6 g

Beans & Broccoli Soup

Servings: 3
Cooking Time: 15 Mins.
Ingredients:
- ¾ lb. broccoli, chopped
- 1 tbsp. olive oil
- 1 onion, chopped
- 2 garlic cloves, minced
- 4 C. vegetable broth
- 3 C. canned cannellini beans, rinsed and drained
- Salt and ground black pepper, as required

Directions:
1. In a pan of boiling water, add the broccoli and cook for about 3-4 minutes.
2. Drain the broccoli well.

3. In a large soup pan, heat the oil over medium heat and sauté onion for about 5 minutes.

4. Add the garlic and sauté for about 1 minute.

5. Add the broth and beans and bring to a boil.

6. Remove from the heat and set aside to cool slightly.

7. In a blender, add the soup and broccoli in batches and pulse until smooth.

8. Return the soup in the pan and cook for about 3-4 minutes.

9. Stir in the salt and black pepper and serve hot.

Nutrition:

- Per Serving : Protein 17.7 g | Fiber 13 g | Carbs 37.5 g | Fat 6.3 g

Chocolate–peanut Butter Smoothie Bowls

Servings:4
Cooking Time: 10 Minutes
Ingredients:

- 3 frozen bananas
- ½ cup diced avocado
- 2 cups plain Greek yogurt
- 1½ cups milk of choice
- 3 tablespoons peanut butter
- 3 tablespoons unsweetened dark cocoa powder
- 1 tablespoon chia seeds
- 1 tablespoon ground flaxseed
- 1 teaspoon vanilla extract
- OPTIONAL TOPPINGS
- Fresh fruit
- Chia seeds
- Hemp seeds
- Shredded coconut flakes
- Granola
- Nuts of choice

Directions:

1. Nuts of choice

2. Place the bananas, avocado, yogurt, milk, peanut butter, cocoa powder, chia, flaxseed, and vanilla into a blender and puree until smooth.

3. Pour into bowls and garnish with the optional toppings.

Nutrition:

- Per Serving : Protein 20 g | Fiber 7 g | Carbs 38 g | Fat 17 g

Banana Curry

Servings: 3
Cooking Time: 15 Mins.
Ingredients:

- 2 tbsp. olive oil
- 2 onions, chopped
- 8 garlic cloves, minced

- 1 tsp. ground turmeric
- 1 tsp. ground cinnamon
- Salt and ground black pepper, as required
- 2/3 C. fat-free plain yogurt
- 1 C. tomato puree
- 2 bananas, peeled and sliced
- 3 tomatoes, peeled, seeded and chopped finely

Directions:

1. In a large pan, heat the oil over medium heat and sauté onion for about 4-5 minutes.

2. Add the garlic and spices and sauté for about 1 minute.

3. Add the yogurt and tomato sauce and bring to a gentle boil.

4. Stir in the bananas and simmer for about 3 minutes.

5. Stir in the tomatoes and simmer for about 1-2 minutes.

6. Serve hot.

Nutrition:

- Per Serving : Protein 9 g | Fiber 9.5 g | Carbs 49.7 g | Fat 12.2 g

Lentil Fritters

Servings: 2
Cooking Time: 10 Minutes
Ingredients:

- ½ cup of chopped coriander
- 1 sliced scallion
- ½ tsp. of sesame seeds
- 1.7 oz. of gram flour
- 10.5 oz. of cooked basic lentils
- 1 tbsp. of rapeseed oil
- 2 carrots
- ½ tsp. of sesame oil
- 2 courgettes
- 1 lime's juice

Directions:

1. Cut the courgettes & carrots into ribbons & mix with lime juice, sesame oil & coriander.

2. Mix the lentils with flour & scallion. Let it rest for a few minutes.

3. In a pan, heat the oil. Add the spoonful of lentil mixture & make it into cakes.

4. Serve with ribbon sides.

Nutrition:

- Per Serving : Protein 0.1 g | Fiber 11 g | Carbs 41 g | Fat 12 g

Minestrone Soup

Servings:4
Cooking Time: 35 Minutes
Ingredients:
- 1 cup high-fiber small pasta shells
- 1 teaspoon canola or vegetable oil
- ½ white or Spanish onion, diced
- 2 celery stalks, diced
- 1 garlic clove, minced
- 1 tablespoon Italian seasoning
- 6 cups vegetable stock
- 1 (28-ounce) can diced tomatoes
- 1 tablespoon tomato paste
- 1 (15-ounce) can kidney beans, drained and rinsed
- 1 cup frozen mixed carrots and green beans
- Salt
- Freshly ground black pepper
- Freshly grated Parmesan cheese (optional)

Directions:
1. Freshly grated Parmesan cheese (optional)
2. Bring a large saucepan of water to a boil over high heat and cook the pasta according to the package instructions until al dente, about 8 minutes. Drain, transfer to a bowl, and set aside.
3. In a large stockpot over medium heat, warm the oil. Add the onion, celery, garlic, and Italian seasoning and cook until the onions are translucent, about 4 minutes. Raise the heat to medium-high. Add the vegetable stock, diced tomatoes, and tomato paste and bring to a boil. Lower the heat to medium-low, cover, and simmer, stirring occasionally, for 15 to 20 minutes.
4. Add the kidney beans, frozen mixed carrots and green beans, and cooked pasta, and continue to simmer until heated through, about 5 minutes. Season with salt and pepper as desired. Spoon into bowls, garnish with grated Parmesan (if using), and serve.
5. Store leftover soup in an airtight container in the refrigerator for up to 5 days or in the freezer for up to 3 months.

Nutrition:
- Per Serving : Protein 1 g | Fiber 13 g | Carbs 14 g | Fat 63 g

Peach & Oat Smoothie

Servings: 2
Cooking Time: 10 Mins.
Ingredients:
- 2 C. frozen peaches, pitted
- ½ C. rolled oats
- ¼ tsp. ground cinnamon
- 1½ C. plain yogurt
- ½ C. fresh orange Juice

Directions:

1. Add all the ingredients in a high-power blender and pulse until creamy.
2. Pour the smoothie into two glasses and serve immediately.

Nutrition:
- Per Serving : Protein 15 g | Fiber 5 g | Carbs 56 g | Fat 4.1 g

Strawberry, Blueberry & Banana Smoothie

Servings: 1
Cooking Time: 0minutes
Ingredients:
- Half cup of frozen blueberries
- 1 tbsp. of cashew butter
- 1 frozen ripe banana
- 1 tbsp. of hulled hemp seeds
- Half cup of frozen strawberries
- ¾ cup of chilled cashew milk, unsweetened

Directions:
1. Add all ingredients to a blender. Pulse until smooth.
2. Serve by pouring in a chilled glass.

Nutrition:
- Per Serving : Protein 6 g | Fiber 8 g | Carbs 45 g | Fat 16 g

Quinoa & Kale Salad

Servings: 4
Cooking Time: 20 Mins.
Ingredients:
- For Salad:
- 1½ C. water
- ¾ C. uncooked quinoa, rinsed
- 8 oz. fresh kale, tough ribs removed and chopped finely
- 2 C. seedless cucumber, peeled and chopped
- 1 large tomato, chopped
- 1/3 C. onion, chopped
- For Vinaigrette:
- ¼ C. fresh lemon juice
- ¼ C. olive oil
- 1 garlic clove, minced
- 1 tsp. Dijon mustard
- 1 tsp. maple syrup
- 4-6 large basil leaves, chopped finely
- Salt and ground black pepper, as required

Directions:
1. For salad: in a medium saucepan, add the water and quinoa over high heat and bring to a boil.
2. Adjust the heat to low and cook, covered for about 15 minutes.
3. Remove from the heat and set aside, covered for about 5 minutes.

4. Uncover the pan and with a fork, fluff the quinoa.

5. Transfer the quinoa into a large bowl and set aside to cool

6. For vinaigrette: in a blender, add all the ingredients and pulse until well combined.

7. In a bowl, add the kale and half of the vinaigrette and with your clean hands, massage the kale for about 3 minutes.

8. In the bowl of quinoa, add the kale, edamame tomato, onion and remaining vinaigrette and toss to coat well.

Nutrition:

- Per Serving : Protein 2.5 g | Fiber 9.4 g | Carbs 45.2 g | Fat 23.5 g

Amarnath Porridge

Servings: 2
Cooking Time: 25 Mins.

Ingredients:

- 2 C. water
- 2/3 C. amaranth
- Pinch of salt
- 1/3 C. unsweetened coconut milk
- 2 tsp. maple syrup
- 2 tbsp. fresh blueberries

Directions:

1. In a small pan, place the water, amaranth and salt over medium-high heat and bring to a rolling boil.

2. Now adjust the heat to low and simmer, covered for about 20-25 minutes or until the amaranth has thickened, stirring twice.

3. Stir in the coconut milk and maple syrup and remove from the heat.

4. Serve hot with the topping of blueberries.

Nutrition:

- Per Serving : Protein 9.5 g | Fiber 6.8 g | Carbs 50 g | Fat 4.9 g

Bean & Spinach Enchiladas

Servings: 6
Cooking Time: 3 Hours & 35 Minutes

Ingredients:

- 10 oz. of squeezed thawed spinach
- 1 cup of corn
- ½ tsp. of ground cumin
- 8 oz. of sharp Cheddar, grated
- ½ cup of grape tomatoes halved
- 8 corn (6") tortillas, warmed
- 1 can of (~16 oz.) black beans, rinsed
- Salt & black pepper
- 3 ½ cups of jarred salsa
- 6 cups of chopped romaine lettuce
- 4 radishes, sliced thin
- 2 tbsp. of olive oil
- ½ cucumber, sliced

- 3 tbsp. of lime juice

Directions:

1. Mash beans (only half) mix with cheddar (1 cup), corn, rest of the beans, salt, spinach, pepper & cumin.

2. In a slow cooker (4-6 qt.), spread one salsa jar.

3. In each tortilla, fill the bean mixture & roll.

4. Place in the slow cooker. Add cheddar & all the salsa on top.

5. Cook for 2 ½-3 hours.

6. Add the rest of the ingredients to a bowl, with salt & pepper, toss & serve with rolls.

Nutrition:

- Per Serving : Protein 28 g | Fiber 12 g | Carbs 60 g | Fat 28 g

Turkey Chili

Servings:4
Cooking Time: 35 Minutes

Ingredients:

- 1 pound lean ground turkey, formed into a large patty
- 1 white or Spanish onion, diced
- 1 cup diced celery
- 2 garlic cloves, minced
- 2 tablespoons chili powder
- 1 tablespoon ground cumin
- Pinch crushed red chili flakes
- 1 red or orange bell pepper, seeded and diced
- 1 cup sliced button mushrooms
- 1 (15-ounce) can baked beans in molasses
- 1 (15-ounce) can no-salt-added kidney beans, drained and rinsed
- 1 (15-ounce) can no-salt-added diced tomatoes
- 1 (6-ounce) can tomato paste
- Salt
- Freshly ground black pepper

Directions:

1. Freshly ground black pepper

2. In a large saucepan over medium heat, place the turkey patty. Cook until the meat browns, about 4 minutes. Flip the turkey and cook until browned, another 4 minutes. Using a spatula, break up the meat into small pieces.

3. Add the onion, celery, garlic, chili powder, cumin, and chili flakes and cook for 2 to 3 minutes.

4. Raise the heat to medium-high, add the bell pepper, mushrooms, baked beans, kidney beans, tomatoes, and tomato paste, and bring to a boil. Lower the heat to medium-low and simmer, stirring frequently to prevent burning, for 15 to 20 minutes. Taste and season with salt and pepper. Serve warm.

5. Store leftovers in an airtight container in the refrigerator for up to 5 days or in the freezer for up to 4 months.

Nutrition:

- Per Serving : Protein 40 g | Fiber 21 g | Carbs 67 g | Fat 10 g

Chicken & Beans Stuffed Bell Peppers

Servings: 4
Cooking Time: 40 Mins.
Ingredients:
- 2 garlic cloves, minced
- 2 tsp. fresh lemon zest, grated finely
- 2 tsp. fresh thyme, minced
- 1 tsp. ground cumin
- 3 tsp. olive oil, divided
- 2 tbsp. fresh lemon juice
- 14 oz. skinless, boneless chicken breasts, cut into thin strips
- 4 large bell peppers
- 1 large onion, sliced
- ¾ C. tomatoes, peeled, seeded and sliced
- 1 C. canned black beans, rinsed and drained

Directions:
1. In a large bowl, add the garlic, lemon zest, thyme, cumin, 1btsp. of oil and lemon juice and mix until well combined.
2. Add the chicken strips and coat with marinade generously.
3. Cover and refrigerate to marinate for about 2 hours.
4. Preheat your oven to 400 ºF. Line a roasting pan with a piece of foil.
5. Arrange the bell peppers into the prepared roasting pan.
6. Roast for about 15-20 minutes, flipping occasionally.
7. Remove the bell peppers from oven and immediately transfer into a paper bag.
8. Seal the top of the paper bag by rolling it closed tightly. Set aside for at least 10 minutes.
9. Remove the bell peppers from bag.
10. With a knife, carefully slice the top.
11. Carefully peel off the skin of each bell pepper and discard the seeds and pith. Set aside.
12. For stuffing mixture: in a large wok, heat remaining oil over medium-high heat and sauté onion for about 8-10 minutes.
13. Transfer the onion into a bowl.
14. In the same wok, add the chicken and cook for about 8 minutes.
15. Stir in the tomatoes, beans and cooked onion and cook for about 1-2 minutes.
16. Arrange the bell peppers onto serving plates.
17. Stuff the bell peppers with chicken mixture evenly and serve.

Nutrition:
- Per Serving : Protein 28 g | Fiber 7.4 g | Carbs 22 g | Fat 7.9 g

Mustardy Salmon With Lentils & Beetroot

Servings: 2
Cooking Time: 30 Minutes
Ingredients:
- 1 tsp. of wholegrain mustard
- ½ tsp. of honey
- 2 tbsp. of olive oil
- 2 salmon fillets
- 1 small pack of dill, chopped
- 8.8 oz. cooked puy lentils
- 2 tbsp. toasted pumpkin seeds
- 8.8 oz. cooked beetroot, cut into wedges
- 2 tbsp. of crème fraîche
- 1-2 tbsp. of capers
- ½ lemon, zest & wedged

Directions:
1. Let the oven preheat to 400°F.
2. Mix seasonings, mustard & oil (1 tbsp.). Spread all over the fish.
3. In a dish, add the beetroot & lentils, add the rest of the oil & seasonings.
4. Bake the fish & lentil mixture for 10 minutes.
5. Add the rest of the ingredients to the lentil mixture.
6. Serve with salmon.

Nutrition:
- Per Serving : Protein 58 g | Fiber 15 g | Carbs 42 g | Fat 49 g

Raspberry Oat Smoothie

Servings: 2
Cooking Time: 10 Mins.
Ingredients:
- 1¼ C. fresh raspberries
- 2 bananas, peeled and sliced
- ½ C. oats
- 1 scoop unsweetened protein powder
- 1 tbsp. maple syrup
- 1½ C. unsweetened almond milk
- ¼ C. ice cubes

Directions:
1. Add all the ingredients in a high-power blender and pulse until creamy.
2. Pour the smoothie into two glasses and serve immediately.

Nutrition:
- Per Serving : Protein 18.3 g | Fiber 10.9 g | Carbs 58.2 g | Fat 5.4 g

Beet & Berries Smoothie Bowl

Servings: 1
Cooking Time: 10 Mins.
Ingredients:
- For Smoothie Bowl:
- 1 C. beets, peeled and chopped
- 1 C. fresh strawberries
- ¼ C. unsweetened protein powder
- ½ C. unsweetened almond milk
- 4 ice cubes
- For Topping:
- ¼ C. mixed berries (blueberries, raspberries)
- 1 tsp. unsweetened coconut, shredded

Directions:
1. For smoothie bowl: add all the ingredients in a high-power blender and pulse until smooth.
2. Pour the smoothie into a serving bowl and top with topping ingredients.
3. Serve immediately.

Nutrition:
- Per Serving : Protein 30.1 g | Fiber 9.9 g | Carbs 35.4 g | Fat 4.3 g

Mixe Veggie Soup

Servings: 3
Cooking Time: 25 Mins.
Ingredients:
- ½ tbsp. olive oil
- 2 tbsp. onion, chopped
- 2 tsp. garlic, minced
- ½ C. carrots, peeled and chopped
- ½ C. green cabbage, chopped
- 1/3 C. fresh beans, chopped
- 3 C. homemade vegetable broth
- ½ tbsp. fresh lemon juice
- 3 tbsp. water
- 2 tbsp. arrowroot starch
- Salt and ground black pepper, as required

Directions:
1. Heat the oil in a large, heavy-bottomed pan over medium heat and sauté the onion and garlic for about 4-5 minutes.
2. Add the carrots, cabbage, and beans and cook for about 4-5 minutes, stirring frequently.
3. Stir in the broth and bring to a boil.
4. Cook for about 4-5 minutes.
5. Meanwhile, in a small bowl, dissolve the arrowroot starch in water.
6. Slowly add the arrowroot starch mixture, stirring continuously.
7. Cook for about 7-8 minutes, stirring occasionally.

8. Stir in the lemon juice, salt, and black pepper and remove from the heat.
9. Serve hot.
Nutrition:
- Per Serving : Protein 9.2 g | Fiber 7 g | Carbs 22.5 g | Fat 4.2 g

Apple-cinnamon Oats

Servings: 1
Cooking Time: 0minutes
Ingredients:
- 1/4 cup of yogurt
- Half tsp. of pumpkin pie spice
- 1/4 cup of pumpkin puree
- 2/3 cup of almond milk, unsweetened
- 1 packet of instant oats
- 1 tsp. of maple syrup

Directions:
1. In a mason jar, add all ingredients. Shake well & keep in the fridge overnight.
2. Serve.

Nutrition:
- Per Serving : Protein 5 g | Fiber 6 g | Carbs 32 g | Fat 4 g

Pork Sausage & Green Lentil Braise

Servings: 6
Cooking Time: 25 Minutes
Ingredients:
- 1.4 oz. of butter
- 2 thyme sprigs
- 2 onions, chopped
- 3 garlic cloves, minced
- 1 tbsp. of olive oil
- 2 bacon rashers, chopped
- 1 carrot, chopped
- 6 thick pork sausages
- 2 celery stalks, chopped
- 2 cups of red wine
- 14 oz. of 2 cans green lentils, rinsed

Directions:
1. Sauté bacon, onion & garlic for 4-6 minutes in butter (half).
2. Add celery & carrot, cook for 8 to 10 minutes.
3. Add red wine simmer for 6 to 8 minutes.
4. Add lentils & thyme, simmer for half an hour. Add the rest of the butter.
5. Grill sausages for 6-8 minutes, serve with lentils.

Nutrition:
- Per Serving : Protein 5 g | Fiber 12 g | Carbs 15 g | Fat 5 g

Orange & Beet Salad

Servings: 4
Cooking Time: 10 Mins.

Ingredients:

- 4 large oranges, peeled, seeded and sectioned
- 2 beets, trimmed, peeled and sliced
- 6 C. fresh arugula
- ¼ C. walnuts, chopped
- 3 tbsp. olive oil
- Pinch of salt

Directions:

1. In a salad bowl, place all ingredients and gently toss to coat.
2. Serve immediately.

Nutrition:

- Per Serving : Protein 5.2 g | Fiber 6.9 g | Carbs 27.5 g | Fat 15.6 g

Chickpeas Falafel

Servings: 4
Cooking Time: 30 Mins.

Ingredients:

- 1 C. dried chickpeas, rinsed, and soaked for 12-24 hours in the refrigerator
- ½ C. onion, chopped roughly
- 4 garlic cloves, peeled
- ½ C. fresh cilantro
- ½ C. fresh parsley
- 1 tbsp. olive oil
- ½ tsp. ground cumin
- Salt and ground black pepper, as required
- 8 C. lettuce, torn

Directions:

1. Preheat your oven to 375 ºF. Place a rack in the middle of the oven. Generously, grease a large rimmed baking sheet.
2. For falafel: in a food processor, add all the ingredients except for lettuce and pulse until smooth.
3. Take about 2 tbsp. of the mixture and shape it into a ½-inch thick patty.
4. Repeat with the remaining mixture.
5. Arrange the patties onto the prepared baking sheet in a single layer.
6. Bake for approximately 25-30 minutes, flipping once halfway through.
7. Divide salad ingredients and falafel patties into serving bowls evenly.
8. Serve immediately.

Nutrition:

- Per Serving : Protein 9.1 g | Fiber 8.7 g | Carbs 31 g | Fat 6 g

Wild Rice & Squash Pilaf

Servings: 8

Cooking Time: 45 Mins.

Ingredients:

- 1 medium butternut squash, peeled and cubed
- 1/3 C. olive oil
- Salt, as required
- 2 C. wild rice, rinsed
- 6 C. water
- 1 medium onion, chopped
- 2 garlic cloves, minced
- ¼ C. fresh lime juice
- ¼ C. fresh orange juice
- 1 tsp. fresh lime zest, grated
- ½ tsp. ground cumin
- 1 C. fresh cranberries
- ¾ C. walnuts, chopped
- 3 tbsp. fresh parsley, chopped

Directions:

1. Preheat your oven to 400 ºF.
2. In a bowl, add the squash cubes, 1 tbsp. of oil and salt and toss to coat well
3. Divide the squash cubes onto 2 baking sheets and spread in a single layer.
4. Roast for about 20 minutes.
5. Meanwhile, in a medium wok, heat 1 tbsp. of oil over medium heat and sauté the onion and garlic for about 3-4 minutes.
6. In a bowl, add the remaining oil, lime juice, orange juice, lime zest and spices and beat until well combined.
7. In a medium pan, add the water and rice over medium-high heat and bring to a boil.
8. Now adjust the heat to low and simmer, covered for about 40 minutes.
9. Remove the pan of rice from heat and drain completely.
10. Transfer the cooked rice into a bowl.
11. Add the cooked onion mixture, squash cubes, cranberries, walnuts, parsley and dressing and gently stir to combine.
12. Serve immediately.

Nutrition:

- Per Serving : Protein 10.3 g | Fiber 7.3 g | Carbs 48.9 g | Fat 8.7 g

Avocado Matcha Banana Bread

Servings: 1 Loaf
Cooking Time: 0minutes

Ingredients:

- 1 ½ cups of all-purpose flour
- 1 egg
- 1 ½ tbsp. of matcha powder
- 1 teaspoon vanilla extract
- 1 tsp. of baking soda
- ½ tsp. of kosher salt
- 2 tsp. of black sesame seeds

- ¾ cup of granulated sugar
- 1 avocado
- 2 ripe bananas
- ¼ cup of vegetable oil

Directions:

1. Let the oven preheat to 350°F. Oil spray a 9 by 5" loaf pan.
2. Add all dry ingredients to a bowl & mix.
3. Add egg, avocado & vanilla to a food processor & pulse until smooth.
4. Mash the bananas. Mix with oil & avocado mixture.
5. Add the wet to dry ingredients.
6. Pour in a pan sprinkle with black seeds.
7. Bake for 50 to 55 minutes.

Nutrition:

- Per Serving : Protein 6 g | Fiber 8 g | Carbs 14 g | Fat 6 g

Lamb With Lentils, Feta & Mint

Servings: 4
Cooking Time: 30 Minutes

Ingredients:

- 1/4 cup of olive oil
- ½ cup of Kalamata olives, chopped
- 1 tbsp. of lemon juice
- 5 oz. of feta, crumbled
- 7 oz. of 2 lamb back straps, trimmed
- 9 oz. of cherry tomatoes
- 1 tbsp. of chopped rosemary
- 2 tbsp. of mint leaves
- 14 oz. of canned lentils, rinsed
- 1 tsp. of dried mint

Directions:

1. Let the oven preheat to 400 F.
2. Coat the tomatoes in oil (2 tsp.), roast for 15 minutes, after 10 minutes, add olives.
3. Season the lamb with salt, pepper, oil (2 tsp.) & rosemary. Brown in the pan for 3 minutes on each side.
4. Cover them in foil loosely.
5. Simmer the lentils in water for 5 minutes, drain & toss with oil (2 tbsp.), salt, pepper & lemon juice.
6. Serve the lamb with lentils & the rest of the ingredients.

Nutrition:

- Per Serving : Protein 14 g | Fiber 9 g | Carbs 13 g | Fat 6 g

Eggless Tomato Omelet

Servings: 4
Cooking Time: 12 Mins.

Ingredients:

- 1 C. chickpea flour
- ¼ tsp. ground turmeric
- Pinch of ground cumin
- Pinch of salt

- 1½-2 C. water
- 1 medium onion, chopped finely
- 2 medium tomatoes, peeled, seeded and chopped finely
- 2 tbsp. fresh cilantro, chopped
- 2 tbsp. olive oil, divided

Directions:

1. In a large bowl, add the flour, spices, and salt and mix well.
2. Slowly add the water and mix until well combined.
3. Fold in the onion, tomatoes and cilantro.
4. In a large non-stick frying pan, heat ½ tbsp. of the oil over medium heat.
5. Add ½ of the tomato mixture and tilt the pan to spread it.
6. Cook for about 5-7 minutes.
7. Place the remaining oil over the omelette and carefully flip it over.
8. Cook for about 4-5 minutes or until golden brown.
9. Repeat with the remaining mixture.

Nutrition:

- Per Serving : Protein 10.6 g | Fiber 10.2 g | Carbs 35.7 g | Fat 10.3 g

Lentils & Chickpeas Salad

Servings: 6
Cooking Time: 35 Mins.

Ingredients:

- For Lentils:
- 4 C. water
- 2 C. dried lentils, rinsed
- 2 large garlic cloves, halved lengthwise
- 2 tbsp. olive oil
- For Dressing:
- 1 garlic clove, minced
- ¼ C. fresh lemon juice
- 2 tbsp. olive oil
- 1 tsp. maple syrup
- 1 tsp. Dijon mustard
- Salt and ground black pepper, as required
- For Salad:
- 1½ (15-oz.) cans chickpeas, rinsed and drained
- 2 large avocados, peeled, pitted and chopped
- 2 C. radishes, trimmed and sliced
- ¼ C. fresh mint leaves, chopped

Directions:

1. For lentils: in a medium pot, add all ingredients over medium-high heat and bring to a boil.
2. Now adjust the heat to low and simmer for about 25-35 minutes or until the lentils are cooked through and tender.
3. Drain the lentils and discard the garlic cloves.
4. For dressing: add all ingredients in a small bowl and beat until well combined.
5. In a large serving bowl, add lentils, chickpeas, radishes, avocados and mint and mix.

6. Add the dressing and toss to coat well.
7. Serve immediately.
Nutrition:
- Per Serving : Protein 24.9 g | Fiber 29.2 g | Carbs 66.4 g | Fat 22.2 g

Quinoa, Oats & Seeds Porridge

Servings: 3
Cooking Time: 15 Mins.
Ingredients:
- 2 C. unsweetened almond milk
- 2 C. water
- 1 C. old-fashioned oats
- ¼ C. dried quinoa, rinsed
- 1 tbsp. flax seeds
- 1 tbsp. chia seeds
- 3 tbsp. maple syrup
- ½ tsp. vanilla extract
- 3 tbsp. almonds, chopped
- ¼ C. fresh strawberries, hulled and sliced
- ¼ C. fresh blueberries

Directions:
1. In a saucepan, mix together all the ingredients except the berries and almonds over medium heat and bring to a gentle boil.
2. Cook for about 20 minutes, stirring occasionally.
3. Stir in chopped dates and immediately remove from heat.
4. Serve warm with the garnishing of berries and almonds.
Nutrition:
- Per Serving : Protein 8.9 g | Fiber 7.5 g | Carbs 48 g | Fat 9.6 g

Avocado Mint Smoothie

Servings: 2
Cooking Time: 10 Mins.
Ingredients:
- 1 avocado, peeled, pitted and chopped
- 12-14 fresh mint leaves
- 2 tbsp. fresh lime juice
- ½ tsp. vanilla extract
- 1½ C. unsweetened almond milk
- ¼ C. ice, crushed

Directions:
1. Add all the ingredients in a high-power blender and pulse until creamy.
2. Pour the smoothie into two glasses and serve immediately.
Nutrition:
- Per Serving : Protein 3.3 g | Fiber 8.9 g | Carbs 11.7 g | Fat 18.5 g

Tempeh & Veggie Hash

Servings: 3
Cooking Time: 25 Mins.
Ingredients:
- 2½ C. sweet potato, peeled and cubed
- 1/3 C. onion, chopped finely
- 1 C. tempeh, cubed
- 1 C. Brussels sprout, trimmed and quartered
- 2 garlic cloves, minced
- Salt and ground black pepper, as required
- 1½ C. fresh kale, tough ribs removed and chopped
- 3 poached eggs

Directions:
1. In a saucepan of boiling water, add the sweet potato cubes and cook for about 8 minutes.
2. Drain the sweet potato cubes completely.
3. Heat the olive oil in a wok over medium-high heat and sauté the onion for about 4-5 minutes.
4. Add in remaining ingredients except for kale and cook for about 6-7 minutes, stirring occasionally.
5. Add cooked sweet potato and kale and cook for about 5 minutes, stirring twice.
6. Serve hot.
Nutrition:
- Per Serving : Protein 21.4 g | Fiber 7.9 g | Carbs 48.1 g | Fat 10.5 g

Rice & Beans Stuffed Bell Peppers

Servings: 4
Cooking Time: 58 Mins.
Ingredients:
- 1½ C. water
- 1 C. brown rice, rinsed and drained
- 1 tbsp. olive oil
- 1 (15-oz.) can kidney beans, rinsed and drained
- 7 oz. frozen corn
- Salt and ground black pepper, as required
- 2 tbsp. fresh parsley, chopped
- 4 large bell peppers, tops and seeds removed

Directions:
1. In a saucepan, add water and rice and bring to a boil.
2. Reduce the heat and simmer, covered for about 30 minutes or until all the liquid is absorbed.
3. Remove from the heat and set aside, covered for about 5 minutes.
4. With a fork, fluff the rice.
5. Preheat your oven to 375 ºF. Grease a large baking sheet.
6. In a large non-stick wok, heat oil over medium heat and cook cooked rice, beans, corn and spices for about 2-3 minutes.
7. Stir in parsley and remove from heat.
8. Stuff the bell peppers with rice mixture evenly.
9. Arrange the bell peppers onto prepared baking sheet.

10. Bake for approximately 15-20 minutes.

11. Serve hot.

Nutrition:

- Per Serving : Protein 11.7 g | Fiber 10.2 g | Carbs 71.4 g | Fat 5.8 g

Spelt Bread

Servings: 8

Cooking Time: 50 Mins.

Ingredients:

- 3 C. spelt flour
- 1 tsp. baking soda
- 1 tsp. salt
- 2 tbsp. maple syrup
- 2½ tbsp. olive oil
- 1 C. plus 1 tbsp. water

Directions:

1. Preheat your oven to 375 °F. Lightly flour a baking sheet.

2. In a bowl, put flour, baking soda and salt and mix well.

3. In another small bowl, add the maple syrup, oil and water and mix well.

4. Add the oil mixture into the bowl of flour mixture and mix until a smooth dough forms.

5. Place the dough onto a lightly floured surface and with your hands, gently knead the dough for about 2-3 minutes.

6. With your hands, make a 6-inch round loaf from dough.

7. Arrange the loaf onto the prepared baking sheet and with a sharp knife, score the top in a semicircle

8. Bake for approximately 50 minutes or until a wooden skewer inserted in the center of loaf comes out clean.

9. Remove from oven and place the baking sheet onto a wire rack to cool for at least 10 minutes.

10. Then invert the bread onto the rack to cool completely before serving.

11. Cut the bread loaf into desired-sized slices and serve.

Nutrition:

- Per Serving : Protein 6.7 g | Fiber 9.7 g | Carbs 36.5 g | Fat 1.4 g

Mango, Orange & Cucumber Smoothie

Servings: 2

Cooking Time: 10 Mins.

Ingredients:

- ½ C. mango chunks
- 2 oranges, peeled
- 2 C. cucumber, chopped
- 2 C. spinach

Directions:

1. Add all the ingredients in a high-power blender and pulse until creamy.

2. Pour the smoothie into two glasses and serve immediately.

Nutrition:

- Per Serving : Protein 11.9 g | Fiber 14.7 g | Carbs 72.3 g | Fat 5.9 g

Avocado Lime Smoothie

Servings: 2

Cooking Time: 10 Mins.

Ingredients:

- 1 large avocado, pitted and sliced
- 1 tbsp. fresh lime juice
- 1 C. unsweetened almond milk
- ½ C. water
- ¼ C. ice cubes

Directions:

1. Add all the ingredients in a high-power blender and pulse until creamy.

2. Pour the smoothie into two glasses and serve immediately.

Nutrition:

- Per Serving : Protein 2.3 g | Fiber 7.1 g | Carbs 9.5 g | Fat 16.1 g

Slow Cooker Black Bean Soup

Servings: 6

Cooking Time: 11 Hours

Ingredients:

- 1 green bell pepper, chopped
- 3 tbsp. of fresh cilantro, chopped
- 3 garlic cloves, minced
- 1 onion, chopped
- 4 cups of vegetable broth
- 1 pound of dried black beans, rinsed
- 1 tbsp. of ground cumin
- 1 avocado, diced
- 2 tbsp. of lime juice
- 1 tsp. of salt
- 6 tsp. of light sour cream

Directions:

1. Soak the beans in water for 12 hours. Drain.

2. In a slow cooker, add all ingredients except for sour cream & lime juice. Cook for 10 hours on low, add lime juice.

3. Pulse with a stick blender to a chunky consistency.

4. Serve with sour cream on top.

Nutrition:

- Per Serving : Protein 5 g | Fiber 9 g | Carbs 29 g | Fat 4 g

Pear & Raspbberry Salad

Servings: 4
Cooking Time: 10 Mins.
Ingredients:
- 4 C. romaine lettuce, torn
- 4 pears, cored and sliced
- 1 C. fresh raspberries, hulled and sliced
- ¼ C. low-fat feta cheese
- 3 tbsp. olive oil
- 2 tbsp. fresh lime juice
- 1 tbsp. maple syrup

Directions:
1. In a salad bowl, place all ingredients and toss to coat well.
2. Serve immediately.

Nutrition:
- Per Serving : Protein 2.7 g | Fiber 8.8 g | Carbs 41 g | Fat 13.1 g

Charred Broccoli Salad With Arugula

Servings: 4-6
Cooking Time: 10 Minutes
Ingredients:
- 3 tbsp. of olive oil
- 1 anchovy fillet, oil-packed
- 2 garlic cloves
- 1 1/2 tsp. of Dijon mustard
- 2/3 cup of mayonnaise
- 2 heads of broccoli, broken into florets
- 1/4 cup of chopped chives
- 1/4 cup of buttermilk
- 1 cup of parsley
- 1 cup of tarragon leaves
- 3.5 oz. of smoked cheddar, shaved
- 1 lemon's juice
- 4 cups of baby arugula
- Salt & pepper

Directions:
1. Boil broccoli for 2 minutes in salted water until tender.
2. Add to cold water & drain. Add to a skillet sauté in hot oil for 5-10 minutes.
3. Sprinkle salt on top.
4. Add the rest of the ingredients to a bowl except for arugula. Whisk well
5. Add broccoli & arugula. Toss & serve.

Nutrition:
- Per Serving : Protein 4 g | Fiber 10 g | Carbs 7 g | Fat 6 g

Apple, Orange & Swiss Chard Juice

Servings: 2
Cooking Time: 10 Mins.
Ingredients:
- 3 C. Swiss chard
- 3 apples, cored and quartered
- 2 oranges, peeled and sectioned

Directions:
1. Add all ingredients into a juicer and extract the juice according to the manufacturer's method.
2. Through a cheesecloth-lined strainer, strain the juice and transfer into 2 glasses.
3. Serve immediately.

Nutrition:
- Per Serving : Protein 3.6 g | Fiber 13.4 g | Carbs 69.8 g | Fat 1 g

Chapter 4: Low-residue Recipes

Tuna Omelet

Servings: 2
Cooking Time: 5 Mins.
Ingredients:

- 4 eggs
- ¼ C. unsweetened almond milk
- Salt and ground black pepper, as required
- 1 (5-oz.) can water-packed tuna, drained and flaked
- 1 tbsp. olive oil
- ½ C. tomato, peeled, seeded and chopped
- ¼ C. low-fat cheddar cheese, shredded

Directions:

1. In a bowl, add the eggs, almond milk, salt, and black pepper, and beat well.
2. Add the tuna and stir to combine.
3. In a large non-stick frying pan, heat oil over medium heat.
4. Place the egg mixture in an even layer and cook for about 1-2 minutes, without stirring.
5. Carefully lift the edges to run the uncooked portion flow underneath.
6. Spread the tomato over the egg mixture and sprinkle with the cheese.
7. Cover the frying pan and cook for about 30-60 seconds.
8. Remove the lid and fold the omelette in half.
9. Remove from the heat and cut the omelette into 2 portions.
10. Serve immediately.

Nutrition:

- Per Serving : Protein 31.4 g | Fiber 0.5 g | Carbs 3.1 g | Fat 20.2 g

Carrot & Beet Soup

Servings: 4
Cooking Time: 30 Mins.
Ingredients:

- 4 C. low sodium vegetable broth
- 1 carrot, peeled and sliced
- 6 oz. canned cooked beets
- Salt, as required

Directions:

1. In a small saucepan, add carrot and broth over medium-high heat and bring to a boil.
2. Now adjust the heat to low and cook, covered, for about 15 minutes.
3. Add beets and cook for about 8-10 minutes.
4. Remove the soup pan from heat and with an immersion blender, blend the soup until smooth.
5. Serve hot.

Nutrition:

- Per Serving : Protein 0.8 g | Fiber 1.2 g | Carbs 9.7 g | Fat 0.1 g

Herbed Swordfish

Servings: 2
Cooking Time: 8 Mins.
Ingredients:

- 2 tbsp. orange zest, grated
- 1 tbsp. fresh thyme, chopped
- 1 tbsp. fresh parsley, chopped
- 1 tsp. olive oil
- 2 (6-oz.) swordfish steaks

Directions:

1. Preheat your oven to broiler.
2. In a bowl, add orange zest, herbs and oil and mix well.
3. Rub the fish steaks with herb mixture generously.
4. Arrange the fish steaks onto a broiler pan and broil for about 3-4 minutes per side.
5. Serve hot.

Nutrition:

- Per Serving : Protein 43.5 g | Fiber 1.2 g | Carbs 2.5 g | Fat 11.2 g

Simple Strip Steak

Servings: 2
Cooking Time: 8 Mins.
Ingredients:

- 2 tsp. olive oil
- 2 (4-oz.) strip steaks, trimmed
- Salt and ground black pepper, as required

Directions:

1. In a large heavy-bottomed wok, heat the oil over high heat and cook the steaks with salt and black pepper for about 3-4 minutes per side.
2. Transfer the steaks onto a cutting board for about 5 minutes before slicing.
3. Cut the steaks into desired-sized slices against the grain and serve.

Nutrition:

- Per Serving : Protein 34.4 g | Fiber 0 g | Carbs 0 g | Fat 12.8 g

Vanilla Pancakes

Servings: 6
Cooking Time: 18 Mins.
Ingredients:
- 1 C. unsweetened almond milk
- 2 tsp. apple cider vinegar
- 1 C. buckwheat flour
- 2 tbsp. wheat germ
- 1 tbsp. baking powder
- ¼ tsp. salt
- ¼ C. maple syrup
- 1 tsp. vanilla extract
- 1 tbsp. extra-virgin olive oil

Directions:
1. In a medium bowl, mix together the almond milk and vinegar. Set aside.
2. In a large bowl, mix together the flour, wheat germ, baking powder, and salt.
3. Add the coconut milk mixture, maple syrup, and vanilla extract and beat until well combined.
4. In a non-stick wok, heat the oil over medium heat.
5. Place desired amount of the mixture and spread in an even circle.
6. Cook for about 1-2 minutes.
7. Flip and cook for about 1 minute.
8. Repeat with the remaining mixture.
9. Serve warm.

Nutrition:
- Per Serving : Protein 3.4 g | Fiber 2.1 g | Carbs 25.7 g | Fat 3.8 g

Turkey & Veggies Bake

Servings: 6
Cooking Time: 1 Hour
Ingredients:
- 2 large zucchinis, peeled, seed and sliced
- 2 medium tomatoes, peeled, seed and sliced
- 1 lb. lean ground turkey
- 1 C. sugar-free tomato sauce
- ½ C. low-fat cheddar cheese, shredded
- 2 C. low-fat cottage cheese, shredded
- 1 egg yolk
- 1 tbsp. fresh rosemary, minced
- Salt and ground black pepper, as required

Directions:
1. Preheat your oven to 500 ºF. Grease a large roasting pa
2. Arrange zucchini and tomato slices into prepared roasting pan and spray with some cooking spray.
3. Roast for about 10-12 minutes.
4. Remove from oven and set aside.
5. Now preheat your oven to 350 ºF.

6. Meanwhile, heat a non-stick wok over medium-high heat and cook the turkey for about 8-10 minutes or until browned.
7. Stir in tomato sauce and cook for about 2-3 minutes.
8. Remove from the heat and place the turkey mixture into a 13x9-inch shallow baking dish.
9. In a bowl, add the remaining ingredients and mix until well combined.
10. Place the roasted vegetables over turkey mixture, followed by the cheese mixture evenly.
11. Bake for approximately 35 minutes.
12. Remove from oven and set aside for about 5-10 minutes.
13. Cut into equal-sized 8 wedges and serve.

Nutrition:
- Per Serving : Protein 29.7 g | Fiber 2 g | Carbs 9.3 g | Fat 11.1 g

Broth Braised Asparagus Tips

Servings: 2
Cooking Time: 5minutes
Ingredients:
- 1 tbsp. of olive oil
- 1 cup of asparagus tips
- ½ cup of chicken broth
- One slice of lemon peel

Directions:
1. Boil the broth with oil.
2. Add the rest of the ingredients. Cook for 3 to 4 minutes.
3. Serve.

Nutrition:
- Per Serving : Protein 0.1 g | Fiber 1 g | Carbs 7 g | Fat 0.2 g

Rosemary Beef Tenderloin

Servings: 12
Cooking Time: 50 Mins.
Ingredients:
- 1 (3-lb.) beef tenderloin
- 1 tbsp. fresh rosemary, minced
- Salt and ground black pepper, as required
- 1 tbsp. olive oil

Directions:
1. Preheat your oven to 425 ºF. Grease a large shallow roasting pan.
2. Place the roast into the prepared roasting pan.
3. Rub the roast with rosemary, salt, and black pepper, and drizzle with oil.
4. Roast the beef for about 45-50 minutes.
5. Remove from oven and place the beef tenderloin onto a cutting board for about 10 minutes.
6. Cut the beef tenderloin into desired-sized slices and serve.

Nutrition:

- Per Serving : Protein 32.8 g | Fiber 0.1 g | Carbs 0.2 g | Fat 11.6 g

Ground Chicken With Tomatoes

Servings: 4
Cooking Time: 13 Mins.
Ingredients:
- 2 tbsp. olive oil
- 1¼ lb. ground chicken
- 2 tomatoes, peeled, seeded and chopped
- 2 tbsp. fresh parsley, chopped
- Salt and ground black pepper, as required

Directions:
1. In a wok, heat the oil over medium heat and cook the ground chicken for about 6-8 minutes.
2. Add in tomatoes and cook for about 4-5 minutes, stirring frequently.
3. Stir in parsley, salt and black pepper and serve hot.

Nutrition:
- Per Serving : Protein 25.3 g | Fiber 0.8 g | Carbs 2.6 g | Fat 18.6 g

Pumpkin Pancakes

Servings: 10
Cooking Time: 40 Mins.
Ingredients:
- 2 eggs
- 1 C. buckwheat flour
- 1 tbsp. baking powder
- ½ tsp. salt
- 1 C. pumpkin puree
- ¾ C. plus 2 tbsp. fat-free milk
- 3 tbsp. maple syrup
- 2 tbsp. olive oil
- 1 tsp. vanilla extract

Directions:
1. In a blender, add all ingredients and pulse until well combined.
2. Transfer the mixture into a bowl and set aside for about 10 minutes.
3. Heat a greased non-stick wok over medium heat.
4. Place about ¼ C. of the mixture and spread in an even circle.
5. Cook for about 2 minutes per side.
6. Repeat with the remaining mixture.
7. Serve warm.

Nutrition:
- Per Serving : Protein 3.6 g | Fiber 2 g | Carbs 16.5 g | Fat 4.4 g

Strawberry Cheesecake Smoothie

Servings:2
Cooking Time: 5 Minutes

Ingredients:
- 2 cups frozen strawberries
- 1 cup milk
- 1 cup cottage cheese
- 3 tablespoons honey or maple syrup
- 1 teaspoon vanilla extract

Directions:
1. teaspoon vanilla extract
2. a blender or food processor, puree the strawberries, milk, cottage cheese, honey, and vanilla until smooth. Serve immediately.

Nutrition:
- Per Serving : Protein 18 g | Fiber 3 g | Carbs 50 g | Fat 4 g

Celery Juice

Servings: 2
Cooking Time: 10 Mins.
Ingredients:
- 8 celery stalks with leaves
- 2 tbsp. fresh ginger, peeled
- 1 lemon, peeled
- ½ C. filtered water
- Pinch of salt

Directions:
1. Add all ingredients in a high-power blender and pulse until well combined.
2. Through a fine mesh strainer, strain the juice and transfer into 2 glasses.
3. Serve immediately.

Nutrition:
- Per Serving : Protein 1 g | Fiber 2 g | Carbs 6.5 g | Fat 0.5 g

Turkey Stuffed Bell Peppers

Servings: 5
Cooking Time: 28 Mins.
Ingredients:
- 5 large bell peppers, tops and seeds removed
- 1 tbsp. olive oil
- 1 lb. lean ground turkey
- ½ tsp. dried oregano
- ½ tsp. dried thyme
- Salt and ground black pepper, as required
- 1 large zucchini, peeled, seeded and chopped
- 3 tbsp. tomato paste

Directions:
1. Preheat your oven to 350 ºF. Grease a small baking dish.
2. In a large pan of boiling water, place the bell peppers and cook for about 4-5 minutes.
3. Remove from the water and place onto a paper towel, cut side down.

4. Meanwhile, in a large non-stick wok, heat the olive oil over medium heat and cook the ground turkey, oregano, salt, and pepper for about 8-10 minutes.

5. Add the zucchini and cook for about 2-3 minutes.

6. Remove from the heat and drain any juices from the beef mixture

7. Add the tomato paste and stir to combine.

8. Arrange the bell peppers into the prepared baking dish, cut side upward

9. Stuff the bell peppers with the beef mixture evenly.

10. Bake for approximately 15 minutes.

11. Serve hot.

Nutrition:

- Per Serving : Protein 19.9 g | Fiber 2 g | Carbs 12.3 g | Fat 9.7 g

Green Bean Potato Salad

Servings: 4-6
Cooking Time: 10minutes
Ingredients:

- 6 red potatoes, small & peeled, cubed
- 1 small onion, sliced thin
- 1 tsp. of sugar
- 1/3 Cup of olive oil
- 1 tbsp. of garlic powder
- 1/4 Cup of red wine vinegar
- 1 ½ Pound of fresh green beans
- 1/4 Cup of rice vinegar

Directions:

1. Boil the green beans & potatoes for 7 minutes, till tender-crisp.

2. Drain & add to the cold water. Drain.

3. Add onions, beans & potatoes. Add the rest of the ingredients to a bowl, whisk & pour on the salad. Toss & serve.

Nutrition:

- Per Serving : Protein 2 g | Fiber 3 g | Carbs 12 g | Fat 3 g

Stuffed Mushrooms

Servings:4
Cooking Time: 25 Minutes
Ingredients:

- 4 portabella mushrooms (about 1 pound)
- Salt
- Freshly ground black pepper
- 1 tablespoon olive oil
- 1 cup finely chopped baby spinach
- ¼ cup finely chopped green onion
- 1 garlic clove, minced
- ½ cup bread crumbs
- ¼ cup grated Parmesan cheese

Directions:

1. ¼ cup grated Parmesan cheese

2. Preheat the oven to 350°F. Grease a 9-by-13-inch baking dish.

3. Clean the mushrooms with a damp paper towel. Remove the stems and set the caps aside. Finely chop the stems and set aside.

4. Place the caps upside down in the prepared baking dish. Lightly season with salt and pepper.

5. In a large sauté pan or skillet over medium heat, warm the oil. Add the spinach, onion, and garlic and cook until the vegetables are tender, 4 to 5 minutes.

6. Remove from heat and stir in the bread crumbs. Season lightly with salt and pepper.

7. Spoon the mixture into the mushroom caps and top with the Parmesan cheese.

8. Bake for 15 to 20 minutes, or until the mushrooms are tender.

Nutrition:

- Per Serving : Protein 7 g | Fiber 3 g | Carbs 16 g | Fat 6 g

Cheddar Scramble

Servings: 6
Cooking Time: 8 Mins.
Ingredients:

- 2 tbsp. olive oil
- 12 large eggs, beaten lightly
- Salt and ground black pepper, as required
- 4 oz. low-fat cheddar cheese, shredded

Directions:

1. In a large wok, heat the oil over medium heat.

2. Add the eggs, salt and black pepper and cook for about 3 minutes, stirring continuously.

3. Remove from the heat and immediately stir in the cheese.

4. Serve immediately.

Nutrition:

- Per Serving : Protein 17.4 g | Fiber 7.1 g | Carbs 27.1 g | Fat 0.5 g

Ground Turkey In Tomato Sauce

Servings: 8
Cooking Time: 45 Mins.
Ingredients:

- 2 tbsp. olive oil
- 2 lb. lean ground turkey
- 3 C. tomatoes, peeled, seeded and chopped finely
- 2 oz. sugar-free tomato paste
- 2 C. homemade chicken broth
- Salt and ground black pepper, as required

Directions:

1. In a large Dutch oven, heat the oil over medium heat and cook the turkey and cook for about 4-5 minutes.

2. Stir in the tomatoes and tomato paste and cook for about 3-4 minutes.

3. Add the broth and bring to a boil.

4. Now adjust the heat to low and simmer, covered for about 30 minutes.

5. Stir in the salt and black pepper and serve hot.

Nutrition:

- Per Serving : Protein 24.4 g | Fiber 1.1 g | Carbs 4.2 g | Fat 12.1 g

Thyme Tenderloin Fillets

Servings: 6
Cooking Time: 14 Mins.
Ingredients:

- 4 (6-oz.) beef tenderloin fillets
- Salt and ground black pepper, as required
- 2 tbsp. olive oil
- 1 tbsp. fresh thyme, chopped

Directions:

1. Season the beef fillets with salt and black pepper evenly and set aside.
2. Heat oil in a cast-iron sauté pan over medium heat and sauté the thyme for about 1 minute.
3. Add the fillets and cook for about 5-7 minutes per side.
4. Remove the fillets from wok and place onto a cutting board for about 10 minutes before slicing.
5. Cut each fillet into desired-sized slices and serve.

Nutrition:

- Per Serving : Protein 32.9 g | Fiber 0.2 g | Carbs 0.3 g | Fat 15.1 g

Spinach, Mushroom, And Bacon Quiche

Servings:4
Cooking Time: 55 Minutes
Ingredients:

- 1 (9-inch) premade pie shell
- 3 large eggs
- 1½ cups milk of choice
- Pinch salt
- Pinch freshly ground black pepper
- 4 slices bacon or ½ cup precooked bacon bits
- 1 cup shredded cheese of choice, divided
- 1 (10-ounce) package frozen spinach, thawed and squeezed dry
- ½ cup sliced mushrooms

Directions:

1. ½ cup sliced mushrooms
2. Preheat the oven to 375°F.
3. Parbake the pie shell for 5 to 7 minutes. This will prevent the crust from getting soggy after you add the egg mixture. Set aside.
4. In a medium bowl, whisk together the eggs, milk, salt, and pepper. Set aside.
5. Line a plate with paper towels. In a large sauté pan or skillet over medium heat, cook the bacon until crisp, 5 to 7

minutes. Transfer the bacon to the lined plate. When cool, crumble into bits.

6. Sprinkle the pie shell with ½ cup of the cheese. Add the spinach, mushrooms, and bacon.
7. Pour the egg mixture into the pie shell (it should be about ⅔ full). Sprinkle the remaining ½ cup of cheese over the top of the egg mixture.
8. Bake for 30 to 40 minutes, or until the pastry is golden and the egg mixture is just set but still wobbly. Cut into wedges and serve warm, or refrigerate for 1 hour and serve cold.
9. To store, cover the pan with plastic wrap and refrigerate for up to 5 days.

Nutrition:

- Per Serving : Protein 22 g | Fiber 2 g | Carbs 35 g | Fat 31 g

Tomato & Basil Scramble

Servings: 2
Cooking Time: 5 Mins.
Ingredients:

- 4 eggs
- Salt and ground black pepper, as required
- ¼ C. fresh basil, chopped
- ½ C. tomatoes, peeled, seeded and chopped
- 1 tbsp. olive oil

Directions:

1. In a large bowl, add eggs, salt and black pepper and beat well.
2. Add the basil and tomatoes and stir to combine.
3. In a large non-stick wok, heat the oil over medium-high heat.
4. Add the egg mixture and cook for about 3-5 minutes, stirring continuously.
5. Serve immediately.

Nutrition:

- Per Serving : Protein 11.6 g | Fiber 0.7 g | Carbs 2.6 g | Fat 15.9 g

Turkey Burgers

Servings: 10
Cooking Time: 16 Mins.
Ingredients:

- 2 lb. lean ground turkey
- 9 oz. low-fat Halloumi cheese, grated
- 2 eggs
- 1 tbsp. fresh rosemary, chopped finely
- 1 tbsp. fresh parsley, chopped finely
- Salt and ground black pepper, as required

Directions:

1. Preheat the grill to medium-high heat. Grease the grill grate.
2. In a large bowl, add all the ingredients and mix until well combined.

3. Make 10 equal-sized patties from the mixture.

4. Place the burgers onto the grill and cook for about 5-8 minutes per side or until done completely.

Nutrition:

- Per Serving : Protein 28 g | Fiber 0.2 g | Carbs 1 g | Fat 10.3 g

Apricot Honey Oatmeal

Servings: 2
Cooking Time: 0 Minutes

Ingredients:

- 1/4 tsp. of cinnamon
- 1/4 Cup of peeled & chopped apricots
- 1 Cup of water
- ½ cup of rolled oats
- 1 tbsp. of honey

Directions:

1. Add all ingredients to a bowl & microwave for 2 minutes.
2. Mix well & serve.

Nutrition:

- Per Serving : Protein 1 g | Fiber 3 g | Carbs 9 g | Fat 2.2 g

Tuna Salad

Servings: 4
Cooking Time: 15 Mins.

Ingredients:

- For Dressing:
- 2 tbsp. fresh dill, minced
- 2 tbsp. olive oil
- 1 tbsp. fresh lime juice
- Salt and ground black pepper, as required
- For Salad:
- 2 (6-oz.) cans water-packed tuna, drained and flaked
- 6 hard-boiled eggs, peeled and sliced
- 1 C. tomato, peeled, seeded and chopped
- 1 large seedless cucumber, peeled, seeded and sliced

Directions:

1. For dressing: in a small bowl, add all the ingredients and beat until well combined.
2. For salad: in another large serving bowl, add all the ingredients and mix well.
3. Divide the tuna mixture onto serving plates.
4. Drizzle with dressing and serve.

Nutrition:

- Per Serving : Protein 31.2 g | Fiber 1.1 g | Carbs 5.9 g | Fat 14.5 g

Chicken In Yogurt Sauce

Servings: 6
Cooking Time: 28 Mins.

Ingredients:

- 2 tbsp. olive oil
- 1½ lb. chicken breasts, cut into ¾-inch chunks
- 2 tomatoes, peeled, seeded and chopped finely
- Salt and ground black pepper, as required
- 1 C. fat-free plain yogurt
- 2 tbsp. fresh cilantro, chopped

Directions:

1. In a large wok, heat oil over medium-high heat and cook the tomatoes for about 2-3 minutes, crushing with the back of spoon.
2. Stir in the chicken salt and black pepper and cook for about 4-5 minutes.
3. Stir in the yogurt and cook for about 8-10 more minutes, stirring occasionally.
4. Stir in the cilantro and serve hot.

Nutrition:

- Per Serving : Protein 34.8 g | Fiber 0.5 g | Carbs 4.4 g | Fat 13.2 g

Simple Butternut Squash

Servings: 6
Cooking Time: 45 Mins.

Ingredients:

- 5 C. butternut squash, peeled, seeded and cubed
- 2 tbsp. olive oil
- Salt, as required

Directions:

1. Preheat your oven to 425 ºF. Arrange pieces of foil into 2 baking sheets.
2. In a large bowl, add all the ingredients and toss to coat well.
3. Arrange the squash pieces onto the prepared baking sheets in a single layer.
4. Roast for about 40-45 minutes.
5. Serve hot.

Nutrition:

- Per Serving : Protein 1.2 g | Fiber 2.3 g | Carbs 13.6 g | Fat 4.8 g

Chicken & Aspargus Stew

Servings: 6
Cooking Time: 20 Mins.

Ingredients:

- 1 tbsp. olive oil
- 1 lb. skinless, boneless chicken breasts, cubed
- 2 C. homemade chicken broth
- 3 C. asparagus tips
- Salt and ground black pepper, as required

Directions:

1. In a wok, heat the oil over medium heat and cook the chicken for about 4-5 minutes.
2. Add broth and bring to a boil.
3. Adjust the heat low and cook for about 8-10 minutes.

4. Add the asparagus, salt, and black pepper, and cook for about 4-5 minutes or until desired doneness

5. Serve hot.

Nutrition:

- Per Serving : Protein 21.5 g | Fiber 1.9 g | Carbs 4.3 g | Fat 5.5 g

Lemony Shrimp

Servings: 4
Cooking Time: 7 Mins.

Ingredients:

- 1 tbsp. olive oil
- 1 lb. medium shrimp, peeled and deveined
- Salt and ground black pepper, as required
- 1 tbsp. fresh lemon juice

Directions:

1. In a non-stick sauté pan, heat oil over medium heat and cook the shrimp, salt and black pepper for about 3 minutes per side, stirring occasionally.

2. Stir in the lemon juice and immediately remove from the heat.

3. Serve hot.

Nutrition:

- Per Serving : Protein 48.7 g | Fiber 0 g | Carbs 0.2 g | Fat 9.8 g

Pasta With Asparagus

Servings: 4
Cooking Time: 10 Mins.

Ingredients:

- 2 tbsp. olive oil
- 1 lb. asparagus tips
- Salt and ground black pepper, as required
- ½ lb. cooked hot pasta, drained

Directions:

1. In a large cast-iron wok, heat the oil over medium heat and cook the asparagus, salt and black pepper for about 8-10 minutes, stirring occasionally.

2. Place the hot pasta and toss to coat well.

3. Serve immediately.

Nutrition:

- Per Serving : Protein 8.9 g | Fiber 2.1 g | Carbs 35.2 g | Fat 8.4 g

Tomato Sauce Glazed Chicken Thighs

Servings: 4
Cooking Time: 10 Mins.

Ingredients:

- 2 tbsp. fresh cilantro, minced
- ½ C. sugar-free tomato sauce
- 2½ tbsp. apple cider vinegar
- 1 tbsp. olive oil
- Salt and ground black pepper, as required
- 4 (4-oz.) skinless, boneless chicken thighs

Directions:

1. In a glass baking dish, add all the ingredients except for chicken thighs and mix well.

2. Add the chicken thighs and coat with the mixture generously.

3. Refrigerate to marinate overnight.

4. Preheat the broiler of oven. Line a large baking sheet with a greased piece of foil.

5. Remove the chicken thighs from bowl, reserving the remaining marinade

6. Arrange the chicken thighs onto prepared baking sheet in a single layer and broil for about 5 minutes per side.

7. Meanwhile, transfer the reserved marinade into a small pan over medium heat and cook for about 8-10 minutes.

8. Serve the chicken thighs with the topping of glaze.

Nutrition:

- Per Serving : Protein 25.7 g | Fiber 0.5 g | Carbs 2 g | Fat 7.6 g

Yellow Squash Soup

Servings: 6
Cooking Time: 33 Mins.

Ingredients:

- 2 tbsp. olive oil
- 6 C. yellow squash, peeled, seeded and cubed
- 4 thyme sprigs
- 4 C. homemade vegetable broth
- Salt and ground black pepper, as required
- 2 tbsp. fresh lemon juice

Directions:

1. In a large soup pan, heat oil over medium heat cook the yellow squash cubes for about 5 minutes.

2. Stir in the thyme, broth, salt and black pepper and bring to a boil.

3. Now adjust the heat to low and cook, covered for about 15-20 minutes.

4. Remove from the heat and discard the thyme sprigs.

5. Set the pan aside to cool slightly.

6. In a large blender, add the soup in batches and pulse until smooth.

7. Return the soup into the same pan over medium heat.

8. Stir in the lemon juice and cook for about 2-3 minutes or until heated completely.

9. Serve hot.

Nutrition:

- Per Serving : Protein 4.6 g | Fiber 1.3 g | Carbs 4.5 g | Fat 5.8 g

Chicken & Potato Bake

Servings: 4
Cooking Time: 53 Mins.
Ingredients:
- 13 tbsp. fresh lemon juice
- 3 tbsp. olive oil, divided
- 1 tsp. dried parsley
- 1 tsp. dried oregano
- Salt, as required
- 4 (4-oz.) skinless chicken thighs
- 8 baby potatoes, halved

Directions:
1. In a large bowl, add the lemon juice, 2 tbsp. of oil, dried herbs and salt and mix well.
2. Reserve half of the marinade into a bowl.
3. In the bowl of remaining marinade, add the chicken thighs and mix well.
4. Cover the bowl and refrigerate overnight, turning the chicken thighs occasionally.
5. Preheat oven to 430 °F.
6. In a large oven-proof skillet, heat the remaining oil over medium-high heat and sear the chicken thighs for about 4 minutes per side.
7. With a spoon, remove the excess fat from skillet, leaving about 1 tbsp. inside.
8. Place the potatoes and reserved marinade and gently, toss to combine.
9. Cover the skillet with a lid and transfer into the oven.
10. Bake for about 35 minutes.
11. Now, set the oven to broiler.
12. Remove the lid of skillet and broil for about 5-10 minutes or until chicken and potatoes are crispy and golden browned
13. Remove from oven and set aside, covered for about 5-10 minutes before serving.

Nutrition:
- Per Serving : Protein 25.6 g | Fiber 2.9 g | Carbs 40 g | Fat 15.3 g

Eggs In Tomato Sauce

Servings: 4
Cooking Time: 50 Mins.
Ingredients:
- 1 tbsp. olive oil
- 2½ C. tomatoes, seeded and chopped finely
- 4 large egg
- 3 oz. low-fat feta cheese, crumbled
- Salt and ground black pepper, as required

Directions:
1. In a large cast iron wok, heat the oil over medium-low heat and cook the tomatoes for about 4-6 minutes, stirring frequently.
2. With the spoon, spread the mixture in an even layer.

3. Carefully crack the eggs over tomato mixture and sprinkle with the feta cheese and black pepper.
4. Cover the pan tightly and cook for about 10-15 minutes or until desired doneness of the eggs.
5. Serve hot.
Nutrition:
- Per Serving : Protein 10.3 g | Fiber 1.3 g | Carbs 5.6 g | Fat 13.2 g

Shrimp With Bell Peppers

Servings: 5
Cooking Time: 10 Mins.
Ingredients:
- 2 tbsp. olive oil
- 3 C. bell peppers, seeded and julienned
- 1 lb. medium shrimp, peeled and deveined
- ¼ C. homemade chicken broth
- Salt and ground black pepper, as required

Directions:
1. In a large non-stick sauté pan, heat olive oil over medium heat and cook the bell peppers for about 3-4 minutes.
2. Add shrimp, salt and black pepper and stir fry for about 3-4 minutes.
3. Stir in broth and cook for about 1-2 minutes.
4. Serve hot.
Nutrition:
- Per Serving : Protein 20.2 g | Fiber 0.9 g | Carbs 2.6 g | Fat 6.8 g

Watermelon & Orange Juice

Servings: 2
Cooking Time: 10 Mins.
Ingredients:
- 1 C. fresh orange juice
- 4 C. seedless watermelon, chopped
- 5-6 fresh mint leaves
- 1-2 tbsp. honey

Directions:
1. Add all ingredients in a high-power blender and pulse for about 15-20 seconds.
2. Through a cheesecloth-lined sieve, strain the juice and pour into two glasses.
3. Serve immediately.
Nutrition:
- Per Serving : Protein 2.9 g | Fiber 1.9 g | Carbs 44.9 g | Fat 0.7 g

Zucchini Lasagna

Servings: 10
Cooking Time: 40 Minutes
Ingredients:

- 1 tsp. of powdered onion
- 1 tsp. of powdered garlic
- Salt & pepper, to taste
- 1 tbsp. of chopped chives
- 9 lasagna sheets
- 1 tbsp. of dried oregano
- 8.8 oz. of ricotta
- 1.7 oz. of shredded cheddar
- 12 oz. of passata
- 28 oz. of grated zucchini

Directions:

1. Let the oven preheat to 400°F.
2. Sauté the zucchini, onion & garlic powder for 3 minutes in hot oil.
3. Add cheddar & ricotta (3/4 tub), salt & pepper.
4. Cook the lasagna sheets for 5 to 6 minutes.
5. Layer the cooked sheets with zucchini & cheese mix, add chives & oregano on each later, lastly, add a layer of passata.
6. Keep doing the layers.
7. Add some cheese on top. Bake at 350° F for half an hour.
8. Serve.

Nutrition:

- Per Serving : Protein 4 g | Fiber 3 g | Carbs 21 g | Fat 6 g

Zucchini Waffles

Servings: 2
Cooking Time: 10 Mins.
Ingredients:

- 1 egg, beaten
- ¼ C. part-skim Mozzarella cheese, shredded
- 2 tbsp. low-fat Parmesan cheese, grated
- ½ of small zucchini, peeled, seeded, grated and squeezed
- ¼ tsp. dried basil, crushed
- Salt and ground black pepper, as required

Directions:

1. Preheat a mini waffle iron and then grease it.
2. In a medium bowl, put all ingredients and with a fork, mix until well combined.
3. Place half of the mixture into preheated waffle iron and cook for about 4-5 minutes.
4. Repeat with the remaining mixture.
5. Serve warm.

Nutrition:

- Per Serving : Protein 6.1 g | Fiber 0.3 g | Carbs 1.3 g | Fat 4.1 g

Prawn & Vegetable Pasta

Servings: 4
Cooking Time: 30minutes
Ingredients:

- 3 tbsp. of olive oil
- 2 cups of baby spinach
- 2 minced garlic cloves
- 6 oz. of pasta
- ½ cup of fresh basil, sliced
- 1 tsp. of oregano
- 1.5 cups of cherry tomatoes
- 1 large zucchini, spiralized
- 18 medium prawns
- Salt & pepper, to taste

Directions:

1. Cook pasta as per package Directions.
2. Sauté oregano, olive oil & garlic for 1 minute. Add tomatoes & cook for 5 minutes.
3. Add spinach cook until it wilts.
4. In a different pan cook, the prawns with 1 tbsp. of oil for 1 to 2 minutes on one side. Turn the heat off.
5. Add basil, zucchini noodles & pasta with spinach & tomatoes. Toss for 2 minutes.
6. Adjust seasoning. Serve with prawns.

Nutrition:

- Per Serving : Protein 10 g | Fiber 3 g | Carbs 14 g | Fat 5 g

Apple & Pear Pita Pockets

Servings: 1
Cooking Time: 0 Minutes
Ingredients:

- 1 pita bread
- ½ pear, peeled & chopped
- ½ apple, peeled & chopped
- 1/4 Cup of cottage cheese

Directions:

1. In a bowl, mix cheese, apple & pear.
2. Cut the pita bread in half but not all the way through.
3. Stuff with apple/pear mixture. Drizzle with honey & serve.

Nutrition:

- Per Serving : Protein 1 g | Fiber 1.2 g | Carbs 18 g | Fat 2 g

Brazilian Fish Stew

Servings: 4
Cooking Time: 20 Minutes
Ingredients:

- 1 to 1 1/2 pounds of firm white fish
- One lime's juice & zest
- ½ tsp. of salt
- Sauce

- 1 onion, diced
- 4 garlic cloves, chopped
- ½ tsp. of salt
- 2 to 3 tbsp. of olive oil
- 1 cup carrot, diced
- 1 red bell pepper, chopped
- ½ jalapeno, minced (optional)
- 1 cup of chicken stock
- 1 tbsp. of tomato paste
- ½ cup of chopped herbs
- 2 tsp. of paprika
- 1 tsp. of ground cumin
- 1 1/2 cups of chopped tomatoes
- 1 can of (14 oz.) coconut milk

Directions:
1. Coat the fish in the lime juice (1 tbsp.), zest & salt.
2. In a pan, sauté onion & salt for 2 to 3 minutes. Add jalapeno, carrot, garlic & bell pepper for 4 to 5 minutes.
3. Add stock, spices & tomato paste. Simmer for 5 minutes.
4. Add coconut milk salt. Stir & add fish; cook for 4 to 6 minutes.
5. Adjust seasoning & serve.

Nutrition:
- Per Serving : Protein 44 g | Fiber 1.2 g | Carbs 12.6 g | Fat 19.7 g

Beef With Carrot

Servings: 6
Cooking Time: 15 Mins.
Ingredients:
- 2 tbsp. olive oil
- 1 lb. beef tenderloin, trimmed and cut into thin strips
- 3 large carrots, peeled and sliced
- ¼ C. homemade chicken broth
- 1 tbsp. fresh lemon juice
- Salt and ground black pepper, as required

Directions:
1. Heat the oil in a large non-stick wok over high heat and sear the beef strips for about 4-5 minutes or until cooked through.
2. With a slotted spoon, transfer the beef into a bowl.
3. In the same wok, add the carrot and cook for about 3-5 minutes.
4. Stir the cooked beef, broth, lemon juice, salt and black pepper and cook for about 3-5 minutes or until desired doneness, stirring occasionally.
5. Serve hot.

Nutrition:
- Per Serving : Protein 22.4 g | Fiber 0 g | Carbs 3.6 g | Fat 11.7 g

Chicken Pasta Salad

Servings: 4

Cooking Time: 15minutes
Ingredients:
- 1 Cup of cooked & cubed chicken
- 1 tsp. of Italian seasoning
- ½ cup of peas
- ½ pound of pasta
- ½ cup of Ranch dressing
- 1 tbsp. of Parmesan cheese, grated

Directions:
1. Cook pasta as per package Directions
2. Drain & add to a bowl with the rest of the ingredients.
3. Toss well & serve.

Nutrition:
- Per Serving : Protein 12 g | Fiber 1 g | Carbs 13 g | Fat 5 g

Chicken & Zucchini Muffins

Servings: 8
Cooking Time: 15 Mins.
Ingredients:
- 4 eggs
- ¼ C. olive oil
- ¼ C. water
- 1/3 C. coconut flour
- ½ tsp. baking powder
- ¼ tsp. salt
- ¾ C. cooked chicken, shredded
- ¾ C. zucchini, grate
- ½ C. low-fat Parmesan cheese, shredded
- 1 tbsp. fresh oregano, minced
- 1 tbsp. fresh thyme, minced
- ¼ C. low-fat cheddar cheese, grated

Directions:
1. Preheat your oven to 400 ºF. Lightly grease 8 cups of a muffin tin.
2. In a bowl, add the eggs, oil and water and beat until well blended.
3. Add the flour, baking powder, and salt, and mix well.
4. Add the remaining ingredients and mix until just blended.
5. Place the muffin mixture into the prepared muffin cups evenly.
6. Bake for approximately 13-15 minutes or until tops become golden brown
7. Remove muffin tin from oven and place onto a wire rack to cool for about 10 minutes.
8. Invert the muffins onto a platter and serve warm.

Nutrition:
- Per Serving : Protein 9.9 g | Fiber 1.9 g | Carbs 4.3 g | Fat 12.6 g

Chicken Parmesan

Servings: 4
Cooking Time: 45minutes
Ingredients:
- 4 chicken legs
- Breadcrumbs, as needed
- ¼ cup of water
- 2 tbsp. of oil
- 1 egg
- 4 slices of cheese
- 1 can of (15 oz.) chopped tomatoes
- ½ tsp. of mix oregano, thyme & basil
- Salt & pepper

Directions:
1. Whisk egg with 1 tbsp. of water.
2. Coat the chicken in egg mixture then in breadcrumbs.
3. Oil spray them generously & bake until cooked at 400°F.
4. Add the rest of the ingredients in a bowl (except for cheese), mix & pour over chicken. Transfer to a pan.
5. Cook for 15-20 minutes more on medium flame.
6. Place cheese on top cook until it melts.

Nutrition:
- Per Serving : Protein 12.2 g | Fiber 3 g | Carbs 17.7 g | Fat 7 g

Ricotta Pancakes

Servings: 4
Cooking Time: 20 Mins.
Ingredients:
- 4 eggs
- ½ C. part-skim ricotta cheese
- ¼ C. unsweetened protein powder
- ½ tsp. baking powder
- Pinch of salt
- ½ tsp. liquid stevia
- 2 tbsp. olive oil

Directions:
1. In a blender, add all the ingredients except for oil and pulse until well combined.
2. In a wok, heat over medium heat.
3. Add the desired amount of the mixture and spread it evenly.
4. Cook for about 2-3 minutes or until golden brown.
5. Flip and cook for about 1-2 minutes or until golden brown
6. Repeat with the remaining mixture.
7. Serve warm.

Nutrition:
- Per Serving : Protein 14.4 g | Fiber 0 g | Carbs 2.1 g | Fat 14 g

Banana Pancakes

Servings: 5

Cooking Time: 25 Mins.
Ingredients:
- ¼ C. coconut flour
- ¼ tsp. baking powder
- ½ tsp. ground cinnamon
- Pinch of salt
- ½ C. unsweetened almond milk
- 2 eggs
- 1 ripe banana, peeled and mashed
- 1 tbsp. maple syrup
- 1 tsp. apple cider vinegar
- ½ tsp. vanilla extract
- 2 tsp. olive oil

Directions:
1. In a large bowl, place flour, baking powder, cinnamon and salt and mix well.
2. In a separate bowl, add almond milk, egg, banana, maple syrup, vinegar and vanilla and beat until well combined.
3. Add egg mixture into the bowl of flour mixture and mix until well combined.
4. In a large frying pan heat oil over medium heat.
5. Add desired amount of mixture and spread in an even layer.
6. Cook for about 2-3 minutes or until golden.
7. Flip the side and cook for 1-2 minutes more.
8. Repeat with the remaining mixture.
9. Serve warm.

Nutrition:
- Per Serving : Protein 3.4 g | Fiber 2 g | Carbs 10 g | Fat 4.7 g

Beef & Veggie Burgers

Servings: 8
Cooking Time: 24 Mins.
Ingredients:
- 1 lb. lean ground beef
- 1 carrot, peeled and chopped finely
- 1 large beet, trimmed, peeled and chopped finely
- 1 tbsp. fresh cilantro, chopped finely
- Salt and ground black pepper, as required
- 3 tbsp. olive oil

Directions:
1. In a large bowl, add all ingredients except for oil and mix until well combined.
2. Make equal-sized 8 patties from mixture.
3. In a large non-stick sauté pan, heat the olive oil over medium heat and cook the patties in 2 batches for about 4-6 minutes per side.
4. Serve hot.

Nutrition:
- Per Serving : Protein 17.5 g | Fiber 0.4 g | Carbs 2 g | Fat 8.8 g

Zucchini & Spinach Frittata

Servings: 4
Cooking Time: 20 Mins.
Ingredients:

- 6 eggs
- ½ C. unsweetened almond milk
- Salt and ground black pepper, as required
- 2 C. fresh baby spinach, chopped
- ¾ C. zucchini, peeled, seeded and chopped
- ¼ C. fresh cilantro, chopped

Directions:
1. Preheat your oven to 400 ºF. Lightly grease a pie dish.
2. In a large bowl, add the eggs, almond milk, salt and black pepper and beat until well combined. Set aside.
3. In another bowl, add the zucchini and cilantro and mix well.
4. In the bottom of prepared pie dish, place the zucchini mixture evenly and top with the egg mixture.
5. Bake for approximately 20 minutes or until a wooden skewer inserted in the center comes out clean.
6. Remove from oven and set aside for about 5 minutes before slicing.
7. Cut into desired-sized wedges and serve warm.

Nutrition:
- Per Serving : Protein 9.1 g | Fiber 0.7 g | Carbs 2.1 g | Fat 7.1 g

Strawberry Spread

Servings: 1 Cup
Cooking Time: 25 Minutes
Ingredients:

- 1 tbsp. of lemon juice
- 2 cups of strawberries
- 1/4 cup of sugar

Directions:
1. In a pan, add berries with the rest of the ingredients.
2. Place on high flame until it boils; turn the heat low while keep stirring for 15 minutes.
3. Cook until the liquid is absorbed. Cool & add to a jar.

Nutrition:
- Per Serving : Protein 0 g | Fiber 1 g | Carbs 5 g | Fat 4 g

Cod En Papillote

Servings:4
Cooking Time: 25 Minutes
Ingredients:

- 2 Yukon Gold potatoes, very thinly sliced
- 1 cup chopped asparagus tips
- 1 red bell pepper, thinly sliced
- ¼ red onion, very thinly sliced
- 4 teaspoons butter
- Salt
- Freshly ground black pepper
- 4 (5-ounce) cod fillets, bones and skin removed
- 4 very thin lemon slices

Directions:
1. very thin lemon slices
2. Preheat the oven to 400°F. Cut 4 (12-inch) sheets of parchment paper and fold them each in half. Open them up and turn them so the fold is horizontal on the counter in front of you.
3. Place ¼ of the potatoes on the bottom half of each piece of parchment. Repeat this process with ¼ of the asparagus, bell pepper, red onion, and butter. Season each portion with salt and pepper.
4. Place 1 cod fillet on top of each pile of vegetables and sprinkle with more salt and pepper. Place 1 slice of lemon on each piece of fish.
5. To seal the packages, fold the top half of the parchment paper over the vegetables and fish. Starting at one corner, fold the edges over, pinching as you go, until the packet is closed. Repeat with the remaining pouches.
6. Bake for 20 to 25 minutes, until the fish is cooked through and the vegetables are tender. Serve hot in the packet, carefully opening the paper to avoid the escaping steam.

Nutrition:
- Per Serving : Protein 35 g | Fiber 4 g | Carbs 20 g | Fat 5 g

Beef Kabobs

Servings: 5
Cooking Time: 12 Mins.
Ingredients:

- 2 tbsp. extra-virgin olive oil
- 2 tbsp. fresh lemon juice
- 1 tbsp. fresh thyme, chopped
- 1 tbsp. fresh oregano, chopped
- 1 tsp. lemon zest, grated
- Salt and ground black pepper, as required
- 1½ lb. beef tenderloin, trimmed and cut into 1-inch cubes

Directions:
1. In a large bowl, add all the ingredients except for beef cubes and mix until well combined.
2. Add the pork cubes and coat with the mixture generously.
3. Cover the bowl and refrigerate to marinate overnight.
4. Preheat the outdoor grill to medium-high heat. Grease the grill grate.
5. Thread the beef cubes onto the pre-soaked bamboo skewers
6. Place the skewers onto the grill and cook for about 10-12 minutes, flipping after every 2-3 minutes.
7. Serve immediately.

Nutrition:

- Per Serving : Protein 33 g | Fiber 0.2 g | Carbs 1 g | Fat 5.2 g

Chicken & Apple Lettuce Wraps

Servings: 2
Cooking Time: 15 Mins.
Ingredients:

- 6 oz. cooked chicken breast, cut into strips
- ½ C. apple, peeled, cored and sliced thinly
- 1 seedless cucumber, sliced thinly
- 1 tbsp. fresh mint leaves, minced
- 4 large lettuce leaves

Directions:
1. In a large bowl, add all ingredients except lettuce leaves and gently toss to coat well.
2. Place the lettuce leaves onto serving plates.
3. Place the chicken mixture over each lettuce leaf evenly and serve immediately.

Nutrition:
- Per Serving : Protein 26 g | Fiber 1.7 g | Carbs 8.8 g | Fat 2.9 g

Lychee Juice

Servings: 2
Cooking Time: 10 Mins.
Ingredients:

- 30 fresh lychees, peeled and pitted
- 1 C. filtered water
- 2 tbsp. simple syrup

Directions:
1. Add all ingredients into a juicer and extract the juice according to the manufacturer's method.
2. Through a cheesecloth-lined strainer, strain the juice and transfer into 2 glasses.
3. Serve immediately.

Nutrition:
- Per Serving : Protein 1.2 g | Fiber 1.9 g | Carbs 40.6 g | Fat 0.6 g

Balsamic Roasted Carrots

Servings:6
Cooking Time: 40 Minutes
Ingredients:

- 2 tablespoons maple syrup
- 2 tablespoons balsamic vinegar
- 1 tablespoon canola oil or grape seed oil
- ½ teaspoon garlic powder
- ¼ teaspoon ground ginger
- Pinch salt
- Pinch freshly ground black pepper
- 10 medium carrots peeled and cut in half lengthwise (or in quarters if they are large)

Directions:

1. medium carrots peeled and cut in half lengthwise (or in quarters if they are large)
2. Preheat the oven to 400°F. Line a baking sheet with parchment paper or aluminum foil.
3. In a small bowl, mix together the maple syrup, balsamic vinegar, oil, garlic powder, ginger, salt, and pepper.
4. Place the carrots on the prepared baking sheet and drizzle with half of the maple syrup mixture. Toss the carrots until they are coated in the glaze. Roast for 15 to 20 minutes, or until the carrots start to caramelize.
5. Flip the carrots, pour the remaining half of the glaze over the top, and roast for another 15 to 20 minutes, until the carrots are tender and cooked through.

Nutrition:
- Per Serving : Protein 1 g | Fiber 3 g | Carbs 15 g | Fat 3 g

Vanilla Soy Pudding

Servings: 4
Cooking Time: 5minutes
Ingredients:

- 1/4 cup of cold water
- ½ tsp. of vanilla
- 1 1/4 cup of vanilla soy milk
- 1/4 oz. of unflavored gelatin
- 1 cup of tofu

Directions:
1. Mix the gelatin with water & stir. Let it rest for 10 minutes.
2. Heat the milk adds to a blender with the rest of the ingredients.
3. Pulse until smooth. Pour in a container keep it in the fridge for 2 hours.
4. Serve.

Nutrition:
- Per Serving : Protein 9 g | Fiber 1.2 g | Carbs 5 g | Fat 5 g

Salmon Parcel

Servings: 6
Cooking Time: 20 Mins.
Ingredients:

- 6 (3-oz.) salmon fillets
- Salt and ground black pepper, as required
- 2 bell peppers, seeded and cubed
- 4 tomatoes, peeled, seeded and cubed
- ½ C. fresh parsley, chopped
- 2 tbsp. olive oil
- 2 tbsp. fresh lemon juice

Directions:
1. Preheat your oven to 400 °F.
2. Arrange 6 pieces of foil onto a smooth surface.
3. Place 1 salmon fillet onto each foil paper and sprinkle with salt and black pepper.

4. In a bowl, add the bell peppers and tomato and mix.
5. Place veggie mixture over each fillet evenly and top with parsley and capers.
6. Drizzle with oil and lemon juice.
7. Fold the foil around the salmon mixture to seal it.
8. Arrange the foil packets onto a large baking sheet in a single layer.
9. Bake for approximately 20 minutes.
10. Serve hot.

Nutrition:
- Per Serving : Protein 17.8 g | Fiber 1.8 g | Carbs 5.5 g | Fat 10.2 g

Lemony Scallops

Servings: 4
Cooking Time: 6 Mins.

Ingredients:
- 2 tbsp. olive oil
- 2 tbsp. fresh rosemary, chopped
- ½ teaspoon lemon zest, grated
- 1 lb. sea scallops
- 1 tbsp. fresh lemon juice
- Salt and ground black pepper, as required

Directions:
1. In a medium sauté pan, heat the oil over medium-high heat and sauté the rosemary and lemon zest for about 1 minute.
2. Add scallops and cook for about 2 minutes per side.
3. Stir in lemon juice, salt and black pepper and serve hot.

Nutrition:
- Per Serving : Protein 19.2 g | Fiber 0.7 g | Carbs 3.9 g | Fat 8.1 g

Shrimp Curry

Servings:4
Cooking Time: 35 Minutes

Ingredients:
- 1½ cups jasmine rice, rinsed
- 2¼ cups water
- ¼ teaspoon vegetable oil
- 1 pound large shrimp, peeled and deveined
- Salt
- Freshly ground black pepper
- 2 tablespoons butter or margarine
- 1 white or Spanish onion, diced
- 1 garlic clove, minced
- 1 (6-ounce) can tomato paste
- 1 tablespoon yellow curry paste
- ½ teaspoon ground ginger
- 1 tablespoon all-purpose flour
- 1 (13½-ounce) can unsweetened coconut milk
- 1 teaspoon lime juice
- 1 teaspoon honey

- ¼ cup chopped fresh cilantro (optional)

Directions:
1. ¼ cup chopped fresh cilantro (optional)
2. In a medium saucepan over high heat, mix the rice with 2¼ cups water and bring to a boil. Lower the heat to medium-low, cover, and cook for 10 minutes. Remove from the heat and let sit, covered, for an additional 10 minutes.
3. In a large sauté pan or skillet over medium heat, warm the oil until it just begins to shimmer. Add the shrimp and season with salt and pepper. Cook, stirring occasionally, until the shrimp are bright pink, 3 to 5 minutes. Remove the shrimp from the pan and set aside.
4. Add the butter and onion to the pan and cook until the onion is fragrant and translucent, 3 to 4 minutes. Add the garlic, tomato paste, curry paste, and ginger and stir to combine. Add the flour and cook, stirring, for 1 to 2 minutes.
5. Slowly whisk in the coconut milk until the sauce is smooth. Simmer until it begins to thicken, 5 to 7 minutes.
6. Add the lime juice and honey and stir. Return the shrimp to the pan and stir to combine. Taste and season with salt and pepper, if needed.
7. Serve warm over the steamed rice. Garnish with the cilantro, if using.

Nutrition:
- Per Serving : Protein 32 g | Fiber 3 g | Carbs 69 g | Fat 27 g

Chicken With Mushrooms

Servings: 6
Cooking Time: 18 Mins.

Ingredients:
- 2 tbsp. olive oil, divided
- 4 (4-oz.) boneless, skinless chicken breasts, cut into small pieces
- Salt and ground black pepper, as required
- 4 C. fresh mushrooms, sliced
- 1 C. homemade chicken broth

Directions:
1. In a large wok, heat 1 tbsp. of oil over medium-high heat and stir fry the chicken pieces, salt, and black pepper for about 4-5 minutes.
2. With a slotted spoon, transfer the chicken pieces onto a plate.
3. In the same wok, heat the remaining oil over medium heat and cook the mushrooms for about 6-7 minutes, stirring frequently.
4. Add the cooked chicken and broth and cook for about 4-5 minutes
5. Add in the salt and black pepper and serve hot.

Nutrition:
- Per Serving : Protein 24.8 g | Fiber 1.6 g | Carbs 0.5 g | Fat 10.4 g

Lemon Pepper Turkey

Servings: 4
Cooking Time: 20 Minutes
Ingredients:

- 1 tbsp. of lemon pepper seasoning
- 1 tsp. of kosher salt
- 2 minced cloves garlic
- 2 lemons
- ½ cup of all-purpose flour
- 2 tbsp. of butter
- 1 lb. turkey breasts, boneless & skinless halved
- 2 tbsp. olive oil
- ½ cup of Chicken broth

Directions:

1. Let the oven preheat to 400°F.
2. In a bowl, add one lemon's zest, flour, salt & lemon pepper.
3. Add turkey & coat well.
4. Bake turkey for 5 minutes with hot oil on one side.
5. Add the rest of the ingredients with one lemon (in slices). Bake it until done.
6. Serve.

Nutrition:

- Per Serving : Protein 14 g | Fiber 1.7 g | Carbs 12 g | Fat 6 g

Maple-mustard Chicken Leg

Servings: 4-6
Cooking Time: 45minutes
Ingredients:

- 8 oz. of small carrots, cut in half
- 2 tbsp. of oil
- 12 oz. of baby potatoes, cut in half
- Salt & pepper, to taste
- 2 tbsp. of Dijon mustard
- 1 tsp. of fresh thyme leaves
- 4 whole chicken legs
- 2 tbsp. of whole-grain mustard
- 1 tbsp. of maple syrup

Directions:

1. Let the oven preheat to 450°F.
2. Toss carrots & potatoes with 1 tbsp. of oil, salt & pepper.
3. Season the chicken with 1 tbsp. of oil, salt & pepper. Place on the baking dish skin side up with vegetables.
4. Add the rest of the ingredients with a pinch of red pepper flakes.
5. Brush the vegetables & chicken.
6. Roast for 35 minutes. Brush with chicken juices & broil for 2-3 minutes. Serve.

Nutrition:

- Per Serving : Protein 21 g | Fiber 2 g | Carbs 13 g | Fat 8.1 g

Avocado Frittata

Servings: 6
Cooking Time: 12 Mins.
Ingredients:

- 8 eggs, beaten well
- 8 tbsp. fat-free milk
- Salt and ground black pepper, as required
- 2 oz. low-fat feta cheese, crumbled
- ½ C. part-skim mozzarella cheese, grated
- 2 tsp. olive oil
- 1 large avocado, peeled, pitted and sliced lengthwise

Directions:

1. Preheat the broiler of oven.
2. Arrange the oven rack about 4-5-inch from the heating element.
3. In a bowl, add the eggs, milk, salt and black pepper and beat until well combined.
4. In a heavy oven-proof frying wok, heat the oil over medium-low heat.
5. Add the eggs and cook for about 2 minutes.
6. Add the mozzarella and cook for about 5 minutes.
7. Arrange the avocado slices over egg mixture and sprinkle with the feta cheese.
8. With a lid, cover the wok and cook for about 3 minutes.
9. Remove the lid and transfer the wok into the oven.
10. Broil for about 2 minutes.
11. Remove from oven and serve hot.

Nutrition:

- Per Serving : Protein 10.8 g | Fiber 2.4 g | Carbs 5.1 g | Fat 16.6 g

Mini Cheesecakes

Servings:12
Cooking Time: 25 Minutes
Ingredients:

- 1 cup graham cracker crumbs or Oreo cookie crumbs
- 3 tablespoons butter or margarine, at room temperature
- 2 (8-ounce) packages cream cheese, at room temperature
- ½ cup sugar
- 1 teaspoon vanilla extract
- ½ teaspoon lemon juice
- 2 large eggs

Directions:

1. large eggs
2. Preheat the oven to 350°F. Place muffin liners in a 12-cup muffin tin.
3. In a medium bowl, mix together the graham cracker crumbs and butter. Press the mixture equally into the lined muffin cups.
4. Bake for 5 minutes. Let cool on a wire rack.
5. Using a hand mixer, stand mixer, or whisk, mix together the cream cheese, sugar, vanilla, lemon juice, and eggs until

smooth. Divide the mixture equally among the 12 muffin cups.

6. Bake for 18 to 20 minutes, or until the cheesecakes are set.

7. Let cool on a wire rack. Peel off the muffin liners before serving.

8. Store these cheesecakes in an airtight container in the refrigerator for up to 5 days or freeze them for up to 3 months.

Nutrition:

- Per Serving : Protein 4 g | Fiber 1 g | Carbs 15 g | Fat 17 g

Avocado Eggs

Servings:4
Cooking Time: 20 Minutes
Ingredients:

- 2 ripe avocados, cut in half and pits removed
- 4 large eggs
- Salt
- Freshly ground black pepper
- 1 cup shredded Cheddar cheese
- 2 green onions, minced

Directions:

1. green onions, minced
2. Preheat the oven to 425°F.
3. Place the avocados cut-side up on a baking sheet.
4. Crack 1 egg into each avocado half.
5. Season with salt and pepper and top with the cheese and green onions.
6. Bake for 15 to 20 minutes, until the eggs are cooked to your preference. Serve warm.

Nutrition:

- Per Serving : Protein 14 g | Fiber 6 g | Carbs 9 g | Fat 27 g

Pasta & Veggies Soup

Servings: 4
Cooking Time: 50 Mins.
Ingredients:

- 5 C. homemade chicken broth
- 1 carrot, peeled and chopped
- 1 potato, peeled and chopped
- 6 oz. asparagus tips
- ½ C. tomato, peeled, seeded and chopped
- ½ C. cooked whole-wheat pasta

Directions:

1. In a medium soup pan, add broth, carrot and potato over medium-high heat and bring to a boil.
2. Now adjust the heat to ow and cook, covered for about 20 minutes.
3. Add asparagus tips and tomatoes and cook for about 10-15 minutes.

4. Stir in cooked pasta and cook for about 5 minutes.
5. Serve hot.

Nutrition:

- Per Serving : Protein 14 g | Fiber 2.1 g | Carbs 35.8 g | Fat 3 g

Potato Soup

Servings: 6
Cooking Time: 35 Mins.
Ingredients:

- 2 tbsp. olive oil
- 1 C. carrot, peeled and chopped
- 1 tsp. fresh rosemary, chopped
- Salt and ground black pepper, as required
- 4 C. homemade chicken broth
- 4 C. potatoes, peeled and cubed
- ¼ C. fat-free plain yogurt
- ½ C. low-fat cheddar cheese

Directions:

1. In a large Dutch oven, heat oil over medium heat and cook the carrots for about 6-8 minutes, stirring occasionally
2. Stir in the rosemary, salt and black pepper and cook for about 1 minute, stirring continuously.
3. Add the potatoes and broth and bring to a boil.
4. Cook partially covered for about 20 minutes.
5. Now adjust the heat to low and stir in the yogurt and cheese.
6. Remove from the heat and with a potato masher, mash half of the potatoes.
7. Serve immediately.

Nutrition:

- Per Serving : Protein 6.7 g | Fiber 2.7 g | Carbs 19 g | Fat 7.3 g

Spinach & Carrot Soup

Servings: 6
Cooking Time: 35 Mins.
Ingredients:

- 2 tbsp. olive oil
- 3 small carrots, chopped
- ¾ lb. fresh spinach, chopped
- 5 C. vegetable broth
- Salt and ground black pepper, as required

Directions:

1. Heat the oil in a large soup pan over medium heat and cook the carrot for about 8-10 minutes, stirring frequently.
2. Add the broth and spinach and bring to a boil.
3. Cook partially covered for about 20 minutes.
4. Stir in salt and black pepper and remove from the heat.
5. With an immersion blender, blend the soup until smooth.
6. Serve immediately.

Nutrition:

- Per Serving : Protein 8.1 g | Fiber 2.3 g | Carbs 7.1 g | Fat 7.5 g

Milky Crepes

Servings: 4
Cooking Time: 16 Mins.
Ingredients:
- 1 C. whole-wheat flour
- ¼ tsp. salt
- 2 eggs
- ½ C. fat-free milk
- ½ C. water
- 1 tbsp. olive oil

Directions:
1. In a bowl, mix together flour and salt.
2. Add eggs and mix until well combined.
3. Slowly add milk and water and beat until well combined.
4. In a non-stick sauté pan, heat oil over medium-high heat.
5. Add about ¼ C. of the mixture and spread in a thin layer.
6. Cook for about 2 minutes.
7. Carefully flip the side and cook for about 1-2 minutes.
8. Repeat with the remaining mixture.
9. Serve warm.

Nutrition:
- Per Serving : Protein 7 g | Fiber 0.8 g | Carbs 25.5 g | Fat 6 g

Beet Soup

Servings: 4
Cooking Time: 5 Mins.
Ingredients:
- 2¼ C. fat-free plain yogurt
- 4 tsp. fresh lemon juice
- 2¼ C. beets, trimmed, peeled and chopped
- 2 tbsp. fresh dill
- Salt, as required

Directions:
1. In a high-speed blender, add all ingredients and pulse until smooth.
2. Transfer the soup into a pan over medium heat and cook for about 3-5 minutes or until heated through.
3. Serve immediately.

Nutrition:
- Per Serving : Protein 6 g | Fiber 2 g | Carbs 15.9 g | Fat 0.4 g

Ground Turkey With Asparagus

Servings: 8
Cooking Time: 20 Mins.
Ingredients:
- 1 tbsp. olive oil
- 1¾ lb. lean ground turkey
- 4 C. asparagus tips

- ¼ C. water
- 2 tbsp. fresh parsley, chopped
- Salt and ground black pepper, as required

Directions:
1. In a large non-stick wok, heat oil over medium heat and cook the turkey and cook for about 8-10 minutes or until browned.
2. Add the asparagus and water and cook for about 5-6 minutes
3. Stir in parsley, salt and black pepper and cook for about 3-4 minutes, stirring continuously.
4. Serve hot.

Nutrition:
- Per Serving : Protein 22.5 g | Fiber 1.9 g | Carbs 4.1 g | Fat 8.9 g

Eggs With Spinach

Servings: 2
Cooking Time: 22 Mins.
Ingredients:
- Olive oil cooking spray
- 6 C. fresh baby spinach
- 2-3 tbsp. filtered water
- 4 eggs
- Ground black pepper, as required
- 2-3 tbsp. feta cheese, crumbled
- 2 tsp. fresh chives, minced

Directions:
1. Preheat your oven to 400 ºF. Lightly grease 2 small baking dishes with cooking spray.
2. In a large frying pan, add the spinach and water over medium heat and cook for about 3-4 minutes, stirring occasionally.
3. Remove from the heat and drain the excess water completely.
4. Divide the spinach into prepared baking dishes evenly.
5. Carefully crack 2 eggs in each baking dish over spinach.
6. Sprinkle with black pepper and top with feta cheese evenly.
7. Arrange the baking dishes onto a large cookie sheet.
8. Bake for approximately 15-18 minutes or until desired doneness of eggs.
9. Remove from oven and serve hot with the garnishing of chives.

Nutrition:
- Per Serving : Protein 15 g | Fiber 1.1 g | Carbs 4.4 g | Fat 11.2 g

Low Fiber Beet Carrot Soup

Servings: 4
Cooking Time: 0minutes
Ingredients:

- 4 cups of vegetable broth
- Salt, to taste
- 1 carrot, sliced
- 1 can of cooked beets (simple, not pickled)

Directions:

1. In a pan, add broth & carrots.
2. Boil & simmer until tender.
3. Add beets & cook for a few minutes. Pulse with a stick blender.
4. Adjust seasoning & serve.

Nutrition:

- Per Serving : Protein 2 g | Fiber 3.1 g | Carbs 22 g | Fat 1 g

Boost Detox Juice

Servings: 2
Cooking Time: 20minutes
Ingredients:

- 1 orange
- 1 green apple peeled & cored
- 1/4 tsp. of chopped ginger
- 3 kale leaves
- 1 carrot, chopped
- 1 cup of baby spinach
- ½ peeled lemon
- 2 cups of water

Directions:

1. Add all ingredients to a blender. Pulse until smooth.
2. Strain well & serve.

Nutrition:

- Per Serving : Protein 3 g | Fiber 4 g | Carbs 17 g | Fat 0.2 g

Creamy Tuscan Chicken Pasta

Servings: 4
Cooking Time: 20 Minutes
Ingredients:

- 1.5 lb. of diced chicken breast, boneless & skinless
- 2 tbsp. of olive oil
- 10 oz. of short pasta
- 3-4 garlic cloves, minced
- 1 tsp. of Italian seasoning
- 2 tbsp. of flour
- Salt and pepper to taste
- ½ cup of Parmesan cheese
- 8 oz. sun-dried (in oil) tomatoes, chopped
- 3 cups of almond milk
- 3 cups of baby spinach

Directions:

1. Cook pasta as per package Directions.
2. Mix the chicken with salt, pepper, oil, garlic & Italian seasoning.
3. Cook chicken in a drizzle of hot oil for 2 to 3 minutes.
4. Add the tomatoes & cook for 5 to 7 minutes.
5. Whisk flour & milk. Add to the pan cook for 3-4 minutes.
6. Add spinach, then add pasta with cheese, stir & serve.

Nutrition:

- Per Serving : Protein 27 g | Fiber 4 g | Carbs 36 g | Fat 13 g

Chicken Kabobs

Servings: 4
Cooking Time: 7 Mins.
Ingredients:

- ¼ C. low-fat Parmesan cheese, grated
- 3 tbsp. olive oil
- 1 C. fresh basil leaves, chopped
- Salt and ground black pepper, as required
- 1¼ lb. boneless, skinless chicken breast, cut into 1-inch cubes

Directions:

1. In a food processor, add the cheese, oil, garlic, basil, salt, and black pepper, and pulse until smooth.
2. Transfer the basil mixture into a large bowl.
3. Add the chicken cubes and mix well.
4. Cover the bowl and refrigerate to marinate for at least 4-5 hours.
5. Preheat the grill to medium-high heat. Generously, grease the grill grate.
6. Thread the chicken cubes onto pre-soaked wooden skewers.
7. Place the skewers onto the grill and cook for about 3-4 minutes.
8. Flip and cook for about 2-3 minutes more.
9. Remove from the grill and place onto a platter for about 5 minutes before serving.
10. Serve hot.

Nutrition:

- Per Serving : Protein 31.5 g | Fiber 0.3 g | Carbs 0.1 g | Fat 15.3 g

Lychee & Dill Juice

Servings: 2
Cooking Time: 0minutes
Ingredients:

- 4 to 5 ice cubes
- 1 lime's juice
- 8.8 oz. of lychees, peeled & deseeded
- 1-2 sprigs of dill

Directions:

1. In a blender, add all ingredients with some water.

2. Strain & serve.
Nutrition:
*   Per Serving : Protein 1 g | Fiber 2 g | Carbs 11 g | Fat 1.2 g

Tuna Muffins

Servings: 6
Cooking Time: 30 Mins.
Ingredients:
*   1 (7-oz.) can water-packed tuna, drained
*   3 oz. low-fat cheddar cheese, shredded
*   ½ C. low-fat mayonnaise
*   2 large eggs
*   ¼ C. spinach, chopped finely
*   1 tbsp. fresh parsley, chopped
*   Salt and ground black pepper, as required

Directions:
1. Preheat your oven to 350 ºF. Grease 6 cups of a muffin tin.
2. In a bowl, add all the ingredients and mix until well combined.
3. Place the muffin mixture into the prepared muffin C. evenly.
4. Bake for approximately 25-30 minutes or until top becomes golden-brown.
5. Remove the muffin tin from oven and place onto a wire rack to cool for about 10 minutes.
6. Invert the muffins onto a platter and serve warm.

Nutrition:
*   Per Serving : Protein 15.2 g | Fiber 0.1 g | Carbs 3.4 g | Fat 1.9 g

Turkey Quesadillas

Servings: 4
Cooking Time: 20minutes
Ingredients:
*   ½ onion, sliced
*   Salt & pepper, to taste
*   1 lb. of turkey breasts, boneless & skinless strips
*   2 cups of shredded cheddar
*   2 bell peppers, sliced
*   1 tbsp. of vegetable oil
*   1 tbsp. of olive oil
*   ½ tsp. of dried oregano
*   1 avocado, sliced
*   ½ tsp. of ground cumin
*   4 flour tortillas
*   2 cups of Monterey jack, shredded

Directions:
1. Sauté onion & peppers with salt & pepper for 5 minutes. Take it out on a plate.
2. Season the turkey with salt, and pepper. Cook for 8 minutes & take it out on a plate.

3. Warm the tortilla & top with cheese, onion, peppers & turkey with avocado slices & scallions.
4. Fold & heat the tortillas for 3 minutes on each side.
Nutrition:
*   Per Serving : Protein 7.9 g | Fiber 1 g | Carbs 13 g | Fat 7 g

Avocado Smash Chips

Servings: 5
Cooking Time: 30minutes
Ingredients:
*   1 slice of honey soy tofu, cubed
*   3.5 oz. of cream cheese
*   2 peeled sweet potatoes
*   Salt & pepper, to taste
*   1/4 cup of coriander, chopped
*   1 tsp. of sumac
*   1 avocado
*   1/4 cup of lime juice

Directions:
1. Let the oven preheat to 400°F.
2. Oil spray 2 baking sheets.
3. Cut the sweet potatoes into thin slices. Place on the prepared tray.
4. Spray the slices & bake for 20 minutes.
5. Flip & bake for 10 minutes after oil spraying them.
6. In a bowl, smash the avocado with salt, coriander, lime juice, sumac & pepper.
7. Serve the potato chips with avocado mix & cube of tofu on top.
Nutrition:
*   Per Serving : Protein 3 g | Fiber 2 g | Carbs 14 g | Fat 3 g

Furikake Salmon

Servings: 2
Cooking Time: 15minutes
Ingredients:
*   3 tbsp. of Mirin
*   Salt, pepper, to taste
*   2 tbsp. of sesame oil
*   4 oz. of shiitake mushrooms, sliced without stems
*   2 tbsp. of olive oil
*   3 tbsp. of soy sauce
*   1 shallot, sliced
*   2 cups of shredded cabbage
*   8 to 10 oz. of salmon fillets

Directions:
1. In a bowl, mix mirin, sesame oil & soy sauce.
2. Sauté shallot & cabbage with salt & pepper until it wilts. Toss with a drizzle of soy sauce mixture.
3. In a pan, add one tbsp. of oil. Add salt & pepper.
4. Add mushrooms & salmon, cook on both sides. Add the soy sauce mixture.

5. Serve the salmon with rice, cabbage & the rest of the ingredients.

Nutrition:
- Per Serving : Protein 34 g | Fiber 3 g | Carbs 45 g | Fat 25 g

Pumpkin Waffles

Servings: 2
Cooking Time: 8 Mins.

Ingredients:
- 1 egg, beaten
- ½ C. part-skim mozzarella cheese, shredded
- 1 tbsp. canned solid pumpkin
- ¼ tsp. ground cinnamon

Directions:
1. Preheat a mini waffle iron and then grease it.
2. In a medium bowl, put all ingredients and with a fork, mix until well combined.
3. Place half of the mixture into preheated waffle iron and cook for about 3-4 minutes.
4. Repeat with the remaining mixture.
5. Serve warm.

Nutrition:
- Per Serving : Protein 4.9 g | Fiber 0.4 g | Carbs 1.4 g | Fat 3.5 g

Parmesan Asparagus

Servings: 4
Cooking Time: 10 Mins.

Ingredients:
- 2 tbsp. olive oil
- 1 lb. asparagus tips
- Salt and ground black pepper, as required
- ½ C. low-fat Parmesan cheese, grated freshly

Directions:
1. In a large wok, heat oil and butter over medium heat and cook asparagus for about 10 minutes.
2. Stir in Parmesan, salt and black pepper and serve immediately.

Nutrition:
- Per Serving : Protein 5.2 g | Fiber 1.8 g | Carbs 3.8 g | Fat 9.5 g

Spinach, Cucumber & Parsley Juice

Servings: 2
Cooking Time: 10 Mins.

Ingredients:
- 4 C. baby spinach
- 2 large seedless cucumbers, roughly chopped
- ½ C. fresh parsley
- 1 (1-inch) piece fresh ginger, peeled

Directions:
1. Add all ingredients into a juicer and extract the juice according to the manufacturer's method.

2. Through a cheesecloth-lined strainer, strain the juice and transfer into 2 glasses.
3. Serve immediately.

Nutrition:
- Per Serving : Protein 6.5 g | Fiber 4.1 g | Carbs 26.5 g | Fat 0.5 g

Spinach Waffles

Servings: 4
Cooking Time: 20 Mins.

Ingredients:
- 1 large egg, beaten
- 1 C. part-skim ricotta cheese, crumble
- ½ C. part-skim Mozzarella cheese, shredded
- ¼ C. low-fat Parmesan cheese, grated
- 4 oz. frozen spinach, thawed and squeezed dry
- Salt and ground black pepper, as required

Directions:
1. Preheat a mini waffle iron and then grease it.
2. Add cheeses, spinach, salt and black pepper in a medium mixing bowl and mix until well blended.
3. Place ¼ of the mixture into preheated waffle iron and cook for about 4-5 minutes or until golden brown.
4. Repeat with the remaining mixture.
5. Serve warm.

Nutrition:
- Per Serving : Protein 11.7 g | Fiber 0.6 g | Carbs 4.8 g | Fat 7.1 g

Cucumber Salad

Servings: 4
Cooking Time: 10 Mins.

Ingredients:
- 4 medium seedless cucumbers, peeled, seeded and chopped
- ½ C. low-fat Greek yogurt
- 1½ tbsp. fresh dill, chopped
- 1 tbsp. fresh lemon juice
- Salt and ground black pepper, as required

Directions:
1. In a large bowl, add all the ingredients and mix well.
2. Serve immediately.

Nutrition:
- Per Serving : Protein 4 g | Fiber 1.7 g | Carbs 13.8 g | Fat 0.8 g

Chicken & Potato Curry

Servings: 6
Cooking Time: 35 Mins.
Ingredients:

- 2 tbsp. olive oil
- 4 (4-oz.) boneless, skinless chicken breasts, cubed
- Salt and ground black pepper, as required
- 2 tomatoes, peeled, seeded and chopped
- 1 lb. potato, peeled and cubed
- 2 C. homemade chicken broth

Directions:
1. In a large sauté pan, heat oil over medium-high heat and stir fry the chicken pieces, salt, and black pepper for about 4 minutes.
2. With a slotted spoon, transfer the chicken onto a plate.
3. In the same pan, add the tomatoes and cook for about 2-3 minutes.
4. Add the potatoes and cook for about 2-3 minutes.
5. Add broth and cooked chicken and bring to a boil.
6. Now adjust the heat to medium-low and cook for about 15-20 minutes.
7. Add in the salt and black pepper and serve hot.

Nutrition:

- Per Serving : Protein 25.4 g | Fiber 2.1 g | Carbs 15.1 g | Fat 10.9 g

Citrus Salad

Servings: 6
Cooking Time: 10 Mins.
Ingredients:

- 8 clementines, peeled and sliced in rounds
- 1 orange, peeled and sliced in rounds
- 2 grapefruit, peeled and sliced in rounds
- 2 tsp. lime zest
- 3 tbsp. fresh lime juice
- 1 tbsp. honey

Directions:
1. In a salad bowl, add all d ingredients and gently toss to coat.
2. Serve immediately.

Nutrition:

- Per Serving : Protein 1.5 g | Fiber 2.9 g | Carbs 23.4 g | Fat 0.3 g

Tandoori Chicken Skewers

Servings: 6
Cooking Time: 15minutes
Ingredients:

- 1 cup of yogurt
- 2 tsp. of ground coriander
- 1 lemon's juice
- 18 chicken tenderloins, cut into smaller pieces
- 1 small onion, diced

- 6 cloves garlic, chopped
- 1 piece of (3") ginger, chopped
- 2 tsp. of ground cumin
- 1 tsp. of ground turmeric
- 1 tbsp. of garam masala
- 1 tsp. of kosher salt

Directions:
1. In a bowl, add all ingredients except for chicken. Mix & add chicken, keep in the fridge for 2 hours.
2. Thread the chicken onto soaked skewers and rest for half an hour at room temperature.
3. Preheat the grill & oil spray the grates. Grill the skewers for 4-5 minutes on 1 side. Serve.

Nutrition:

- Per Serving : Protein 23 g | Fiber 1 g | Carbs 8 g | Fat 8 g

Citrus Swordfish

Servings: 2
Cooking Time: 0minutes
Ingredients:

- 1 tbsp. of fresh thyme, chopped
- 2 tbsp. of mix Lemon, lime & orange lime zest
- 2 swordfish steaks (6 oz. each)
- 1 tbsp. of fresh parsley, chopped
- 1 tbsp. of olive oil

Directions:
1. Heat the broiler.
2. Mix the oil with herbs. Rub on the fish.
3. Broil for 3-4 minutes, flip & broil until done.
4. Serve with zest mixture on top.

Nutrition:

- Per Serving : Protein 34 g | Fiber 1 g | Carbs 3 g | Fat 9 g

Chicken Waffles

Servings: 4
Cooking Time: 20 Mins.
Ingredients:

- 1/3 C. unsweetened almond milk
- 4 medium eggs
- ¼ C. cooked chicken, chopped finely
- 4 tbsp. bell peppers, seeded and chopped
- 2 tbsp. part-skim mozzarella cheese, shredded

Directions:
1. Preheat the waffle iron and then grease it.
2. In a medium bowl, add almond milk and eggs and beat well.
3. Add remaining ingredients and stir to combine well.
4. Place the desired amount of the mixture into preheated waffle iron.
5. Cook for about 5 minutes or desired doneness.
6. Repeat with the remaining mixture.
7. Serve warm.

Nutrition:

- Per Serving : Protein 9.3 g | Fiber 0.2 g | Carbs 1.1 g | Fat 5.7 g

One-pot Chicken And Orzo

Servings:6
Cooking Time: 20 Minutes
Ingredients:
- 1 tablespoon canola oil
- 1 cup diced chicken breast
- 1½ cups orzo pasta
- 4 cups Homemade Chicken Stock or store-bought chicken stock
- ½ cup chopped fresh or frozen and thawed asparagus tips
- ½ teaspoon garlic powder
- 1 teaspoon onion powder
- 1½ cups frozen mixed peas and carrots
- Salt
- Freshly ground black pepper
- ½ cup grated Parmesan cheese

Directions:
1. ½ cup grated Parmesan cheese
2. In a large sauté pan or skillet over medium heat, warm the oil until it just begins to shimmer. Add the chicken and cook, stirring occasionally, until it's browned but not yet cooked through, about 5 minutes. Add the orzo and cook until the pasta has slightly softened, about 1 minute.
3. Raise the heat to medium-high, add the chicken stock, asparagus tips, garlic powder, and onion powder, and bring to a boil. Lower the heat to medium-low and simmer until the asparagus is tender and the chicken is cooked through, 8 to 10 minutes.
4. Stir in the frozen peas and carrots and cook until heated through, about 2 minutes.
5. Taste and season with salt and pepper. Sprinkle with the Parmesan cheese. Serve hot.

Nutrition:
- Per Serving : Protein 19 g | Fiber 3 g | Carbs 38 g | Fat 8 g

Yogurt & Cheese Bowl

Servings: 2
Cooking Time: 10 Mins.
Ingredients:
- ½ C. fat-free plain yogurt
- ½ C. low-fat cottage cheese
- 2 tsp. extra-virgin olive oil
- 1 small apple, peeled, cored and sliced

Directions:
1. In a large bowl, add the yogurt, cheese, oil and cinnamon and mix until well combined.
2. Divide the yogurt mixture in 2 serving bowls.
3. Top with apple slices and serve immediately.

Nutrition:
- Per Serving : Protein 13.6 g | Fiber 0.9 g | Carbs 13.3 g | Fat 5.9 g

Egg & Cheese Bowl

Servings: 3
Cooking Time: 10 Mins.
Ingredients:
- 5 hard-boiled eggs, peeled and sliced
- 1/3 C. low-fat cottage cheese
- Salt and ground black pepper, as required
- 1 large tomato, peeled, seeded and chopped

Directions:
1. In a bowl, add cheese, salt and black pepper and whisk until smooth
2. Add egg slices and stir to combine.
3. Top with tomato pieces and serve.

Nutrition:
- Per Serving : Protein 12.9 g | Fiber 0.2 g | Carbs 2 g | Fat 7.8 g

Beet Salad

Servings: 4
Cooking Time: 1 Hour
Ingredients:
- For Salad:
- 4 medium beets, scrubbed
- 4 C. fresh baby spinach
- 4 oz. feta cheese, crumbled
- For Dressing:
- 2 tbsp. extra-virgin olive oil
- 1 tbsp. balsamic vinegar
- 1 tbsp. maple syrup
- Salt and ground black pepper, as required

Directions:
1. Preheat your oven to 400 ºF.
2. Wrap each beet in a piece of foil.
3. Arrange wrapped beets onto a baking sheet and roast for approximately 1 hour.
4. Remove from oven and unwrap the beets.
5. Set aside to cool completely.
6. Then peel the beets and cut into pieces.
7. Meanwhile, for dressing: in a bowl, add all ingredients and beat until well combined.
8. In a salad bowl, add beets, spinach and dressing and toss to coat well.
9. Top with feta and serve.

Nutrition:
- Per Serving : Protein 3.2 g | Fiber 1.3 g | Carbs 7.7 g | Fat 10.2 g

Celery & Carrot Juice

Servings: 2
Cooking Time: 10 Mins.
Ingredients:
- 4 celery stalks, roughly chopped
- 4 carrots, peeled and chopped roughly
- 1 tbsp. fresh lemon juice
- 1 C. filtered water

Directions:
1. Add all ingredients in a high-power blender and pulse until well combined.
2. Through a cheesecloth-lined sieve, strain the juice and pour into two glasses.
3. Serve immediately.

Nutrition:
- Per Serving : Protein 1.2 g | Fiber 3 g | Carbs 13 g | Fat 0.1 g

Spinach Omelet

Servings: 2
Cooking Time: 6½ Mins.
Ingredients:
- 4 large eggs
- 1/3 C. cooked spinach, squeezed
- 2 tbsp. fresh parsley, chopped
- ½ C. low-fat feta cheese, crumbled
- Ground black pepper, as required
- 2 tsp. olive oil

Directions:
1. Preheat the broiler of oven.
2. Arrange a rack about 4-inch from the heating element.
3. Carefully crack the eggs in a medium bowl and with a wire whisk, beat well.
4. Add remaining ingredients except for oil and stir to combine
5. In an ovenproof wok, melt butter over medium heat.
6. Add egg mixture and tilt the wok to spread the mixture evenly.
7. Immediately adjust the heat to medium-low and cook for about 3-4 minutes or until golden-brown.
8. Now transfer the wok under broiler and broil for about 1½-2½ minutes.
9. Cut the omelette into desired-sized wedges and serve.

Nutrition:
- Per Serving : Protein 18.5 g | Fiber 0.6 g | Carbs 3.8 g | Fat 2.2 g

Zucchini Soup

Servings: 8
Cooking Time: 30 Mins.
Ingredients:
- 3 carrots, peeled and chopped
- 4 small zucchinis, peeled, seeded and chopped

- 2 tomatoes, peeled, seeded and chopped
- Salt and ground black pepper, as required
- 8 C. vegetable broth

Directions:
1. In a large soup pan, add all ingredients over high heat and bring to a boil.
2. Reduce the heat to low and simmer, partially covered for about 20 minutes.
3. Remove from the heat and set aside to cool slightly.
4. In a blender add the soup in batches and pulse until smooth.
5. Return the pureed mixture into the pan over medium heat and simmer for about 3-5 minutes.
6. Serve hot.

Nutrition:
- Per Serving : Protein 6 g | Fiber 7.1 g | Carbs 6.3 g | Fat 1.5 g

Scallops With Zucchini

Servings: 3
Cooking Time: 10 Mins.
Ingredients:
- 2 tbsp. olive oil
- 2 C. zucchini, peeled, seeded and chopped
- ¾ lb. scallops
- 1 tsp. fresh lemon juice
- Salt, as required

Directions:
1. In a large sauté pan, heat oil over medium heat and cook the zucchini for about 3-5 minutes, stirring occasionally.
2. Add in the scallops and cook for about 3-4 minutes, flipping occasionally.
3. Stir in the lemon juice and remove from the heat.
4. Serve hot.

Nutrition:
- Per Serving : Protein 20 g | Fiber 0.8 g | Carbs 5.2 g | Fat 10.3 g

Chicken & Spinach Stew

Servings: 8
Cooking Time: 30 Mins.
Ingredients:
- 2 tbsp. olive oil
- 6 (4-oz.) boneless, skinless chicken thighs, trimmed and cut into 1-inch pieces
- 4 tomatoes, peeled, seeded and chopped
- 2 C. homemade chicken broth
- Salt and ground black pepper, as required
- 4 C. fresh spinach, chopped

Directions:
1. Heat oil in a large heavy-bottomed pan over medium heat and cook the chicken for about 4-5 minutes.

2. Add the tomatoes, broth, salt, and black pepper, and bring to gentle simmer.

3. Now adjust the heat to low and simmer, covered for about 10-15 minutes.

4. Stir in the spinach and cook for about 4-5 minutes.

5. Serve hot.

Nutrition:

- Per Serving : Protein 26.8 g | Fiber 1.1 g | Carbs 3.2 g | Fat 10.3 g

Taco Soup

Servings: 8
Cooking Time: 45minutes
Ingredients:

- 1 packet of ranch dressing
- 1 small onion
- 3 cups of water
- 1 pound of lean ground beef
- 1 bag of frozen corn
- 15 oz. canned tomato sauce
- 1 packet of taco seasoning

Directions:

1. Sauté meat until no longer pink.

2. Push to a side & sauté onion until translucent. Drain the fat.

3. Add the rest of the ingredients. Simmer on low flame for half an hour.

4. Serve.

Nutrition:

- Per Serving : Protein 6.5 g | Fiber 1.9 g | Carbs 18.7 g | Fat 7.5 g

Feta Stuffed Chicken Breasts

Servings: 4
Cooking Time: 17 Mins.
Ingredients:

- 4 (5-oz.) skinless, boneless chicken breasts, pounded into 1/8-inch thickness
- 4 tbsp. olive oil, divided
- Salt and ground black pepper, as required
- 4 oz. low-fat feta cheese, crumbled
- 2 tbsp. fresh oregano, minced
- ½ tsp. lemon zest, grated

Directions:

1. Preheat your oven to 450 ºF.

2. Brush the chicken breasts with 2 tbsp. of oil and then season with salt and black pepper.

3. Arrange the chicken breasts onto a smooth surface.

4. Top each chicken breast with feta, followed by oregano and lemon zest, leaving edges.

5. Roll each breast like a jelly roll to seal the filling securely.

6. With 1 kitchen twine, tie each roll at 1-inch intervals.

7. Heat remaining oil over medium heat and cook the chicken rolls for about 10 minutes or until browned on all sides.

8. Remove the wok of chicken rolls from heat.

9. Arrange the rolls into a baking dish in a single layer.

10. Bake for approximately 5-7 minutes.

11. Serve hot.

Nutrition:

- Per Serving : Protein 35.9 g | Fiber 1.2 g | Carbs 2.7 g | Fat 21.3 g

Tomato Tuna Salad With Eggs

Servings: 3-5
Cooking Time: 0 Minutes
Ingredients:

- 5 tsp. of vinegar
- 1 tbsp. of fresh basil, sliced
- 1 tbsp. of sun-dried tomatoes with 1 tbsp. of oil
- 3 hard-boiled eggs
- 1/8 tsp. of salt
- 5 oz. of tuna, drained

Directions:

1. Cut the eggs in half lengthwise.

2. Take the egg yolk in a bowl with the rest of the ingredients.

3. Mix well & spoon onto the egg whites' halves.

4. Serve.

Nutrition:

- Per Serving : Protein 1 g | Fiber 1 g | Carbs 11 g | Fat 3 g

Apple-cinnamon Muffins

Servings:12
Cooking Time: 25 Minutes
Ingredients:

- 2 cups all-purpose flour
- ½ cup sugar
- 2 teaspoons ground cinnamon
- 1 teaspoon baking powder
- ½ teaspoon baking soda
- ¾ cup unsweetened applesauce
- 2 apples, Honey Crisp, Fuji, Granny Smith, or Gala, peeled and grated
- 1 teaspoon vanilla extract
- 1 large egg
- 4 tablespoons (½ stick) butter or margarine, at room temperature

Directions:

1. tablespoons (½ stick) butter or margarine, at room temperature

2. Preheat the oven to 350°F. Line a 12-cup muffin tin with muffin liners and set aside.

3. In a large mixing bowl, mix together the flour, sugar, cinnamon, baking powder, and baking soda.

4. Make a well in the middle of the flour mixture, add the applesauce, grated apples, vanilla, egg, and butter to the well, and gently whisk to combine. Be careful not to overmix, or the muffins will be tough.

5. Spoon the batter equally into the lined muffin cups. Bake for 20 to 25 minutes, or until a toothpick inserted into the center of a muffin comes out clean. Serve warm or at room temperature.

6. Store the muffins in an airtight container at room temperature for up to 5 days.

Nutrition:
- Per Serving : Protein 3 g | Fiber 1 g | Carbs 25 g | Fat 4 g

Mini Pineapple Upside-down Cakes

Servings:12
Cooking Time: 30 Minutes
Ingredients:
- 12 tablespoons (1½ sticks) butter, at room temperature, divided
- 2 tablespoons sugar, plus ½ cup
- 12 pineapple rings, fresh or canned
- 1½ cups all-purpose flour
- 1 teaspoon baking powder
- Pinch salt
- 1 large egg
- ¼ cup milk of choice
- ¼ cup sour cream or plain Greek yogurt
- 1 teaspoon vanilla extract

Directions:
1. teaspoon vanilla extract
2. Preheat the oven to 350°F. Spray a 12-cup muffin tin with cooking spray.
3. Place 1 teaspoon of butter in each muffin cup. Sprinkle ½ teaspoon of sugar into each muffin cup.
4. Trim the pineapple rings to fit the bottom of the muffin cups and place in the bottom of each one, reserving the trimmed pieces.
5. In a large bowl, mix together the flour, baking powder, and salt and set aside.
6. In a stand mixer with the paddle attachment, beat the remaining 8 tablespoons of butter and the remaining ½ cup of sugar until light and creamy. Add the egg, milk, sour cream, and vanilla and beat until smooth.
7. Add the flour mixture, ¼ cup at a time, and beat until smooth.
8. Chop the remaining pineapple into small pieces and gently fold them into the batter.
9. Spoon the batter equally into the 12 muffin cups.
10. Bake for 25 to 30 minutes, or until a toothpick inserted into one of the cakes comes out clean. Let the cakes cool in the pan for 5 minutes.
11. Place a large cutting board over the muffin tin and carefully flip them both over to release the cakes from the pan. Let cool and serve.

Nutrition:
- Per Serving : Protein 3 g | Fiber 2 g | Carbs 29 g | Fat 13 g

Mushroom Curry

Servings: 6
Cooking Time: 20 Mins.
Ingredients:
- 2 C. tomatoes, peeled, seeded and chopped
- 1½ C. water
- 2 tbsp. olive oil
- 1 tsp. fresh ginger, chopped
- ¼ tsp. ground turmeric
- 2 C. fresh shiitake mushrooms, sliced
- 5 C. fresh button mushrooms, sliced
- ¼ C. fat-free plain yogurt, whipped
- Salt and ground black pepper, as required

Directions:
1. In a food processor, add the tomatoes and ¼ C. of water and pulse until smooth paste forms.
2. In a pan, heat the oil over medium heat and sauté the ginger and turmeric for about 1 minute.
3. Add the tomato paste and cook for about 5 minutes.
4. Stir in the mushrooms, yogurt and remaining water and bring to a boil.
5. Cook for about 10-12 minutes, stirring occasionally.
6. Season with salt and black pepper and serve hot.

Nutrition:
- Per Serving : Protein 3 g | Fiber 1.4 g | Carbs 5.3 g | Fat 5 g

Braised Asparagus

Servings: 2
Cooking Time: 8 Mins.
Ingredients:
- ½ C. homemade chicken broth
- 1 tbsp. olive oil
- 1 (½-inch) piece lemon peel
- 1 C. asparagus tips

Directions:
1. In a small pan add the broth, oil and lemon peel over medium heat and bring to a boil.
2. Add the asparagus and cook, covered for about 3-4 minutes.
3. Discard the lemon peel and serve.

Nutrition:
- Per Serving : Protein 3.7 g | Fiber 1.4 g | Carbs 2.6 g | Fat 7.1 g

Fiesta Chicken Tacos

Servings: 8
Cooking Time: 20minutes
Ingredients:
- 1 tbsp. of olive oil
- ¼ tsp. of salt
- ½ tsp. of ground cumin
- 1 pound of chicken breast, skinless & boneless, cut into thin strips
- 1 cup of each sliced red bell pepper & red onion
- 8 corn tortillas (six inches)
- 1 cup of mixed salad greens

Directions:
1. Season chicken with cumin. Sauté in hot oil for 3 minutes.
2. Take it out on a plate.
3. Sauté the onion & bell pepper in 1 tsp. of oil for 3 minutes.
4. Add chicken back in the pan add salt.
5. Warm the tortillas & add chicken mixture (1/3 cup) with 2 tbsp. of mixed greens.
6. Roll & serve.

Nutrition:
- Per Serving : Protein 30.3 g | Fiber 3.8 g | Carbs 36.1 g | Fat 6.4 g

Lemony Trout

Servings: 8
Cooking Time: 25 Mins.
Ingredients:
- 2 (1½-lb.) trout, gutted and cleaned
- Salt and ground black pepper, as required
- 1 lemon, sliced
- 2 tbsp. fresh dill, minced
- 2 tbsp. olive oil
- 2 tbsp. fresh lemon juice

Directions:
1. Preheat your oven to 475 ºF. Arrange a wire rack onto a foil-lined baking sheet.
2. Sprinkle the trout with salt and black pepper from inside and outside generously.\Fill the cavity of each fish with lemon slices and dill.
3. Place the trout onto prepared baking sheet and drizzle with the melted butter and lemon juice.
4. Bake for approximately 25 minutes.
5. Remove the baking sheet from oven and transfer the trout onto a serving platter.
6. Serve hot.

Nutrition:
- Per Serving : Protein 36.7 g | Fiber 0.2 g | Carbs 0.7 g | Fat 16.9 g

Aloo Masala

Servings: 2
Cooking Time: 20minutes
Ingredients:
- 17.6 oz. peeled potato, cut into chunks
- 1/4 cup of smooth cashew butter
- 2 tbsp. of raisins
- 1 tsp. of powdered garlic
- 4 peeled carrots, cut into chunks
- 2 tsp. of garam masala
- ½ cup of coriander leaves
- 1 tsp. of ground cumin
- 3.5 oz. of baby spinach
- 1 tbsp. of brown sugar
- 1 cup of vegetable stock
- Salt and black pepper, to taste
- 1 lemon, sliced into wedges

Directions:
1. Sauté garlic & onion in hot oil for 1 minute.
2. Add cumin, vegetables, salt, pepper & garam masala, cook for 2 to 3 minutes.
3. Add raisins, stock & sugar; cook for 10-12 minutes.
4. Add spinach, coriander & nut butter. Cook for 2-3 minutes.
5. Serve with lemon wedges.

Nutrition:
- Per Serving : Protein 0.1 g | Fiber 3 g | Carbs 189 g | Fat 12 g

Spinach In Yogurt Sauce

Servings: 4
Cooking Time: 8 Mins.
Ingredients:
- 2 tbsp. olive oil
- 2 (10-oz.) packages frozen spinach, thawed and squeezed dry
- ½ C. fat-free plain yogurt
- Salt and ground black pepper, as required
- 1 tsp. fresh lemon juice

Directions:
1. In a wok, heat oil over medium heat and cook the spinach for about 1-2 minutes.
2. Stir in yogurt and cook for about 3-5 minutes.
3. Stir in the salt, black pepper and lemon juice and remove from heat.
4. Serve immediately.

Nutrition:
- Per Serving : Protein 4.3 g | Fiber 2.3 g | Carbs 5.8 g | Fat 6.1 g

Chicken & Asparagus Frittata

Servings: 4
Cooking Time: 12 Mins.
Ingredients:

- ½ C. cooked chicken, chopped
- 1/3 C. low-fat Parmesan cheese, grated
- 6 eggs, beaten lightly
- Salt and ground black pepper, as required
- 1/3 C. boiled asparagus, chopped
- ¼ C. tomatoes, peeled, seeded and chopped
- ¼ C. part-skim mozzarella cheese, shredded

Directions:

1. Preheat the broiler of oven.
2. In a bowl, add the Parmesan cheese, eggs, salt and black pepper and beat until well combined.
3. In a large ovenproof wok, melt butter over medium-high heat and cook the chicken and asparagus for about 2-3 minutes
4. Add the egg mixture and tomatoes and stir to combine.
5. Cook for about 4-5 minutes.
6. Remove from the heat and sprinkle with the mozzarella cheese.
7. Now transfer the wok under broiler and broil for about 3-4 minutes or until slightly puffed.
8. Cut into desired-sized wedges and serve immediately.

Nutrition:

- Per Serving : Protein 16.8 g | Fiber 0.4 g | Carbs 1.7 g | Fat 7.3 g

Vanilla Crepes

Servings: 4
Cooking Time: 18 Mins.
Ingredients:

- 2 tbsp. arrowroot powder
- 2 tbsp. almond flour
- ½ tsp. ground cinnamon
- 4 eggs
- 1 tsp. vanilla extract
- Olive oil cooking spray

Directions:

1. In a bowl, add the arrowroot powder, almond flour and cinnamon and mix well.
2. In another bowl, add the eggs and vanilla extract and beat until well combined.
3. Add the egg mixture into the bowl of flour mixture and mix until well combined.
4. Lightly grease a large non-stick sauté pan with cooking spray and heat over medium-high heat.
5. Add the desired amount of mixture and tilt the pan to spread in an even and thin layer.
6. Cook for about 1 minute or until bottom becomes golden brown.

7. Carefully flip the side and cook for about 1 minute more or until golden brown.
8. Repeat with the remaining mixture.
9. Serve warm.

Nutrition:

- Per Serving : Protein 5.6 g | Fiber 0.5 g | Carbs 5.3 g | Fat 6.3 g

Potato & Zucchini Frittata

Servings: 6
Cooking Time: 26 Mins.
Ingredients:

- 2 tbsp. olive oil
- 1 large potato, peeled and cut into thin slices
- 2 zucchinis, peeled, seeded and sliced
- 8 eggs
- Salt and ground black pepper, as required

Directions:

1. Preheat your oven to broiler.
2. In a large ovenproof wok, heat oil over medium-low heat.
3. Add potato and cook for about 7-8 minutes.
4. Add zucchini and cook for about 3-4 minutes.
5. Meanwhile, in a bowl, add eggs, salt and black pepper and beat until well combined.
6. Pour egg mixture over veggies evenly. Immediately adjust the heat to low.
7. Cook for about 10 minutes or until just done.
8. Transfer the wok under the broiler and broil for about 3-4 minutes or until top becomes golden brown.
9. Cut the frittata in desired-sized slices. Serve with the garnishing of parsley.

Nutrition:

- Per Serving : Protein 8.7 g | Fiber 1.3 g | Carbs 7.6 g | Fat 10.7 g

Parsley Scallops

Servings: 4
Cooking Time: 7 Mins.
Ingredients:

- 1¼ lb. fresh sea scallops, side muscles removed
- Salt and ground black pepper, as required
- 2 tbsp. olive oil
- 1 tbsp. fresh parsley, minced

Directions:

1. Sprinkle the scallops with salt and black pepper.
2. In a large wok, heat the oil over medium-high heat and cook the scallops for about 2-3 minutes per side.
3. Stir in the parsley and remove from the heat.
4. Serve hot.

Nutrition:

- Per Serving : Protein 23.8 g | Fiber 0 g | Carbs 3.4 g | Fat 8.1 g

Fried Eggs With Tomatoes

Servings: 2
Cooking Time: 6 Mins.
Ingredients:
- 2 tbsp. olive oil
- 2 eggs
- 1 tomato, peeled, seed and chopped
- Salt and ground black pepper, as required

Directions:
1. In a large cast-iron wok, heat the oil over medium heat
2. Crack an egg into a small bowl
3. Carefully pour the egg into the wok and cook for about 2½-3 minutes, gently tilting the pan occasionally
4. Carefully transfer the cooked egg onto a plate.
5. Repeat with the remaining egg.
6. Divide the tomatoes onto each plate with eggs.
7. Sprinkle each egg with salt, black pepper and serve.

Nutrition:
- Per Serving : Protein 5.8 g | Fiber 0.4 g | Carbs 1.6 g | Fat 18.4 g

Cucumber & Tomato Salad

Servings: 5
Cooking Time: 10 Mins.
Ingredients:
- 2 C. seedless cucumbers, peeled, seeded and chopped
- 2 C. tomatoes, peeled, seeded and chopped
- 2 tbsp. extra-virgin olive oil
- 2 tbsp. fresh lime juice
- Salt, as required

Directions:
1. In a large serving bowl, add all the ingredients and toss to coat well.
2. Serve immediately.

Nutrition:
- Per Serving : Protein 0.9 g | Fiber 1.1 g | Carbs 4.4 g | Fat 5.8 g

Citrus Carrots

Servings: 6
Cooking Time: 2- Mins.
Ingredients:
- 1½ lb. carrots, peeled and sliced into ½-inch pieces diagonally
- ½ C. water
- 2 tbsp. olive oil
- Salt, as required
- 3 tbsp. fresh orange juice

Directions:
1. In a large wok, add the carrots, water, boil and salt over medium heat and bring to a boil.
2. Now adjust the heat to low and simmer| covered for about 6 minutes.

3. Add the orange juice and stir to combine.
4. Now adjust the heat to high and cook, uncovered for about 5-8 minutes, tossing frequently.
5. Serve immediately.

Nutrition:
- Per Serving : Protein 1 g | Fiber 2.2 g | Carbs 12 g | Fat 4.7 g

Watermelon & Plum Juice

Servings: 2
Cooking Time: 10 Mins.
Ingredients:
- 3 C. seedless watermelon, cut into chunks
- 4 plums, pitted and halved
- 6-8 ice cubes

Directions:
1. Add all ingredients in a high-power blender and pulse until well combined.
2. Through a cheesecloth-lined sieve, strain the juice and pour into two glasses.
3. Serve immediately.

Nutrition:
- Per Serving : Protein 2.3 g | Fiber 2.7 g | Carbs 33.1 g | Fat 0.7 g

Turkey Meatloaf

Servings: 8
Cooking Time: 40 Mins.
Ingredients:
- For Meatloaf:
- 2 lb. lean ground turkey
- 1 C. low-fat cheddar cheese, shredded
- Salt, as required
- 1 egg
- 2 oz. sugar-free tomato sauce
- For Topping:
- 2 oz. tomato sauce
- ½ C. low-fat cheddar cheese, shredded

Directions:
1. Preheat your oven to 400 ºF. Greased a 9x13-inch casserole dish.
2. For meatloaf: add all ingredients in a bowl and mix until well combined.
3. Place the mixture into the prepared casserole dish evenly and press to smooth the surface.
4. Coat the top of meatloaf with tomato sauce evenly and sprinkle with cheese.
5. Bake for approximately 40 minutes.
6. Remove the meatloaf from oven and place onto a wire rack to cool slightly.
7. Cut the meatloaf into desired-sized slices and serve warm.

Nutrition:

- Per Serving : Protein 28.4 g | Fiber 0.8 g | Carbs 1.1 g | Fat 15.7 g

Simple Tilapia

Servings: 5
Cooking Time: 7 Mins.
Ingredients:
- 2 tbsp. olive oil
- 5 (5-oz.) tilapia fillets
- 4 tbsp. homemade chicken broth
- Salt and ground black pepper, as required

Directions:
1. In a large sauté pan, heat oil over medium heat and cook the tilapia fillets for about 3 minutes.
2. Flip the side and cook for about 1-2 minutes.
3. Add the broth and cook for about 2-3 more minutes.
4. Serve hot.

Nutrition:
- Per Serving : Protein 26.6 g | Fiber 0 g | Carbs 0.1 g | Fat 7 g

Pan Seared Salmon

Servings: 4
Cooking Time: 9 Mins.
Ingredients:
- 4 (4-oz.) skinless, boneless salmon fillets
- Salt and ground black pepper, as required
- 2 tbsp. olive oil

Directions:
1. Sprinkle the salmon fillets with salt and black pepper evenly.
2. In a non-stick wok, heat oil over medium heat.
3. In the wok, place the salmon fillets, skin side down and cook for about 3-5 minutes, without stirring.
4. Flip the salmon fillets and cook for about 3-4 minutes.
5. Serve hot.

Nutrition:
- Per Serving : Protein 22.1 g | Fiber 0 g | Carbs 0 g | Fat 19 g

Haddock In Tomato Sauce

Servings: 3
Cooking Time: 20 Mins.
Ingredients:
- 1 tbsp. olive oil
- 2½ C. tomatoes, peeled, seeded and chopped
- 3 tbsp. fresh cilantro, chopped
- 1 tbsp. balsamic vinegar
- 3 (4-oz.) haddock fillets
- Salt and ground black pepper, as required

Directions:
1. Preheat your oven to 325 ºF.

2. In a medium, ovenproof non-stick sauté pan, heat oil over medium heat and cook the tomatoes for about 2 minutes, stirring continuously.
3. Stir in cilantro and vinegar and cook for about 2-3 minutes.
4. Add haddock fillets, salt and black pepper and stir to combine with sauce.
5. Transfer the sauté pan into the oven and bake for approximately 12-15 minutes.
6. Serve hot.

Nutrition:
- Per Serving : Protein 28.8 g | Fiber 1.7 g | Carbs 5.9 g | Fat 6 g

Banana Muffins

Servings: 12
Cooking Time: 20minutes
Ingredients:
- 2/3 Cups of skim milk
- 4 eggs
- 1 Cup of white flour
- 1/4 Cup of canola oil
- 1 1/2 Cup of cereal
- 1 Cup of mashed ripe banana
- ½ tsp. of salt
- ½ cup of brown sugar
- 2 tsp. of baking powder

Directions:
1. Let the oven preheat to 400°F.
2. Add milk & cereal to a bowl, mix & let it rest. Add bananas, oil, eggs & sugar, mix well.
3. In a bowl, add salt, flour & baking powder. Mix & add to the wet ingredients.
4. Add to the oil sprayed muffin tray. Bake for 15 to 18 minutes.
5. Serve.

Nutrition:
- Per Serving : Protein 4 g | Fiber 3 g | Carbs 18.9 g | Fat 4 g

Vanilla Waffles

Servings: 2
Cooking Time: 10 Mins.
Ingredients:
- ¼ C. coconut flour
- 6 egg whites
- 1 tbsp. pure maple syrup
- 1 tsp. baking powder
- ¼ C. fat-free milk
- ¼ tsp. vanilla extract

Directions:
1. Preheat the waffle iron and lightly grease it.

2. In a large bowl, add the flour and baking powder and mix well.

3. Add the remaining ingredients and mix until well combined.

4. Place half of the mixture in the preheated waffle iron.

5. Cook for about 3-5 minutes or until waffles become golden brown.

6. Repeat with the remaining mixture.

7. Serve warm.

Nutrition:

- Per Serving : Protein 12.1 g | Fiber 0.7 g | Carbs 11.2 g | Fat 0.5 g

Brown Rice Greek Salad

Servings: 4
Cooking Time: 0minutes
Ingredients:

- ½ cup of canned white beans, rinsed
- 1/4 Cup of avocado, diced
- ½ cup of fresh spinach
- ½ cup of Brown rice, cooked
- 1 tsp. of red wine vinegar
- 2 tbsp. of Feta cheese, crumbled
- ½ cup of tomatoes, no seeds
- ½ cup of English Cucumber, no seeds
- 1 tbsp. of red onion, chopped
- 2 tbsp. of olive oil
- Salt and pepper, to taste

Directions:

1. Add all ingredients to a bowl. Toss & adjust seasoning.
2. Serve.

Nutrition:

- Per Serving : Protein 0.1 g | Fiber 1.2 g | Carbs 18.7 g | Fat 2 g

Salmon Cakes

Servings:6
Cooking Time: 20 Minutes
Ingredients:

- ½ pound salmon, bones and skin removed, diced
- 2 garlic cloves, minced
- 1 large egg
- ¾ cup bread crumbs
- ¼ cup minced chives
- 1 tablespoon lemon juice
- 1 teaspoon hot sauce
- ½ teaspoon Dijon mustard
- ½ teaspoon salt
- ½ teaspoon freshly ground black pepper
- ¼ teaspoon paprika
- 1 tablespoon vegetable oil
- 6 white burger buns, toasted

Directions:

1. white burger buns, toasted

2. In a large bowl, mix together the salmon, garlic, egg, bread crumbs, chives, lemon juice, hot sauce, Dijon mustard, salt, pepper, and paprika until just combined.

3. Form the mixture into 6 patties.

4. In a large sauté pan or skillet over medium heat, warm the oil until it begins to shimmer. Add the salmon patties and cook until the salmon begins to turn pink and the bottom is browned, 7 to 10 minutes. Flip and cook until the patties are firm and golden on both sides, another 7 to 10 minutes. The salmon should be pale pink.

5. Serve the patties hot, sandwiched between the toasted buns.

6. Leftover salmon cakes can be stored in an airtight container in the refrigerator for up to 5 days or in the freezer for up to 3 months.

Nutrition:

- Per Serving : Protein 13 g | Fiber 1 g | Carbs 29 g | Fat 6 g

Ciabatta Pizza

Servings: 4
Cooking Time: 20minutes
Ingredients:

- 2 cups of tomato sauce
- 2 cups of mozzarella cheese
- 1 small zucchini, cut into ¼" rounds
- 1-pound loaf of ciabatta
- ½ cup of sliced mushrooms
- 2 tbsp. of basil

Directions:

1. Let the oven preheat to 400°F.

2. Slice the bread loaf lengthwise & take some of the bread out from inside.

3. Place on a baking sheet. Add sauce on top & spread.

4. Add zucchini & mushrooms on top, end with cheese & basil.

5. Bake for 12-15 minutes.

Nutrition:

- Per Serving : Protein 13 g | Fiber 2 g | Carbs 36.5 g | Fat 8 g

Low & Slow Pulled Pork

Servings: 10
Cooking Time: 5 Hours
Ingredients:

- 1 cup of dark brown sugar
- 1 tbsp. of Creole seasoning
- ½ cup of granulated garlic
- ½ cup of kosher salt
- 5 pounds of pork blade roast
- 1/2cup of paprika

- 2 tbsp. of dried minced onion
- 1 tbsp. of red pepper
- 1 tbsp. of ground cumin
- 1 tbsp. of black pepper
- 1/4 cup of Worcestershire sauce
- 1 minced garlic clove
- 3/4 cup of cider vinegar
- 1 tbsp. of lemon juice
- ½ cup of ketchup
- 1 tbsp. of brown sugar
- ½ tsp. of dry mustard
- 2 tbsp. of onions
- 1 dash of red pepper
- Apple juice, as needed

Directions:

1. In a bowl, mix paprika (half cup), Creole seasoning (1 tbsp.), cumin (1 tbsp.), dark brown sugar (1 cup), granulated onion, red pepper, granulated garlic & salt (half cup). Mix & store in a container.

2. In a pan, add the rest of the ingredients except for pork. Let it come to a boil, turn the heat low & simmer for 40 minutes. Divide this into 2 containers.

3. Season the pork with spice rub generously. Wrap in plastic wrap & keep in the fridge overnight.

4. Place the meat at room temperature for 45 minutes before cooking.

5. Smoke the meat for 2 hours at 225-250°F.

6. Spray the meat with apple juice & place wrap in the aluminum foil.

7. Smoke for 2 more hours, smoke until the internal temperature reaches 195 F.

8. Cool for half an hour, shred & serve with sauce.

Nutrition:

- Per Serving : Protein 17 g | Fiber 1.2 g | Carbs 11 g | Fat 8 g

Cinnamon Waffles

Servings: 4
Cooking Time: 40 Mins.

Ingredients:

- 1¼ C. unsweetened almond milk
- 1 tbsp. apple cider vinegar
- 1 tbsp. ground flaxseed
- 3 tbsp. water
- 1 C. buckwheat flour
- 1 tbsp. Erythritol
- 1¼ tsp. baking powder
- 1 tsp. baking soda
- ¼ tsp. salt
- ¼ tsp. ground cinnamon

Directions:

1. In a bowl, mix together almond milk vinegar. Set aside for 5 minutes.

2. In a bowl, add ground flaxseed and mix well. Set aside for about 5 minutes or until thicken.

3. In a separate bowl, add buckwheat flour, coconut sugar, cinnamon, baking powder, baking soda and salt and mix well.

4. In the bowl of flaxseed mixture, add almond milk mixture and stir to combine.

5. Add flour mixture and mix until just combined. Set aside for about 5-10 minutes.

6. Preheat the waffle iron and then grease it.

7. Place the desired amount of the mixture into the preheated waffle iron and cook for about 5 minutes per side or until golden brown.

8. Repeat with the remaining mixture.

9. Serve warm.

Nutrition:

- Per Serving : Protein 4.4 g | Fiber 2.4 g | Carbs 23.2 g | Fat 2.6 g

Tex-mex Chili

Servings: 6
Cooking Time: 30 Minutes

Ingredients:

- 2 packets of Taco Seasoning
- 1 can diced tomato with chilies
- 21 oz. of black bean
- 1 pound of lean ground beef & ground turkey
- 22 oz. of pepper & onion blend

Directions:

1. Brown the meats & drain all fat.

2. Add the rest of the ingredients simmer for 20 minutes. Do not add extra water.

3. Serve.

Nutrition:

- Per Serving : Protein 18 g | Fiber 1.2 g | Carbs 17 g | Fat 6 g

Molasses Cookies

Servings:2
Cooking Time: 10 Minutes

Ingredients:

- ¼ cup sugar
- 12 tablespoons (1½ sticks) butter or margarine
- 1 cup brown sugar
- ¼ cup molasses
- 1 large egg
- 2 cups all-purpose flour
- 2 teaspoons baking soda
- 1 teaspoon ground cinnamon
- ½ teaspoon ground ginger
- Pinch ground cloves
- Pinch salt

Directions:

1. Pinch salt
2. Preheat the oven to 375°F. Line a baking sheet with parchment paper. Put the sugar in a small bowl and set aside.
3. In a stand mixer fitted with the paddle attachment, beat the butter and brown sugar on medium speed until light and fluffy.
4. Add the molasses and egg and beat until well combined. With the mixer on low, add the flour, baking soda, cinnamon, ginger, cloves, and salt and mix until well combined.
5. Take about 2 tablespoons of dough and roll it into a 1-inch ball. Roll the ball in the sugar, and place it on the prepared baking sheet. Repeat with the rest of the dough, spacing the balls 2 inches apart. The cookies will spread while baking.
6. Bake for 8 to 10 minutes. Let cool on a wire rack.
7. The cookies can be stored in an airtight container at room temperature for up to 5 days or frozen for up to 3 months.
Nutrition:
- Per Serving : Protein 1 g | Fiber 1 g | Carbs 20 g | Fat 6 g

Apple Porridge

Servings: 6
Cooking Time: 25 Mins.
Ingredients:
- 3 C. apples, peeled, cored and shredded
- 1¾ C. fat-free milk
- 1 tsp. vanilla extract
Directions:
1. In a non-stick saucepan, stir together all ingredients over medium heat and bring to a gentle simmer.
2. Now adjust heat to low and simmer for about 15-20 minutes.
3. Serve warm.
Nutrition:
- Per Serving : Protein 2.5 g | Fiber 0.7 g | Carbs 10.6 g | Fat 0.1 g

Eggs With Zucchini

Servings: 4
Cooking Time: 15 Mins.
Ingredients:
- 2 tbsp. olive oil, divided
- 1 lb. zucchini, peeled, seeded and sliced thinly
- 1 tsp. fresh rosemary, chopped finely
- Sat, as required
- 4 large eggs
- Salt and ground black pepper, as required
Directions:
1. In a large wok, heat 1 tbsp. of oil over medium-high heat and cook zucchini, for about 5-8 minutes.
2. Add rosemary and salt and stir to combine.
3. With a wooden spoon, make a large well in the center of wok by moving the veggie mixture towards the sides.

4. Now adjust the heat to medium and pour remaining oil in the well.
5. Carefully crack the eggs in the well and sprinkle with salt and black pepper.
6. Cook for about 1-2 minutes.
7. Cover the wok and cook for about 2-3 minutes more.
8. Serve hot.
Nutrition:
- Per Serving : Protein 7.7 g | Fiber 3 g | Carbs 4.4 g | Fat 12.9 g

Salmon & Spinach Soup

Servings: 8
Cooking Time: 35 Mins.
Ingredients:
- 2 C. carrots, peeled and chopped
- 8 C. homemade chicken broth
- 1½ lb. salmon fillets, cubed
- 8 C. fresh baby spinach
- 1 C. fresh cilantro, chopped
- Salt, as required
Directions:
1. In a large soup pan, add carrot and broth and bring to a boil.
2. Now adjust the heat to medium-low and simmer for about 15 minutes.
3. Stir in salmon cubes, spinach, cilantro and salt and simmer, covered for about 10-15 minutes.
4. Serve hot.
Nutrition:
- Per Serving : Protein 22.5 g | Fiber 1.3 g | Carbs 4.8 g | Fat 6.8 g

Salmon & Tomato Salad

Servings: 2
Cooking Time: 10 Mins.
Ingredients:
- ¼ C. part-skim mozzarella cheese, cubed
- ¼ C. tomato, peeled, seeded and chopped
- 1 tbsp. fresh dill, chopped
- 1 tsp. fresh lemon juice
- Salt, as required
- 6 oz. cooked salmon, chopped
Directions:
1. In a small bowl, add all the ingredients and stir to combine.
2. Serve immediately.
Nutrition:
- Per Serving : Protein 18 g | Fiber 0.5 g | Carbs 1.9 g | Fat 6 g

Apple Cider Sausage

Servings: 8
Cooking Time: 25 Minutes
Ingredients:

- 1 peeled red apple (cut into wedges)
- 1.7 oz. of chopped yellow squash
- 1 tsp. of garlic powder
- 1 ½ cups of dry cider
- ¼ cup of cream
- 8 chicken sausages
- 1 tbsp. of dried Italian herbs
- 1 tbsp. of olive oil
- ¾ cup of chicken stock
- 2 carrots, peeled
- 1 tbsp. of arrowroot flour

Directions:

1. Sauté the sausage in a splash of hot oil until golden brown; take them out on a plate.
2. Add the carrots & apple squash to the same pan cook until tender.
3. Add garlic powder, cider, herbs & stock. Stir & add flour cook until it thickens.
4. Add sausages & cook for 5 to 10 minutes.
5. Add cream & simmer for 5-10 minutes more.

Nutrition:

- Per Serving : Protein 9 g | Fiber 3 g | Carbs 12 g | Fat 0.2 g

Shrimp Lettuce Wraps

Servings: 6
Cooking Time: 4 Minutes.
Ingredients:

- 1 tbsp. extra-virgin olive oil
- 1½ lb. shrimp, peeled, deveined and chopped
- Salt and ground black pepper, as required
- 12 butter lettuce leaves
- 1 C. carrot, peeled and julienned

Directions:

1. In a large wok, heat the oil over medium heat and cook the shrimp with salt and black pepper for about 3-4 minutes.
2. Remove from the heat and set aside to cool slightly.
3. Arrange the lettuce leaves onto serving plates.
4. Place the shrimp over lettuce leaves evenly and top with carrot.
5. Serve immediately.

Nutrition:

- Per Serving : Protein 26 g | Fiber 0.5 g | Carbs 3.8 g | Fat 4.3 g

Beef & Zucchi Soup

Servings: 6
Cooking Time: 20 Minutes.
Ingredients:

- 6 C. homemade beef broth
- 1 lb. cooked beef, sliced thinly
- 1 lb. zucchini, peeled, seeded and chopped
- ¼ C. fresh parsley, chopped
- 2 tbsp. fresh lemon juice
- Salt and ground black pepper, as required

Directions:

1. In a soup pan, add broth, beef and zucchini and bring to a boil.
2. Now adjust the heat to medium-low and simmer for about 10 minutes.
3. Stir in parsley, lemon juice, salt and black pepper and cook for about 5 minutes.
4. Serve hot.

Nutrition:

- Per Serving : Protein 28.8 g | Fiber 0.9 g | Carbs 3.7 g | Fat 6.3 g

Zucchini Bread

Servings: 24
Cooking Time: 55 Minutes.
Ingredients:

- 3 C. all-purpose flour
- 2 tsp. baking soda
- 1 tsp. ground cinnamon
- 1 tsp. ground nutmeg
- 2 C. Erythritol
- 1 C. olive oil
- 3 eggs, beaten
- 2 tsp. vanilla extract
- 2 C. zucchini, peeled, seeded and grated

Directions:

1. Preheat your oven to 325 ºF. Arrange a rack in the center of oven. Grease 2 loaf pans.
2. In a medium bowl, mix together the flour, baking soda and spices.
3. In another large bowl, add the Erythritol and oil and beat until well combined.
4. Add the eggs and vanilla extract and beat until well combined.
5. Add the flour mixture and mix until just combined.
6. Gently, fold in the zucchini.
7. Place the mixture into the bread loaf pans evenly.
8. Bake for approximately 45-50 minutes or until a toothpick inserted in the center of bread comes out clean.
9. Remove the bread pans from oven and place onto a wire rack to cool for about 15 minutes.
10. Then invert the breads onto the wire rack to cool completely before slicing.
11. With a sharp knife, cut each bread loaf into desired-sized slices and serve.

Nutrition:

- Per Serving : Protein 16.3 g | Fiber 0.6 g | Carbs 28.4 g | Fat 9.2 g

Kiwi Juice

Servings: 2
Cooking Time: 10 Minutes.
Ingredients:
- 4 medium kiwis, peeled and chopped
- 4 C. chilled filtered water

Directions:
1. Add all ingredients in a high-power blender and pulse until well combined.
2. Through a cheesecloth-lined sieve, strain the juice and pour into four glasses.
3. Serve immediately.

Nutrition:
- Per Serving : Protein 1.7 g | Fiber 3 g | Carbs 22.3 g | Fat 0.8 g

Banana Porridge

Servings: 4
Cooking Time: 10 Minutes.
Ingredients:
- 4 small bananas, peeled, sliced and mashed
- 1 tbsp. low-fat butter, softened
- ¼ tsp. ground cinnamon

Directions:
1. In a large bowl, add mashed bananas, almond butter and cinnamon and stir to combine.
2. Serve immediately.

Nutrition:
- Per Serving : Protein 2 g | Fiber 0.1 g | Carbs 30.7 g | Fat 3.9 g

Egg Potato Bites

Servings: 12
Cooking Time: 25minutes
Ingredients:
- 8 oz. of cooked & peeled potato, chopped
- 1 cup of cottage cheese, pureed
- 8 eggs
- Salt, to taste
- 2 oz. of Swiss cheese

Directions:
1. Let the oven preheat to 325°F. Oil spray a 12 cup muffin tin.
2. In a bowl, mix the cottage cheese, potatoes, salt & egg. Add to the cups, sprinkle with cheese on top.
3. Bake for half an hour.

Nutrition:
- Per Serving : Protein 8 g | Fiber 1 g | Carbs 3 g | Fat 4 g

Chicken & Veggie Frittata

Servings: 8

Cooking Time: 43 Minutes.
Ingredients:
- 1 tsp. olive oil
- 4 C. fresh spinach, chopped
- 1 C. bell pepper, seeded and chopped
- 2 C. cooked chicken, chopped
- 2 large eggs
- 4 large egg whites
- 1¼ C. unsweetened almond milk
- 1 C. low-fat cheddar cheese, shredded
- Salt and ground black pepper, as required
- 1 tbsp. low-fat Parmesan cheese, shredded

Directions:
1. Preheat your oven to 350 ºF. Grease a 9-inch pie plate.
2. In a wok, heat oil over medium heat and cook spinach and bell pepper and sauté for about 2-3 minutes.
3. Stir in chicken and transfer the mixture into the prepared pie dish evenly.
4. Add eggs, egg whites, almond milk, cheddar cheese, salt, and black pepper in a mixing bowl and beat until well combined.
5. Pour egg mixture over the chicken mixture evenly and top with Parmesan cheese.
6. Bake for approximately 40 minutes or until top becomes golden-brown.
7. Remove the pie dish from oven and set aside for about 5 minutes
8. Cut into 8 equal-sized wedges and serve.

Nutrition:
- Per Serving : Protein 17.5 g | Fiber 0.4 g | Carbs 2.1 g | Fat 8.3 g

Simple Salmon With Dill Sauce

Servings: 6
Cooking Time: 40 Minutes
Ingredients:
- 2 tbsp. of soy sauce
- ½ cup of chopped cucumber
- Black pepper, to taste
- 2 pounds of salmon fillet
- ½ cup of sour cream
- Olive oil, to taste
- 1 tsp. of fresh dill

Directions:
1. Let the oven preheat to 450°F.
2. Pour the soy sauce on the fish & season with salmon. Roast for 10 minutes for each" of thickness,
3. Mix the rest of the ingredients & serve with salmon.

Nutrition:
- Per Serving : Protein 31 g | Fiber 0 g | Carbs 5 g | Fat 17 g

Prawn & Tomato Spaghetti

Servings: 6
Cooking Time: 20 Minutes
Ingredients:

- 1 tbsp. of olive oil
- 2 tbsp. of chopped parsley leaves
- 4 garlic cloves, sliced
- 6 tomatoes, chopped without seeds
- 13 oz. of spaghetti
- 20 green prawns, peeled & deveined

Directions:

1. Cook noodles as per package Directions. Drain all but a half cup of water.
2. Sauté garlic in hot oil for 1 minute.
3. Add prawns cook for 2 to 3 minutes.
4. Add tomatoes & cook for 2 minutes.
5. Add parsley & pasta. Toss & serve.

Nutrition:

- Per Serving : Protein 33 g | Fiber 1.2 g | Carbs 50 g | Fat 6.5 g

Cioppino

Servings: 6-8
Cooking Time: 45minutes
Ingredients:

- 1/4 cups of olive oil
- 2 shallots, minced
- 2 garlic cloves, sliced
- 1 lb. of shrimp, peeled & deveined
- 1 tsp. of dried oregano
- 1 bulb fennel, sliced
- 12 littleneck clams, cleaned
- Salt & pepper, to taste
- 1 1/2 cups of dry white wine
- 1 can of (28-oz.) crushed tomatoes
- 1 bottle of (8-oz.) clam juice
- 2 cups of water
- 1 lb. of halibut, 1-inch pieces without skin
- 2 dried bay leaves
- 12 mussels, cleaned

Directions:

1. Sauté shallots & fennels for 6 minutes till soft in hot oil.
2. Add pepper flakes, garlic, salt, pepper & oregano for 1 minute.
3. Add wine, cook for 3-5 minutes & deglaze. Add tomatoes, water, clam juice & bay leaves. Cook for 20 minutes.
4. Take the bay leaves.
5. Add clams & cook for 5 minutes. Add mussels, then add shrimps, add fish.
6. Do not mix; cook for 5 minutes after covering it.

7. Do not use mussels that have not opened. Add salt & pepper. Serve.
Nutrition:

- Per Serving : Protein 28 g | Fiber 2 g | Carbs 13 g | Fat 6 g

Chicken With Green Beans

Servings: 6
Cooking Time: 18 Minutes.
Ingredients:

- 2 tbsp. olive oil
- 1 lb. boneless, skinless chicken breasts, sliced thinly
- 1 lb. canned green beans, drained
- Salt and ground black pepper, as required
- ¼ C. homemade chicken broth

Directions:

1. Heat oil in a sauté pan over medium-high heat and cook the chicken for about 4-5 minutes, stirring frequently.
2. Add the green beans and cook for about 2-3 minutes.
3. Stir in the salt, black pepper, and broth, and bring to a boil
4. Now adjust the heat to medium and cook for about 3-5 minutes or until all the liquid is absorbed, stirring occasionally.
5. Serve immediately.

Nutrition:

- Per Serving : Protein 26.7 g | Fiber 0.4 g | Carbs 0.9 g | Fat 12.4 g

Shrimp & Tomato Bake

Servings: 6
Cooking Time: 25 Minutes.
Ingredients:

- 2 tbsp. olive oil
- 1½ lb. large shrimp, peeled and deveined
- ¾ tsp. dried oregano, crushed
- ¼ C. fresh parsley, chopped
- ½ C. homemade chicken broth
- 2 C. tomatoes, peeled, seeded and chopped
- 4 oz. low-fat feta cheese, crumbled

Directions:

1. Preheat your oven to 350 °F.
2. In a sauté pan, heat oil over medium-high heat and cook the shrimp and oregano for about 2 minutes.
3. Stir in the parsley and salt and immediately transfer into a casserole dish evenly.
4. In the same wok, add broth over medium heat and simmer for about 2-3 minutes or until reduced to half.
5. Stir in tomatoes and cook for about 2-3 minutes.
6. Place the tomato mixture over the shrimp mixture evenly and top with cheese.
7. Bake for approximately 15-20 minutes or until top becomes golden brown.

8. Serve hot.

Nutrition:
- Per Serving : Protein 25.7 g | Fiber 0.9 g | Carbs 5.4 g | Fat 7 g

Very Berry Khatta

Servings: 1
Cooking Time: 0minutes

Ingredients:
- 1 orange wedge
- ¼ cup of grape juice
- Crushed ice, as needed
- 4 mulberries
- 2 lime slices
- 2 tbsp. of kala khatta syrup
- Black salt, as needed

Directions:
1. Crush 2 mulberries with orange & half of the lime.
2. Add the rest of the ingredients. Adjust seasoning.
3. Serve.

Nutrition:
- Per Serving : Protein 0 g | Fiber 1 g | Carbs 3 g | Fat 0 g

Beef & Spinach Burgers

Servings: 4
Cooking Time: 12 Minutes.

Ingredients:
- 1 lb. lean ground beef
- 1 C. fresh baby spinach leaves, chopped
- ½ C. sun-dried tomatoes, peeled, seeded and chopped
- 1 egg, beaten
- ¼ C. low-fat feta cheese, crumbled
- Salt and ground black pepper, as required
- 2 tbsp. olive oil

Directions:
1. In a large bowl, add all the ingredients except for oil and mix until well combined.
2. Make 4 equal-sized patties from the mixture
3. In a cast-iron wok, heat oil over medium-high heat and cook the patties for about 5-6 minutes per side or until desired doneness.
4. Serve immediately.

Nutrition:
- Per Serving : Protein 25.6 g | Fiber 0.7 g | Carbs 1.5 g | Fat 17.1 g

Tomato, Carrot & Celery Juice

Servings: 3
Cooking Time: 10 Minutes.

Ingredients:
- 6 tomatoes
- 2 carrots, peeled
- 1 celery stalk

- ¼ C. filtered water
- Pinch of salt and ground black pepper
- 2-3 ice cubes

Directions:
1. Add all ingredients in a high-power blender and pulse until well combined.
2. Through a cheesecloth-lined strainer, strain the juice and transfer into 3 glasses.
3. Serve immediately.

Nutrition:
- Per Serving : Protein 2.5 g | Fiber 3.4 g | Carbs 13.7 g | Fat 0.5 g

Asparagus & Bean Frittata

Servings: 4
Cooking Time: 15minutes

Ingredients:
- 1 Cup of diced onion
- 2 tbsp. of olive oil
- 1 minced garlic clove
- 14 oz. of canned beans, rinsed
- 1/4 Cup of Parmesan cheese
- 1 Cup of chopped red pepper
- 1 Cup of cooked asparagus, chopped
- 4 eggs
- ½ tsp. of salt

Directions:
1. Let the oven preheat to 350°F.
2. Heat one tbsp. of oil on medium flame. Sauté the vegetables & beans for 10 minutes.
3. Whisk eggs with salt & pepper.
4. Add the rest of the oil with eggs. Cook for 10 to 15 minutes on low.
5. Add cheese on top, broil for 3 minutes. Slice & serve.

Nutrition:
- Per Serving : Protein 2 g | Fiber 2 g | Carbs 9.8 g | Fat 4.2 g

Lemony Salmon

Servings: 4
Cooking Time: 14 Minutes.

Ingredients:
- 1 tbsp. fresh lemon zest, grated
- 2 tbsp. extra-virgin olive oil
- 2 tbsp. fresh lemon juice
- Salt and ground black pepper, as required
- 4 (6-oz.) boneless, skinless salmon fillets

Directions:
1. Preheat the grill to medium-high heat. Grease the grill grate.
2. In a bowl, place all ingredients except for salmon fillets and mix well.

3. Add the salmon fillets and coat with garlic mixture generously.

4. Place the salmon fillets onto grill and cook for about 6-7 minutes per side.

5. Serve hot.

Nutrition:

• Per Serving : Protein 33.2 g | Fiber 0.2 g | Carbs 1 g | Fat 21.5 g

Pasta Bake

Servings: 4
Cooking Time: 45minutes

Ingredients:

• 7 oz. of canned asparagus, sliced
• 1 tsp. of mixed herbs
• 14 oz. of pasta
• 2 cups of chicken stock
• 2 oz. of white bread crumbs
• 18 oz. of peeled pumpkin, cut into chunks
• 2 tbsp. of oil
• 5 oz. of grated cheese

Directions:

1. Let the oven preheat to 420°F.

2. Toss the pumpkin with 1 tbsp. of oil & roast until golden & tender.

3. Cook the pasta until done.

4. In a bowl, add olive oil & breadcrumbs; stock mix well.

5. Add the rest of the ingredients. Mix.

6. Add to the baking dish bake for half an hour. Serve.

Nutrition:

• Per Serving : Protein 3 g | Fiber 5 g | Carbs 18.7 g | Fat 6 g

Honey Salmon

Servings: 4
Cooking Time: 9 Minutes.

Ingredients:

• 1 tbsp. honey
• 1 tbsp. fresh lemon juice
• 2 tbsp. olive oil
• 4 (4-oz.) skinless salmon fillets
• 2 tbsp. fresh parsley, chopped

Directions:

1. In a bowl, mix together honey and lemon juice. Set aside.

2. In a large non-stick sauté pan, heat olive oil over medium-high heat and cook the salmon fillets for about 3-4 minutes per side.

3. Stir in honey mixture and immediately remove from heat.

Nutrition:

• Per Serving : Protein 22.2 g | Fiber 0.1 g | Carbs 4.5 g | Fat 19.1 g

Shrimp & Tomato Salad

Servings: 5
Cooking Time: 3 Minutes.

Ingredients:

• 1 lb. shrimp, peeled and deveined
• 1 lemon, quartered
• 2 tbsp. olive oil
• 2 tsp. fresh lemon juice
• Salt and ground black pepper, as required
• 3 tomatoes, peeled, seeded and sliced
• ¼ C. fresh cilantro, chopped finely

Directions:

1. In a pan of lightly salted water, add the quartered lemon and bring to a boil.

2. Add the shrimp and cook for about 2-3 minutes or until pink and opaque.

3. With a slotted spoon, transfer the shrimp into a bowl of ice water to stop the cooking process.

4. Drain the shrimp completely and then pat dry with paper towels.

5. In a small bowl, add the oil, lemon juice, salt, and black pepper, and beat until well combined.

6. Divide the shrimp, tomato, olives, and cilantro onto serving plates.

7. Drizzle with oil mixture and serve.

Nutrition:

• Per Serving : Protein 21.4 g | Fiber 1.2 g | Carbs 5 g | Fat 8 g

Detox Soup

Servings: 8
Cooking Time: 35minutes

Ingredients:

• 1 yellow onion, diced
• 4 carrots, chopped
• 6 cloves of minced garlic minced
• 2" of ginger peeled & chopped
• 1 tbsp. of olive oil
• 4 celery stalks, chopped
• 1 can of (14 oz.) chickpeas, rinsed
• 1 can of 14 oz. tomatoes
• 8 oz. of mushrooms
• 1 small head of broccoli, broken into florets
• ¼ cup of chopped fresh parsley
• 1 tbsp. of turmeric powder
• 1 tsp. of cinnamon
• 2 cups of spinach
• 1 bay leaf
• salt and pepper to taste
• 8 cups of vegetable
• 1 cup of chopped purple cabbage
• 1 lemon's juice

Directions:

1. Sauté the garlic, onion & ginger in hot oil for a few seconds.
2. Add mushrooms, celery, tomatoes, carrots & broccoli, cook for 3 minutes
3. Add the spices and chickpeas & stock. Let it come to a boil, reduce heat & simmer for 15 minutes.
4. Add lemon juice, spinach, parsley & cabbage. Simmer for 5 minutes.
5. Serve.

Nutrition:

- Per Serving : Protein 3 g | Fiber 4 g | Carbs 13 g | Fat 4 g

Lemon Cheese Waffles

Servings: 2
Cooking Time: 8 Minutes.

Ingredients:

- ½ C. part-skim mozzarella cheese, shredded
- 1 large egg
- 2 tbsp. blanched almond flour
- ¼ tsp. baking powder
- 1 tsp. fresh lemon juice
- 2-3 drops liquid stevia

Directions:

1. Preheat a mini waffle iron and then grease it.
2. In a medium bowl, put all ingredients and with a fork, mix until well combined.
3. Place half of the mixture into preheated waffle iron and cook for about 3-4 minutes.
4. Repeat with the remaining mixture.
5. Serve warm.

Nutrition:

- Per Serving : Protein 6.7 g | Fiber 0.8 g | Carbs 2.2 g | Fat 7.1 g

Shrimp With Asparagus

Servings: 6
Cooking Time: 11 Minutes.

Ingredients:

- 3 tbsp. olive oil, divided
- 1 lb. asparagus tips
- 1 lb. shrimp, peeled and deveined
- 1 tbsp. dried parsley
- Salt and ground black pepper, as required

Directions:

1. Heat 1 tbsp. of oil in a large sauté pan over medium heat and stir-fry the asparagus for about 4-5 minutes.
2. With a slotted spoon, transfer the asparagus onto a plate.
3. Heat remaining oil in the same sauté pan and stir-fry shrimp for about 2 minutes.
4. Stir in parsley, salt, and black pepper, and cook for about 1 minute.
5. Add in the cooked asparagus and cook for about 2-3 minutes.

6. Serve hot.

Nutrition:

- Per Serving : Protein 19.1 g | Fiber 1.2 g | Carbs 3.6 g | Fat 8.3 g

Mango Juice

Servings: 2
Cooking Time: 10 Mins.

Ingredients:

- 4 C. mangoes, peeled, pitted and chopped
- 2 C. filtered water

Directions:

1. Add all ingredients in a high-power blender and pulse until well combined.
2. Through a cheesecloth-lined sieve, strain the juice and pour into four glasses
3. Serve immediately.

Nutrition:

- Per Serving : Protein 1.4 g | Fiber 2.6 g | Carbs 24.7 g | Fat 0.6 g

Tomato Soup

Servings: 4
Cooking Time: 45 Minutes.

Ingredients:

- 1 tbsp. olive oil
- 1 carrot, peeled and chopped roughly
- 5 large tomatoes, peeled, seeded and chopped roughly
- 3½ C. homemade vegetable broth
- ¼ C. fresh basil, chopped
- Salt and ground black pepper, as required

Directions:

1. In a large soup pan, heat oil over medium heat and cook the carrot for about 4-5 minutes, stirring frequently.
2. Stir in the tomatoes, basil, broth, salt and black pepper and bring to a boil.
3. Now adjust the heat to low and simmer uncovered for about 30 minutes.
4. Remove the soup pan from heat and with an immersion blender, blend the soup until smooth.
5. Serve hot.

Nutrition:

- Per Serving : Protein 6.7 g | Fiber 2.8 g | Carbs 13.8 g | Fat 5.2 g

Tofu & Spinach Scramble

Servings: 2
Cooking Time: 7 Minutes.
Ingredients:

- 1 tbsp. olive oil
- ¼ lb. medium-firm tofu, drained, pressed and crumbled
- 1/3 C. homemade vegetable broth
- 2¾ C. fresh baby spinach, chopped
- Salt, as required
- 1 tsp. fresh lemon juice

Directions:
1. Heat olive oil in a frying pan over medium-high heat and cook the tofu for about 2-3 minutes, slowly adding the broth.
2. Add the spinach and stir fry for about 3-4 minutes or until all the liquid is absorbed.
3. Stir in salt and lemon juice and serve immediately.

Nutrition:
- Per Serving : Protein 1 g | Fiber 0.7 g | Carbs 2.7 g | Fat 9.8 g

Chicken & Orzo Soup

Servings: 4
Cooking Time: 20 Minutes.
Ingredients:

- 6 C. homemade chicken broth
- 1/3 C. whole-wheat orzo
- 6 large egg yolks
- 1½ C. cooked chicken, shredded
- ¼ C. fresh lemon juice
- Salt and ground black pepper, as required

Directions:
1. In a large pan, add the broth over medium-high heat and bring to a boil.
2. Add the pasta and cook for about 8-9 minutes.
3. Add the egg mixture to the pan, stirring continuously.
4. Now adjust the heat to medium and cook for about 5-7 minutes, stirring, frequently.
5. Stir in the cooked chicken, salt and black pepper and cook for about 1-2 minutes.
6. Remove from the heat and serve hot.

Nutrition:
- Per Serving : Protein 34.6 g | Fiber 0.6 g | Carbs 11.9 g | Fat 8.7 g

Spinach Scrambled Eggs

Servings: 2
Cooking Time: 5 Minutes
Ingredients:

- 6 eggs
- ½ cup of spinach leaves, chopped
- 3 tbsp. of skim milk
- 1/8 tsp. of each salt & pepper

Directions:
1. Oil spray a pan & place on a medium flame.
2. Whisk eggs in a bowl with milk, salt & pepper.
3. Add eggs to the pan & add spinach. Cook until eggs are done & spinach wilts.
4. Serve.

Nutrition:
- Per Serving : Protein 21 g | Fiber 1.2 g | Carbs 4 g | Fat 14 g

Basil Zoodle Frittata

Servings: 4
Cooking Time: 35minutes
Ingredients:

- 1 tsp. of powdered garlic
- ½ cup of cottage cheese
- 1/4 cup of sliced fine chives
- ½ cup of bread crumbs
- 2 zucchinis, spiralized
- 6 eggs
- 1/4 cup of torn basil leaves
- Salt, a pinch
- 1 tbsp. of olive oil

Directions:
1. Let the oven preheat to 350°F.
2. In the pie dish, press the crumbs into a base
3. Bake for 10 minutes, press down once more.
4. Boil the zucchini, sprinkle some salt & drain. Add to a bowl with the rest of the ingredients.
5. Mix well & place on the baked pie crust.
6. Bake for 20 to 30 minutes. Slice & serve.

Nutrition:
- Per Serving : Protein 2 g | Fiber 3 g | Carbs 18 g | Fat 4 g

Peach Scones

Servings:12
Cooking Time: 20 Minutes
Ingredients:

- 2½ cups all-purpose flour
- ½ cup sugar, plus more for sprinkling
- 1 tablespoon baking powder
- 1 teaspoon ground cinnamon
- ½ teaspoon baking soda
- ¾ teaspoon salt
- 8 tablespoons (1 stick) cold butter, cut into cubes
- 1 cup canned peaches packed in water, drained and finely diced
- ¾ cup milk, plus more for brushing
- 1 tablespoon vanilla extract

Directions:
1. tablespoon vanilla extract
2. Preheat the oven to 425°F. Line a baking sheet with parchment paper.

3. In a large mixing bowl, mix together the flour, sugar, baking powder, cinnamon, baking soda, and salt.

4. Add the butter and work it into the dry ingredients with a fork or pastry blender until it resembles pea-sized clumps.

5. Add the peaches, milk, and vanilla and mix until a stiff dough forms.

6. Cut the dough in half and form each portion into a disk about 1 inch thick. Run a large knife under cold water and cut each disk into 6 wedges. Transfer the wedges to the prepared baking sheet, brush them with milk, and sprinkle them lightly with sugar.

7. Bake for 15 to 20 minutes, or until the tops are golden. Let cool on a wire rack for 5 minutes before serving.

Nutrition:

- Per Serving : Protein 3 g | Fiber 1 g | Carbs 29 g | Fat 8 g

Apple Blueberry Friends

Servings: 12
Cooking Time: 20minutes
Ingredients:

- ½ cup + ¼ cup of white flour (self-rising)
- Puree of 2 peeled red apples
- Half cup of blueberries
- 1/3 cup of skim milk
- 2 oz. of almond meal
- 1/4 cup of grapeseed oil
- 5 egg whites
- 3 tbsp. of stevia powder
- 1 tsp. of vanilla essence

Directions:

1. Let the oven preheat to 390 F.
2. Add vanilla essence, flours, stevia & almond meal. Mix.
3. Add oil, milk, blueberries & apple, mix well.
4. Whisk the egg whites till soft peaks form & add the rest of the mixture; fold.
5. Add to the prepared pan & bake for 20 to 30 minutes at 356°F.
6. Let it sit for 5 minutes before taking it out of the mold.

Nutrition:

- Per Serving : Protein 0 g | Fiber 1.2 g | Carbs 12 g | Fat 2 g

Chicken & Veggie Quiche

Servings: 4
Cooking Time: 20 Minutes.
Ingredients:

- 6 eggs
- ½ C. unsweetened almond milk
- Ground black pepper, as required
- 1 C. cooked chicken, chopped
- 1 C. fresh baby spinach, chopped
- ¼ C. fresh mushrooms, sliced
- ¼ C. bell pepper, seeded and chopped
- ¼ C. fresh cilantro, chopped
- 2 tbsp. fresh chives, minced

Directions:

1. Preheat your oven to 400 ºF. Lightly grease a pie dish.
2. In a large bowl, add the eggs, almond milk, salt and black pepper and beat well. Set aside.
3. In another bowl, add the chicken, vegetables and herbs and mix well.
4. Place the chicken mixture in the bottom of the prepared pie dish.
5. Place the egg mixture over the chicken mixture evenly.
6. Bake for approximately 20 minutes or until a toothpick inserted in the center comes out clean.
7. Remove from oven and set aside to cool for about 5-10 minutes before slicing.
8. Cut into desired-sized wedges and serve.

Nutrition:

- Per Serving : Protein 18.2 g | Fiber 0.5 g | Carbs 2.6 g | Fat 7.1 g

Nushroom & Pepper Omelet

Servings: 4
Cooking Time: 25 Minutes.
Ingredients:

- 6 large eggs
- Salt and ground black pepper, as required
- ½ C. fat-free milk
- 1/3 C. fresh mushrooms, cut into slices
- 1/3 C. bell pepper, seeded and chopped
- 1 tbsp. chives, minced

Directions:

1. Preheat your oven to 350 ºF. Lightly grease a pie dish.
2. In a bowl, add the eggs, salt, black pepper milk and beat until well combined.
3. In another bowl, mix together the bell pepper and mushrooms.
4. Transfer the egg mixture into the prepared pie dish evenly.
5. Top with vegetable mixture evenly and sprinkle with chives evenly.
6. Bake for approximately 20-25 minutes.
7. Remove from oven and set aside for about 5 minutes.
8. With a knife, cut into equal-sized wedges and serve.

Nutrition:

- Per Serving : Protein 10.8 g | Fiber 0.2 g | Carbs 3.1 g | Fat 7.8 g

Lemony Chicken Thighs

Servings: 6
Cooking Time: 16 Minutes.
Ingredients:
- 2 tbsp. olive oil, divided
- 1 tbsp. fresh lemon juice
- 1 tbsp. lemon zest, grated
- 2 tsp. dried oregano
- 1 tsp. dried thyme
- Salt and ground black pepper, as required
- 1½ lb. skinless, boneless chicken thighs

Directions:
1. Preheat your oven to 420 ºF.
2. Add 1 tbsp. of olive oil, lemon juice, zest, dried herbs, salt and black pepper in a bowl and stir to combine.
3. In the bowl, add chicken thighs and coat with the oil mixture generously.
4. Refrigerate to marinate for at least 25-30 minutes.
5. In an oven-proof wok, heat the remaining oil over medium-high heat and sear the chicken thighs for about 2-3 minutes per side.
6. Immediately transfer the wok into the oven and bake for approximately 10 minutes.
7. Serve hot.

Nutrition:
- Per Serving : Protein 0.3 g | Fiber 1 g | Carbs 0.7 g | Fat 8.8 g

Cucumber & Grapefruit Juice

Servings: 2
Cooking Time: 10 Minutes.
Ingredients:
- 4 seedless cucumbers, peeled and chopped
- 3 grapefruits, peeled and sectioned
- 1 C. cold water

Directions:
1. Place all ingredients in a high-powered blender and pulse until well combined.
2. Through a fine mesh strainer, strain the juice and transfer into two glasses.
3. Serve immediately.

Nutrition:
- Per Serving : Protein 4.1 g | Fiber 3.1 g | Carbs 31.9 g | Fat 0.7 g

Glazed Chicken Thighs

Servings: 5
Cooking Time: 25 Minutes.
Ingredients:
- 2 tbsp. fresh lime juice
- 2 tbsp. maple syrup
- 2 tbsp. olive oil
- Salt and ground black pepper, as required

- 5 (4-oz.) skinless chicken thighs

Directions:
1. In a bowl, add all ingredients except for chicken thighs and sesame seeds and beat until well combined.
2. In a large plastic zipper bag, add marinade and chicken thighs.
3. Seal the bag and shake to coat well.
4. Refrigerate for at least 1 hour, turning bag twice.
5. Preheat your oven to 425 ºF.
6. Remove the chicken from the bag and reserve the excess marinade.
7. Arrange chicken thighs into a 9x13-inch baking dish in a single layer and coat with some of the cooked marinade.
8. Bake for approximately 25 minutes, coating with the reserved marinade slightly after every 10 minutes.
9. Serve hot.

Nutrition:
- Per Serving : Protein 32.8 g | Fiber 0 g | Carbs 5.4 g | Fat 14 g

Chicken Noodle Soup

Servings: 6
Cooking Time: 6 Hours
Ingredients:
- 3 celery stalks, sliced
- 1 tbsp. of thyme
- 3 carrots, sliced
- 1 onion, diced
- 1 lb. chicken breast, boneless & skinless
- 2 minced garlic cloves
- 8 cups of chicken stock
- 1 tbsp. of rosemary
- 1 tsp. of salt
- 8 oz. of egg noodles

Directions:
1. Add all ingredients to a slow cooker, except
2. Cook for 6 to 8 hours on low or 3 to 4 hours on high.
3. In the last 14 minutes, take the chicken out & shred it.
4. Add to the cooker with noodles. Cook for 14-15 minutes. Serve.

Nutrition:
- Per Serving : Protein 24 g | Fiber 1 g | Carbs 15 g | Fat 6.2 g

Pasta With Zucchini

Servings: 8
Cooking Time: 15 Minutes.
Ingredients:
- 3 tomatoes
- 1 lb. whole-wheat pasta
- ¼ C. olive oil
- 1 lb. zucchini, peeled, seeded and sliced
- 1 tsp. dried oregano, crushed

- ¾ C. low-fat feta cheese, crumbled

Directions:

1. In a large pan of salted boiling water, add the tomatoes and cook for about 1 minute.
2. With a slotted spoon, transfer the tomatoes into a bowl of ice water.
3. In the same pan of boiling water, add the pasta and cook for about 8-10 minutes.
4. Drain the pasta well.
5. Meanwhile, peel the blanched tomatoes and remove the seeds.
6. Then chop the tomatoes well.
7. In a large skillet, heat oil over medium heat and sauté the mushrooms and garlic for about 4-5 minutes.
8. Add the tomatoes and oregano and cook for about 3-4 minutes.
9. Add the pasta and cheese and stir to combine.
10. Serve hot.

Nutrition:

- Per Serving : Protein 9.5 g | Fiber 1.3 g | Carbs 25.3 g | Fat 10.5 g

Cucumber & Celery Juice

Servings: 2
Cooking Time: 10 Minutes.

Ingredients:

- 1 large seedless cucumber, roughly chopped
- 6 celery stalks, chopped
- 1 (1½-inch) piece fresh ginger, peeled and roughly chopped
- 1 tbsp. fresh lemon juice
- ½ C. filtered water

Directions:

1. Add all ingredients in a high-power blender and pulse until well combined.
2. Through a cheesecloth-lined sieve, strain the juice and pour into two glasses.
3. Serve immediately.

Nutrition:

- Per Serving : Protein 41.6 g | Fiber 1.9 g | Carbs 9.2 g | Fat 0.4 g

Eggs With Beef & Tomatoes

Servings: 4
Cooking Time: 30 Minutes.

Ingredients:

- 3 tbsp. olive oil
- 2 tbsp. fresh cilantro, chopped
- 2 tbsp. fresh parsley, chopped
- 12 oz. lean ground beef
- 3 C. tomatoes, peeled, seeded and chopped
- 4 eggs
- 2 oz. low-fat feta cheese, crumbled

Directions:

1. In a large shallow wok, heat the oil over medium heat and cook the cilantro and parsley, salt and black pepper for about 2 minutes, stirring frequently.
2. Add the ground beef and cook for about 4-5 minutes, stirring frequently.
3. Stir in the tomatoes, salt and black pepper and cook for about 15-20 minutes, stirring occasionally.
4. With a spoon, make 4 wells in the greens mixture.
5. Carefully crack 1 egg into each well and season each egg with a bit of salt.
6. Cover the wok and cook for about 5 minutes or until desired doneness of the egg whites.
7. Remove from the heat and serve hot with the garnishing of remaining cilantro.

Nutrition:

- Per Serving : Protein 35.1 g | Fiber 1.7 g | Carbs 6.2 g | Fat 22 g

Shrimp Soup

Servings: 4
Cooking Time: 23 Minutes.

Ingredients:

- 2 tbsp. olive oil
- 2 C. zucchini, peeled, seeded and sliced
- 3½ C. homemade chicken broth
- 1 lb. shrimp, peeled and deveined
- Salt and ground black pepper, as required
- 2 tbsp. fresh parsley, minced

Directions:

1. In a Dutch oven, heat oil over medium heat and cook the zucchini for about 2-3 minutes, stirring frequently.
2. Pour in the broth and simmer for about 10-15 minutes.
3. Add in the shrimp, salt, and black pepper, and simmer for about 4-5 minutes.
4. Stir in the parsley and serve hot.

Nutrition:

- Per Serving : Protein 30.8 g | Fiber 0.7 g | Carbs 4.5 g | Fat 10.2 g

Shrimp Stew

Servings: 6
Cooking Time: 10 Mins.

Ingredients:

- 2 tbsp. olive oil
- ¼ C. canned roasted red pepper, chopped
- 1½ lb. raw shrimp, peeled and deveined
- 3 C. tomatoes, peeled, seeded and chopped
- 1 C. homemade chicken broth
- 2 tbsp. fresh lime juice
- Salt and ground black pepper, as required
- 2 tbsp. fresh cilantro, chopped

Directions:

1. Heat oil in a pan over medium heat and sauté the red pepper for about 4-5 minutes.

2. Add the shrimp and tomatoes and cook for about 3-4 minutes.

3. Stir in the broth and cook for about 4-5 minutes.

4. Stir in the lime juice, salt, and black pepper, and remove from the heat.

5. Garnish with cilantro and serve hot.

Nutrition:

- Per Serving : Protein 27.5 g | Fiber 1.2 g | Carbs 5.9 g | Fat 7 g

Bean And Couscous Salad

Servings: 4

Cooking Time: 0minutes

Ingredients:

- 1 ½ Cup of boiling water
- 2 Cups of tomatoes, peeled, chopped without seeds
- 1 Cup of chopped bell peppers, without seeds
- 1 Cup of couscous
- 2 Cups of cooked black beans
- 1/4 tsp. of pepper
- 1 onion, chopped
- 2 minced garlic cloves
- ½ tsp. of salt
- ½ cup of rice vinegar
- 1/4 Cup of olive oil

Directions:

1. Add water & couscous. Let it rest, covered, until all liquid is absorbed.

2. Add the rest of the ingredients, mix & adjust seasoning.

3. Serve.

Nutrition:

- Per Serving : Protein 4 g | Fiber 5 g | Carbs 17 g | Fat 2 g

Classic French Toast

Servings:4

Cooking Time: 40 Minutes

Ingredients:

- 1 teaspoon butter or margarine
- 3 large eggs
- ½ cup milk
- 2 teaspoons vanilla extract
- 2 teaspoons ground cinnamon

- 8 thick slices day-old white bread of your choice
- ¼ cup confectioners' sugar or maple syrup, for serving

Directions:

1. ¼ cup confectioners' sugar or maple syrup, for serving

2. In a large sauté pan or skillet over medium heat, melt the butter.

3. In a medium bowl, whisk together the eggs, milk, vanilla, and cinnamon until smooth.

4. Pour the egg mixture into a large, shallow dish.

5. Dip a slice of bread into the batter, let it soak for 10 to 15 seconds on each side, and immediately place it in the hot skillet. Cook until both sides are golden brown, 2 to 3 minutes per side. Repeat with the remaining slices of bread. Depending on the size of your skillet, you can likely cook 2 slices at once.

6. Place 2 slices of French toast on each plate and dust each serving with 1 tablespoon of confectioners' sugar or lightly drizzle with 1 tablespoon of maple syrup.

Nutrition:

- Per Serving : Protein 12 g | Fiber 2 g | Carbs 55 g | Fat 8 g

Chicken & Bell Peppe Muffins

Servings: 8

Cooking Time: 20 Minutes.

Ingredients:

- 8 eggs
- Ground black pepper, as required
- 2 tbsp. water
- 8 oz. cooked chicken, chopped finely
- 2 C. bell pepper, seeded and chopped

Directions:

1. Preheat your oven to 350 °F. Grease 8 C. of a muffin tin.

2. In a bowl, add eggs, salt, black pepper and water and beat until well combined.

3. Add the chicken and bell pepper and stir to combine.

4. Transfer the mixture into the prepared muffin C. evenly.

5. Bake for approximately 18-20 minutes or until golden brown.

6. Remove the muffin tin from oven and place onto a wire rack to cool for about 10 minutes.

7. Then invert the muffins onto a platter and serve warm.

Nutrition:

- Per Serving : Protein 14.1 g | Fiber 0.4 g | Carbs 2.7 g | Fat 5.3 g

RECIPES INDEX

H

Haddock In Tomato Sauce 122

Healthy Chopped Salad 58

Healthy Fruit Juice 38

Healthy Jell-o 24

Herbed Beef Broth 25

Herbed Chicken Broth 37

Herbed Pork Bones Broth 35

Herbed Swordfish 94

Hibachi Clear Soup 23

Hibiscus-mint Iced Tea 27

High Fiber Pasta 65

High-fiber Bran Muffins 83

High-fiber Mac And Cheese 72

Homemade Beef Stock 36

Homemade Chicken Stock 30

Homemade Hummus 51

Homemade Iced Tea 27

Honey Salmon 130

Hot Apple Cider 19

I

Iced Green Tea With Mint & Ginger 31

Immune Boon Herbal Tea 25

J

Jambalaya 62

Jell-o Jugglers 27

K

Kidney Beans In Tomato Sauce 65

Kiwi & Avocado Smoothie 57

Kiwi & Orange Salad 43

Kiwi Juice 127

Kiwi, Apple & Cucumber Juice 42

Kiwi, Apple & Grapes Juice 53

L

Lamb Dhal Makhani 74

Lamb With Lentils, Feta & Mint 90

Leeks Clear Soup 34

Lemon Cheese Waffles 131

Lemon Gelatin 21

Lemon Ginger Detox Tea 32

Lemon Pepper Turkey 108

Lemon Tea W Honey & Ginger 26

Lemonade 17

Lemon-rosemary Iced Tea 34

Lemony Chicken Thighs 134

Lemony Fruit Juice 28

Lemony Grapes Juice 23

Lemony Salmon 129

Lemony Scallops 107

Lemony Shrimp 100

Lemony Trout 119

Lentil & Pumpkin & Kale Soup 78

Lentil & Spinach Soup 80

Lentil & Sweet Potato Soup 68

Lentil And Chicken Shepherd's Pie 53

Lentil Burgers With Tomato Sauce 51

Lentil Curry 69

Lentil Fritters 84

Lentil Tomato Salad 73

Lentils & Chickpeas Salad 90

Lentils & Crispy Brussel Sprouts 77

Lentils & Pumpkin Soup 65

Light & Delicious Seafood Soup 29

Lime & Ginger Tea 17

Lime Popsicles 30

Limeade 36

Low & Slow Pulled Pork 123

Low Fiber Beet Carrot Soup 111

Lychee & Dill Juice 111

Lychee Juice 106

M

Mango & Avocado Salad 51

Mango Juice 131

Mango, Orange & Cucumber Smoothie 92

Maple-mustard Chicken Leg 108

Matcha Avocado Smoothie 83

Melon Honey Green Tea 19

Mexican Quinoa Wraps 44

Milky Crepes 110

Minestrone Soup 85

Mini Cheesecakes 108

Mini Pineapple Upside-down Cakes 118

Minty Watermelon Popsicles 21

Mixe Veggie Soup 88

Mixed Berries Gelatin 33

Mocha Protein Overnight Oats 49

Molasses Cookies 124

Moroccan Lamb & Lentil Soup 48

Moroccan Tea 22

Mushroom Clear Soup 26

Mushroom Curry 118

Mussel Broth 37

Mustardy Salmon With Lentils & Beetroot 87

Mutton Soup 35

N

Nushroom & Pepper Omelet 133

Nyquell Herbal Tea 18

O

Oat & Yogurt Bowl 52

One-pot Chicken And Orzo 115

Orange & Avocado Salad 63

Orange & Beet Salad 89

Orange & Carrot Juice 24

Orange & Kale Juice 58

Orange & Kale Salad 70

Orange Juice 18

Orange, Cherries & Carrot Juice 33

Overnight Steel-cut Oats 57

Oxtail Soup 26

P

Pan Seared Salmon 122

Parmesan Asparagus 113

Parsley Scallops 120

Pasta & Chickpeas Curry 41

Pasta & Veggies Soup 109

Pasta Bake 130

Pasta With Asparagus 100

Pasta With Green Peas 67

Pasta With Mushrooms 76

Pasta With Zucchini 134

Peach & Oat Smoothie 85

Peach & Raspberry Smoothie 39

Peach Gelatin 28

Peach Iced Tea 32

Peach Juice 29

Peach Scones 132

Pear & Blueberry Smoothie 60

Pear & Brussels Sprout Salad 79

Pear & Celery Juice 67

Pear & Fennel Juice 42

Pear & Kale Juice 80

Pear & Kale Salad 45

Pear & Raspbberry Salad 93

Pear Juice 33

Pineapple Juice 16

Pineapple Skin Tea 25

Pork Sausage & Green Lentil Braise 88

Pork Sausages With Cider Lentils 40

Potato & Zucchini Frittata 120

Potato Soup 109

Prawn & Tomato Spaghetti 128

Prawn & Vegetable Pasta 102

Prosciutto Pizza With Corn & Arugula 70

Prosciutto, Kale & Bean Stew 53

Pumpkin Oatmeal 42

Pumpkin Overnight Oats 68

Pumpkin Pancakes 96

Pumpkin Waffles 113

Q

Quinoa & Kale Salad 85

Quinoa & Sweet Potato Burgers 73

Quinoa & Veggie Stew 44

Quinoa And Avocado Scramble 63

Quinoa Black Bean Salad 75

Quinoa With Mushrooms 54

Quinoa, Beans & Mango Salad 68

Quinoa, Oats & Seeds Porridge 91

Printed in Great Britain
by Amazon

57272197R00079